*Transportation
for
Marketing and Business
Students*

Transportation
for
Marketing and Business
Students

PAUL T. McELHINEY
Professor of Marketing and Transportation
California State University, Los Angeles

1975

LITTLEFIELD, ADAMS & CO.
Totowa, New Jersey

Library of Congress Cataloging in Publication Data

McElhiney, Paul T.
  Transportation for Marketing and Business Students

  (A Littlefield, Adams Quality Paperback No. 290)
  Includes bibliographies.

  1. Transportation.   2. Shipment of goods.

I. Title.

HE151.M27   380.5   75–9617
ISBN 0–8226–0290–3

Contents

Preface

The purpose of this book is to present a succinct overview of domestic transportation and traffic management for the student of business administration. The aim is to describe the transportation system for the layman and make him aware of how it can be used. Without editorializing heavily, the book presents the outline of subjects that are usually taught in college courses dealing with the economics or principles of transportation. Thus it can serve as a useful study guide for such courses. The treatment includes a chapter on government regulation and one on transportation economics. Matters such as bills of lading and freight rate checking are covered with a view to practical application.

Any errors or omissions, of course, are those of the author. Many thanks are due transportation students at California State University, Los Angeles, who aided in the preparation. Special appreciation is extended to Etild Asjian, Clarence Bolinger, Leonard Coates, Thomas Flescher, David Nakagaki, Michael Trexler, and David Weil.

CHAPTER 1

Modes and Carriers in Transportation

This chapter deals with a definition of transportation and some of the basic concepts and terms involved in it.

DEFINING TRANSPORTATION

From the viewpoint of the businessman, transportation is the movement of goods from where they are not needed to where they are needed. It is also the movement of people to places where employment or entertainment are more easily obtained. The time elapsed in transportation is lost time and should be minimized.

These statements emphasize that commercial transportation is not an end in itself. When it is necessary to move goods or people to a new location the real need is for the goods or people, not the transportation. The demand for transportation is a derived demand, which always arises in response to the need for something else. Because of this, transportation companies are quick to realize a loss of business when there is a downturn in the economy and people cut back their purchases of goods. Carriers like trucklines and airlines, which haul a large proportion of consumer goods, usually feel such a downtrend sooner than do carriers like railroads and bargelines, which carry a large proportion of industrial and producer's goods.

Place Utility

Things can be made more useful or given increased utility in several ways. They can be transported from where they are not needed to where they are needed; this is said to give them *place utility*. They can be stored when they are not needed until they are needed; this is said to give them *time utility*. They can be marketed or sold to someone who will use them; this is said to give them *possession utility*. Usually before any of these things can happen, however, the goods must be put in a more useful form or condition. Logs must be sawed into lumber before they can be transported to the building site and sold to a contractor. Iron ore must be made into steel before it can be made into an automobile that can be driven. Changing the condition of materials is said to give them *form utility*; thus, we attribute form utility to production. Although transportation aids in the creation of all these "utilities," its major role is to create place utility.

Time Utility

Sometimes transportation is also credited with creating time utility. For instance, if medicine is needed in a distant country to halt an epidemic, air transport can get it there in time to be of use. Or, if lumber is not needed in the market for many days it can be sent by a circuitous route that will delay its arrival.

The important factor in both of these cases, however, is not the time-in-transit that the mode of transport can provide, but rather the time at which the need for the good is recognized. This means that someone must plan ahead and allow time for any necessary transportation to take place. How much time depends upon the speed of the transportation mode available.

Frequently, slower means of transportation or circuitous routings are deliberately used to keep goods in transit for longer than necessary. This can be a means of avoiding costly static storage. Though it does create time utility, strictly speaking this is a form of storage-in-motion rather than transportation. Also, when it is successful, the result may be attributed to proper planning. Essentially, therefore, transportation creates place and not time utility. Time utility is created by storage and by the way transport is used. The ideal situation would be for all transportation to be instantaneous, for then needs everywhere could be satisfied immediately, and no advance planning of shipments and inventories would be necessary.

TRANSPORTATION AND GOVERNMENT

In the past, the interest that various national governments had in transportation was probably based more on control and defense than upon economic exchange.

Control

Good transportation permits the central government of a country to extend control to all parts of the territory. It opens remote regions where opposition forces might take refuge and causes all parts of the nation to "look toward" the central government. Someone has suggested that the geographic boundaries of countries are, in part, determined by the speed of transportation available when the country was established. European states, therefore, were small enough to permit communication across them in two or three days' time by horse. In the United States the sizes of the states increases as one goes from east to west; this is partly attributed to the fact that transportation technology was improving as the new territories were opened. This idea, of course, can be accepted only as a partial explanation as it overlooks the quality of the land and whether it can be developed intensively or only extensively.

The geography of transportation routes may also determine the site of the central government. In the development of the American West, some states deliberately planned to put the capital in the center of the state only to find that the natural flow of transportation and communication bypassed it. Utah, for instance, located the seat of government centrally at Fillmore, later to move it to Salt Lake City, which was in the natural mainstream of movement. Similar isolation affects Brazil's new centrally located capital at Brasilia.

Defense

Transportation is so intimately related to national defense that armed forces are classified by the type of transportation they employ: army, navy, and air force. The use that these forces can make of the internal transportation routes of the country determines how defensible it will be. The military must be able to get to all perimeters of the country quickly and with as much security as possible. This is so obvious that the frequent mistakes of diplomats who occasionally re-divide the world into nations are hard to understand. A country such as Pakistan when it was established in two non-contiguous pieces in the 1960's was not only weak from the standpoint of control discussed above but was practically indefensible.

Exchange

Today, when we are concerned about underdeveloped nations, the most important reason for a country to develop its transportation system is to promote economic exchange. This applies both to internal exchange and to foreign trade. That country which would maintain a healthy balance between the two and control its own destiny must control transportation, for transportation can greatly aid one country in exploiting another. Examples of this are seen in the colonial imperialism that European nations practiced in Africa, China, and India in the last century. In each of these countries, railroads were built to take raw materials out of the country, not to tie it together. Consequently, today situations develop in which there are surpluses in one province and starvation in another because the transportation system is incapable of promoting exchange.

An example of a country that preserved national unity by careful control of transportation is Canada. Nearly one hundred years ago the western provinces were becoming large wheat-producing areas. Since western Canadian mountains and valleys run in a north-south direction, the natural transportation tendency was for the harvested wheat to move south to the American railroads which ran east and west just south of the Canadian border. This caused orientation of the economies of the wheat provinces toward the United States and could have had political results. The building of the Canadian railroads just north of the border interrupted the drain-off of wheat and preserved the political integrity of the western region.

MODES OF TRANSPORTATION

Political, economic, and military factors such as those discussed above cause governments to take great interest in transportation. In the United States this interest has caused development of the world's most complex transportation system. Today, five principal modes of transportation—airway, highway, pipeline, railway, and water—are in commercial use. The main difference between these means of transport is the medium through or on which each operates. In each case a vehicle is used that is peculiar to the medium that is used. Obviously, more than five modes are possible. Space travel using a ballistic vehicle in the medium of space and dog team using a sled on a frozen way are other possibilities, though they are not extensively exploited commercially.

Ways

Waterways and airways of course, are nearly identical with the mediums through which the vehicle passes. In both cases, however, the modern way involves complex terminal and navigational facilities which properly become part of the way. In water transport especially, canals, locks, and man-made protected channels often form a large part of the way.

The ways of modern land carriers today are carefully constructed in their entireties. Since we usually take them for granted today, it is hard to imagine that the techniques of building satisfactory railways and roads have only been understood and used for about 150 years. Pipelines are an even newer method of moving things.

The nature of the way determines the method that must be used to schedule traffic over it. Because of their limited flexibility and rigid directional flow, railroad and pipeline traffic must be under the management of a single centralized control center. The opposite applies in water, air, and even highway transport, at least in uncongested situations. In these modes the medium is so widespread and flexible that vehicular movement under individual operator control is usually possible. In airway and highway movement, however, we have recently found that extreme congestion destroys flexibility so that central control can become mandatory here also. This could be true in certain waterway situations as well but the generally slow speeds of the vehicles makes it less critical.

Vehicles

In Latin the original version of our word "vehicle" means "that which carries." Thus, any device a transportation company uses to carry goods or people is a vehicle, whether it is wheeled, hulled, or winged. The nature of the vehicle a mode uses has important implications for the relative cost and efficiency of the mode. Obviously, some vehicles, such as airplanes, steamships, and some trucks, are self-propelled. Others, such as railway freight cars and barges, are not, and require the addition of a power unit such as a locomotive or a towboat.

Vehicles that use detachable power units, such as motor truck semi-tractors, railway locomotives, and towboats, are inherently more efficient than those that do not. Trucking fleets, for instance, are frequently built around some ratio of semi-trailers to tractors, say three to one. Then, while one trailer is being loaded at origin and another unloaded at destination, the power unit can be shuttling a loaded or empty trailer between the two. This flexibility reduces the investment required, since expensive power units are not standing idle while cargo units are being loaded or unloaded. It reduces labor cost because fewer individually operated power units are required. It also permits the establishment of truckload freight rates which are predicated on the assumption that the customer will load and unload the equipment.

Detachable power units also permit the use of multi-vehicle combinations such as trains, barge tows, and motor truck "double bottoms." Multi-vehicle combinations increase the efficiency of the line-haul as well as the terminal activity of the carrier because they add carrying capacity without increasing the operating personnel required. They also make it possible easily and with minimum delay to set out part of the load at a stop intermediate to origin and destination.

TYPES OF CARRIERS

The organizations and companies who use vehicles to perform transportation service over ways are called *carriers*. The carrier is the party who performs the service under the shipping contract; in commercial transportation he is usually the paid servant of the customer or user. Carriers may be classified in several different ways.

Direct and Indirect Carriers

Most transportation companies use their own facilities directly to provide a service for the public. Some companies, however, do not own extensive over-the-road or line-haul equipment but buy service from an underlying carrier and resell it to the public. The most observable example of this is the United States Postal Service. Other indirect carriers are domestic surface-freight forwarders, and air-freight forwarders, the services of which are explained further on in this book.

Private and For-Hire Carriers

Private carriers, obviously, are persons or organizations who haul their own goods in their own vehicles. They are an important part of our transportation system because they represent an alternative that anyone can use. Of the nearly 18 million trucks in the United States, only about 10 percent or less are operated by for-hire carriers; by far the greatest number are owned by private parties. Private railroad transportation is extremely rare, but private barge and steamship carriers are common and some companies are buying their own fleets of aircraft for cargo as well as for passenger carrying.

A for-hire carrier, of course, is a transportation company that sells transportation service for a price as its method of generating revenue. For-hire carriers can be further classified as common and contract carriers.

Common carriers. Common carriers are those that will perform their service for the general public. They cannot refuse service to anyone except for good cause, their rates and charges must be reasonable, and they must treat everyone more or less equally. However, one cannot demand that they perform a service that they are not accustomed to perform.

Contract carriers. Contract carriers have only been recognized as a type of public carrier in the United States since 1935, and then only in trucking and domestic water transport. Contract carriers provide for-hire transportation only under long-term contracts with a few customers. They may refuse service and, under regulation, must not sell service to anyone with whom they do not have a contract; nor can they attempt to attract an unreasonably large number of customers.

Virtually all American railroads and oil pipelines have been declared by law to be common carriers.* One can do business with contract as well as common carriers in the motor bus and truck industry, the airline industry, and in inland and deep-sea water transportation.

CUSTOMERS AND GOODS

Customers

The people who hire carriers to move their goods are generally referred to as shippers. Thus, when we are speaking of customers as a group we call them shippers, but the word shipper also is used specifically to mean the sender of the goods. The term shipper comes down to us from the Anglo-Saxon language. In old England, when water transportation was the principal mode, it meant "to send by ship"; today it is broadened to mean "to commit to transportation." The shipper or sender of goods is also frequently referred to as the *consignor* or one who consigns. Because of the use of this last term, the receiver at the destination end of the journey is called the *consignee*. In the United States the term consignee is used almost exclusively to designate the receiver.

There are other people who use transportation carriers who don't quite fit into either the shipper or consignee category. These are the indirect carriers such as forwarders and consolidators, who use an underlying direct carrier to sell a service of their own.

Goods

The words that signify the products being moved vary from mode to mode. So far, this discussion has used the term "goods" for this purpose, since this word has long meant wares, merchandise, or chattels. In England frequent reference is made to goods wagons, goods trains. The American railroad man or

---

* Petroleum pipelines were declared common carriers at about the turn of the century as part of a government effort to break up oil monopolies. Natural gas and water pipelines are not considered to be for-hire carriers.

trucker refers instead to "freight" and freight cars or freight trains, and when he says "freight" he means products or goods.

This leads to a minor confusion between land and water transportation, for when the steamship man says "freight" he means money. The oldest meaning of the word "freight" is the money that is charged for performing a transportation service. When the water transportation man wishes to signify goods he says "cargo." Cargo is a word that comes from the Spanish verb *cargar* meaning "to load or charge," and has reference to the stowing or loading of a ship.

In most modes, an individual consignment of goods, freight, or cargo is referred to as a "shipment," which ties in with the shipping process and the fact that customers are called shippers. In oil pipeline practice, however, the individual consignment may be referred to as a "tender" because pipeline companies require that the customer must offer or tender them a minimum amount, say 10 thousand or 100 thousand barrels of product, each time he makes a shipment.

COMPARISON OF MODES

Although there is substantial competition between the different types of carriers, each mode has characteristics and advantages that suit it to do a particular job better than the others. In freight transportation, major factors that affect the desirability of one mode over another are cost, speed, and reliability. Reliability includes both on-time performance and delivery of the merchandise without loss or damage. In passenger transportation, a factor of convenience might be included, and probably cost would not be the first factor on the list.

Passenger Transportation

All modes of passenger carriage subject the patron to similar degrees of discomfort. Private automobile travel minimizes this somewhat because the journey is under almost complete management by the passenger himself. Air transport minimizes discomfort by shortening the period it must be endured. Perhaps for these, as well as other reasons, by far the majority of all passenger movement in the United States is by auto, and the major part of commercial passenger transport is by air. Because other factors are more important in freight movement, the relative shares of air and highway transportation of cargo are quite different. Data that illustrate these differences and the factors discussed below are presented in Table 1, page 13.

Freight Transportation

Cost. Airplanes and trucks are relatively low-capacity vehicles in comparison to trains, ships, barges, and pipelines. In addition, they require more crew per unit of cargo and use more horsepower to overcome inertia and produce high speed. It follows that their costs are related to these characteristics and are higher than those of other modes. Therefore, they tend to be well suited to carry relatively small, reasonably valuable shipments.

Rail freight cars, barges, ships, and pipelines are all large-volume vehicles. They employ the multi-vehicle characteristic (or a variation of it) discussed previously. They use less crew and less horsepower in relation to payload. Large capacity thus allows costs to be amortized over a greater number of units. Lower unit costs are attractive to shippers of cheaper commodities and such carriers are well suited for large shipments of bulk goods.

Speed. The speeds of the different modes of transportation vary greatly within a range from over 600 to less than 10 miles per hour. Generalization about a particular mode is difficult because the performance of a certain carrier within a mode may differ from all others and performance may differ from trip to trip. In addition to these qualifications, one must consider the potential speed of the mode in comparison to how this potential is realized in practice and can be utilized by shippers. With these limitations in mind, the following comparisons are made.

Air transport using jet aircraft has a potential line-haul speed in excess of 600 miles per hour. This, of course, is achieved at the expense of a very unfavorable ratio of horsepower to payload: the modern jet airliner requires some 90 thousand horsepower to lift 25 tons of payload off the surface. However, the single-unit air vehicle is quick to handle on the ground, and terminal activity is comparatively uncomplicated. Therefore, to a high degree, the line-haul speed potential of air transport can be realized by the customer. Same-day delivery of cargo moving coast-to-coast across the country is possible with a reasonable amount of traffic management by the shipper.

For land carriers, railroads have a surprisingly high line-haul speed potential. Special passenger train equipment such as the "Turbo-Train" can achieve 170 miles per hour. In practice, ordinary freight diesel-electric locomotives can pull 100 or more conventional freight cars at sustained speeds of about 80 miles per hour. This requires a high-quality roadbed, which is not found everywhere. Horsepower-to-payload ratio is good. On level track, only one-third horsepower is required to pull each ton of a freight train moving at 25 miles per hour. Because trains lose substantial time in complicated terminal activities, however, little of their speed potential is passed on to the customer. Isolated instances of good management produce exceptions such as the piggyback (trailer-container) train that runs between Chicago and Los Angeles in 39 hours.

Since automobiles are capable of very high speeds, it is paradoxical that trucks do not offer as high a line-haul speed potential as railroads. This is partly due to the nature of the highway, where they must mix with other vehicles and, when they observe the law, are restricted in speed. In addition, the gradient and curvature of the highway are the most extreme of any mode. The wheel and tire design of trucks enables them to overcome this, but gives them a high coefficient of friction. Because of friction, horsepower to payload ratio is not as good as rail, and about 300 horsepower are required for around 40 tons of load. Although there is much transcontinental trucking activity, trucks are not well suited to fast long-haul transportation. Where truck line-haul speed potential is realized is on the short haul. Rail terminal activity is so great and airports are so far from the city that a truck shipment going less than 200 miles can nearly arrive at destination before the others get started.

Deep-sea cargo vessels seldom have a speed capability in excess of 30 miles per hour; for years a speed of 8 knots (a knot is one nautical mile per hour, which is equal to 1.15 land miles per hour) was considered sufficient for freighters. Barge tows on the inland waterways make about 4 to 6 miles per hour upstream and perhaps 10 to 12 downstream. A trip from Pittsburgh to New Orleans takes about 10 days. The ratio of power to payload on all water craft is extremely good. American inland water towboats of 6,000 horsepower are capable of pushing barges carrying as much as 50 thousand tons of cargo.

Oil pipeline is probably the slowest of all modes of transportation; the commodity moves through the line at about 5 miles per hour. This unique carrier, the only one in which the cargo moves while the vehicle stands still, has a very favorable horsepower to payload ratio. Continuity of delivery is more important than speed in pipeline transportation; constant-use rates can be established for products that are moving, with consequent reduction of static storage at destination.

Reliability. In theory, railroads are nearly invulnerable to weather, being able to get through when planes, trucks, and even boats have been stalled by storms and fog. In practice, the on-time performance of all American transport modes is reasonably good. Failure to meet timetable schedules is probably caused more by poor dispatching or maintenance failure than by weather.

Much the same is true of shipment damage. Planes supposedly produce the least cargo destruction because they are stable in flight. Rail-switching shock reputedly causes more damage than the moderate swaying of a truck. Water transport has long necessitated formidable packing to protect the goods. These generalizations, however, may no longer be true. Modern carriers have adopted sophisticated techniques to prevent damage such as cushioned underframes (on rail cars), containerization, and inflatable dunnage. Proper packing and loading can do much to prevent damage, and these again are related more to management than to inherent carrier characteristics.

Because of the impact of management, reliability is thus a matter of individual carrier-shipper experience. There are good, fair, and poor carrier companies within each mode. When a shipper finds a carrier who is consistently late or consistently damages the goods, his best alternatives are to try another carrier, another mode, or perhaps to perform the transportation himself.

Chart Comparing Modes

Table 1 on page 13 presents data that support the preceding discussion. Essential to interpretation of this table is the meaning

Table 1. Comparison of Transportation Modes.

1 Mode	2 Miles of Lines	3 Average Length of Haul (miles)	4 Share of Total Freight Ton-Miles	5 Share of Total Passenger-Miles	6 Average Price per Ton-Mile (freight revenue)
Airway	283,861	Cargo 1,147 Passenger 674	18/100%	9%	21 8/10¢
Highway	657,601	Truck 261 Bus 105	22%	Automobile 87% Bus 2%	7 7/10¢
Oil Pipeline	209,478	Crude 297 Product 366	23%	0	27/100¢
Railroad	207,500	Freight 497 Passenger 87	38%	8/10%	1 4/10¢
Waterways Inland Great Lakes Domestic Deep-Sea	25,543	Inland 330 Great Lakes 506 Deep-Sea 1,509	10.6% 5.4%	3/10%	28/100¢

Source: *Transportation Facts and Trends*. Washington, D.C.: Transportation Association of America, 1973.

of the term "ton-mile." A ton-mile is a statistical unit useful for expressing a unit of transportation service; it is not used in practical freight billing or documentation. It means that one ton of freight has been transported one mile. It does not reflect the value of the freight transported or the speed of movement. It is an indicator of relative volume. Column 4 of the table shows the shares of the market that the different modes hold at present. There is undoubtedly some overlapping of the figures, especially those for trucks, as trucks handle part of the haul in many rail, water, and air shipments. There is, of course, overlapping in the average price figures shown in column 6. The rates shown are the average charged per ton-mile for everything the carrier hauls. Obviously each mode charges more than the amount shown for some items and less for others. This means that there are large areas of overlap in which two or more modes compete for the same commodities. Interesting to note also is that the faster carriers and the single-unit carriers tend to charge higher prices than the slower multi-vehicle or multi-unit carriers.

Note that passenger-mile data in column 5 is for total passenger movement, private as well as commercial. In commercial transportation, buses actually originate more passengers than airlines, but airlines generate more passenger-miles because the average length of haul is so much greater.

REFERENCES

The American Waterways Operators, Inc. *Big Load Afloat*. Washington, D.C., 1965.

Becht, J. Edwin. *A Geography of Transportation and Business Logistics*. Dubuque: Wm. C. Brown, 1970.

Grossman, William L. *Fundamentals of Transportation*. New York: Simmons-Boardman, 1959.

Transportation Association of America. *Transportation Facts and Trends*. Washington, D.C. Annual; current as supplemented.

Wolfe, Roy I. *Transportation and Politics*. New York: Van Nostrand, 1963.

CHAPTER 2

Terminal and Line-Haul Problems

The previous chapter described the different modes of transportation and compared them broadly in terms of their cost, speed, and reliability. This chapter compares the ways that different modes solve the problems inherent in a journey. Conclusions are drawn about the effects upon relative costs of the differing speed, volume, and distance factors of the modes.

The word "journey" comes from the French word *jour* meaning "day" and signifies a day's travel. In this book, journey means the complete transportation trip that goods or people take from start to finish when they go somewhere. A journey consists of two basic elements, terminal activity and line-haul movement. One may tend to think that these concepts are clearly separate, with terminal activity performed only before and after the line-haul takes place. There are many overlaps, however. In some cases the line-haul may extend into the terminal, in many cases intermediate terminal activity interrupts the journey, and some carriers integrate terminal activity into the line-haul to save time.

TERMINAL ACTIVITIES

Everyone who travels recognizes that a transportation terminal is a busy place that provides many services for both customers and carriers in addition to the loading and unloading of the vehicles. However, the most important activities that go on at a terminal are consolidation and break-bulk.

Consolidation and Break-Bulk

Consolidation.   Consolidation occurs at the beginning of a journey when all the people or packages that are to travel are gathered up and loaded into the vehicle. This process is obvious in passenger transport and in the handling of small packages as in the postal service. In the interest of efficiency, passengers or parcels that are going to many separate destinations must be brought together in order to fill the equipment and make the journey worthwhile revenue-wise to the carrier.

Break-bulk.   Break-bulk is the opposite activity at the destination of the journey. It involves sorting out all the people or shipments and directing them to their specific destinations. The manner in which consolidation and break-bulk are performed can affect the efficiency of the whole journey. Taking a 200-mile trip by air instead of by car may be foolish if it takes over an hour to get to and from the airports at each end.

Problems of terminal activity.   The freight shipper and the carrier have different views of the terminal problems caused by consolidation and break-bulk. The shipper is eager to see his shipment leave his plant, but may not be much concerned about origin terminal activity because he doesn't see it. He is quick to blame the destination terminal when an expected inbound shipment is late, however, because he is really concerned about total journey time. The carrier would like to impress the shipper that he, too, is primarily concerned about expediting the individual shipment all along the line. As a matter of fact, the carrier's major interest is probably in reducing the turnaround time for his line-haul vehicles. Aircraft, ships, trucks, barges, and railroad cars are either in short supply or very expensive or both. Therefore it is important to run them as much as possible to meet demand and amortize their cost over as many payload units as possible. Because of differences in vehicles, the modes do not face identical obstacles in consolidation and break-bulk.

Trucking Terminal Activity

A reasonably simple example of terminal activity can be seen in the case of a motor-truck common carrier of general freight.

Many such carriers provide a pickup and delivery service for small shipments in which city-van-type trucks are assigned to specific routes throughout an urban area. In the morning such trucks usually cover their routes making deliveries of inbound freight. In the afternoon they retrace the route, collecting shipments destined to all points that the company serves. When the city-van or pickup truck returns to the terminal at nightfall, it is fully loaded with shipments for all points on the trucking company's system. These shipments must be sorted across the freight dock into piles or areas according to destination. This break-bulk and reconsolidation can be quite complex, as each shipment may consist of several packages. Each of these must be identified and placed with the other pieces of the shipment they make up, and in the area of the proper destination. When sufficient freight has accumulated for one destination, it is loaded into a line-haul vehicle. When it is properly loaded and documentation is completed, the line-haul vehicle can depart without further consolidation or break-bulk. Obviously, the mechanics of its trip will be simpler if it contains goods for only one destination and does not have to partly unload at some intermediate way point.

Since such city pickup and cross-dock operation is expensive because of the labor of break-bulk and sorting, trucking companies like to handle loads large enough so that the line-haul truck or "road rig" can get them directly from the customers. Incentive rates are offered to attract shipments of this sort. One large general freight motor carrier found that only 50 percent of its volume was "cross-dock business," as half of its traffic was "loaded to go."

In this example of trucking-terminal activity, only the cargo is consolidated or sorted. The relatively small, single-unit vehicle is individually crewed and operated; when it is loaded, it can begin the line-haul at once without waiting for other line-haul vehicles to accumulate. Even with combinations of a truck and trailer, or a tractor and two or three trailers, this advantage remains greater than in some other modes. In comparison to line-haul vehicles of other modes, the truck or trailer is also inexpensive. A combination of small size and low cost makes it possible for the truck to be kept waiting during loading without incurring exorbitant opportunity costs.

Air Terminal Activity

Like the truck, the airplane is a relatively small, single-unit, individually crewed vehicle. Although commercial planes have increased greatly in size in recent years, weight-bearing capacity has only recently exceeded that of the average rail-freight car. Like the truckline, the airline is primarily a small-shipment carrier. A similar city-van pickup service is provided in most urban areas and the same problems of cross-dock sorting are found in the terminal activity. Differences appear, however, when the loading of the line-haul equipment begins.

Unlike a truck, an airplane cannot be backed up to the loading dock. Because most airlines are combination passenger- and cargo-haulers, loading activity is frequently handled at the passenger gate; even full cargo flights may be loaded some distance from the freight terminal. In addition, fuselage shape makes efficient hand-loading very time-consuming. Finally, the aircraft is an expensive vehicle that is not repaying its great depreciation expense when it is sitting idle on the ground.

Therefore, in their terminal activity the airlines have interposed a containerized step between the destination freight-pile and the line-haul vehicle. As it is sorted from the pickup truck, outbound freight is placed in an inexpensive, light-weight container shaped like the fuselage of the airplane. When several such containers are filled, they can be moved on a special trailer or loader to the aircraft and quickly placed aboard.

Unit Load Concept

Containerization is an example of the unit load concept. This is the idea that in a multiple-part shipment it is much more efficient to put all the packages or pieces together in a block and handle them as a unit rather than handle them separately. This is especially true when repeated consolidation and break-bulk must take place during the journey. Unit loads can be made up in many ways. Cartons may be placed together on a pallet, steel-strapped together, glued together, or placed in containers ranging upwards in dimension to the size of a truck trailer. Since containers are so important in the marine cargo industry their advantages and disadvantages are discussed after "Water Terminal Activity" below.

Rail Terminal Activity

The benefit of the unit load concept is inherent in railroad transportation and especially in the form in which it is sold in the United States today. American railroads provide essentially only one "size" or level of service, and that is carload (abbreviated CL) service. A carload shipment is a consignment moving on one day, usually in one car, from one shipper to one consignee, covered by one bill of lading, loaded by the shipper and unloaded by the consignee, and meeting the minimum weight requirements for a particular carload rate. Since the customers do the consolidation and break-bulk into and out of the equipment, the car moves over the line as a unit load.

In their terminal activity, small-shipment handlers, like trucklines and airlines, who use single-unit vehicles are mostly concerned with the problem of sorting the freight. Railroads, on the other hand, are mostly concerned with sorting vehicles. Rail terminal activity begins when a switch engine (like the motor-freight or air city-van truck) starts its daily rounds to the industrial spur tracks of customers all over the city. The switch crew delivers incoming carloads to customers and picks up the outgoing loads they have ready for shipment. When the switch drag, as this group of cars is sometimes called, returns to the freight yards, it consists of a collection of cars destined for all points the railroad serves. These cars must be sorted in a classification yard into solid blocks or trains going to the individual destinations.

Until recently, railroads also offered a less than carload (LCL) service. Since it combined both the sorting of freight and the sorting of vehicles, it provided one of the worst examples of excessive consolidation and break-bulk. Before the above-described sorting of vehicles could take place, LCL shipments had to go through the same sorting process that those of trucklines and airlines do. By the time the shipment got to the main-line train it had already gone through four consolidations and two break-bulks, and the line-haul movement had not even begun. Small wonder that LCL service could not stand up to truck and air competition. The railroad is a very efficient carrier of volume traffic when consolidation and break-bulk can be minimized.

Water Terminal Activity

Fundamentally, the ship is a single-unit, individually operated vehicle like the truck or airplane. Like all vehicles, the terminal activity it requires is much simpler if it can be fully loaded with a single product, and in fact a high proportion of water transport trips are with cargoes of one or a few bulk products.

An outstanding characteristic of the cargo vessel is its relatively immense size. A river barge can handle a trainload or more of freight, and a modern ocean freighter of moderate size can carry three or four trainloads. When a vessel is used for a general cargo of mixed commodities, this size becomes a handicap because of the excessive consolidation and break-bulk required.

Traditionally, ocean ships have been stowed by hand. This is necessary to keep the load from shifting and to establish a safe center of gravity and center of buoyancy in the vessel. It requires preplanning of where each lot of cargo is to be placed in the ship. Typically, the transit sheds located on steamship piers have not been large enough to hold nearly as much cargo as do the vessels that the pier will accommodate. This means that receipt of inbound cargo must be planned to flow into the shed and across the pier as it is needed by the ship.

The situation is complicated by the fact that a ship that is loading outbound cargo usually must discharge inbound cargo either before or during the loading operation. Because this cargo has been hand-fitted and literally built into the vessel, it comes off the ship in a very mixed order and must be sorted to marks (that is, identified, matched to documentation, and tallied). Limited shed space adds to the inefficiency of the process.

Thus, because of size, the single-vehicle characteristic, which is an advantage to trucklines and airlines, is a detriment to marine transportation. The solution lies in somehow introducing the unit load concept and decentralizing the sorting activity away from where the vessel is loading. Inland water barge lines do this by delivering barges to scattered customers along the waterway for loading and then consolidating them into multi-barge tows for line-haul movement (very similar to the railroad-train concept). Modern deep-sea freighters are achieving the same thing through containerization.

Containerization

Although containerization is giving the water transportation vessel the advantages of the multi-unit vehicle, the exploitation of this new concept is not limited to water transportation. The term "container" may be somewhat misleading to the uninitiated because barrels and cartons and similar devices have been referred to as "shipping containers" for many years. Containerization, however, refers to the use of large uniform boxes or vans that function as detachable parts of transportation vehicles. Since they are considered as vehicles or parts of vehicles, the customer is not charged for the movement of their weight.

If a container could be developed that could be used by all modes of transport, we could develop a true intermodal transportation system. Shipments could be placed in a container at origin by the shipper, then transported over any combination of motor, rail, water, or air lines without handling of the cargo at junction points. Although much progress in containerization has been made by each mode, such standardization does not yet exist.

The common container used by truck lines and railroads is simply the well-known semi-trailer van. These become intermodal when used in rail piggyback service. Although these vans are adequate to protect shipments from the weather, a primary consideration in their construction is light weight and high cubic capacity rather than structural strength. The containers used by steamship companies look very much like truckline semi-trailers, but they are constructed to be lifted by their tops and to be stackable. Consequently, their tare weights are greater than those of truckline vehicles. A recent development in water transport containers has been the lighter-aboard-ship or LASH concept. LASH vessels carry small barges rather than standard truck-type containers; some LASH vessels carry both barges and truckable containers.

Airline containers are much smaller than those of the other modes. They are shaped to conform to the contours of the aircraft and are constructed of light materials such as canvas, fiber glass, or light metal. Also, very few commercial aircraft are capable of carrying rectangular land or water containers, and even then the high tare weight of the containers becomes an important limiting factor.

Some of the advantages of containerization may be summarized as follows:

1. The use of containers allows much faster turnaround time for expensive single-unit vehicles such as steamships and airplanes because containers can be loaded beforehand and time-consuming hand stowage is eliminated.

2. Pickup and delivery of containers by truck makes the street and highway network available to terminal-limited rail, water, and air modes, thus increasing their flexibility.

3. Shipping damage can be sharply reduced if the containers themselves are properly loaded.

4. Pilferage and other loss of cargo can be greatly reduced if the container is used in a true "store-door to store-door" manner.

Containerization, of course, also has disadvantages. These include the following:

1. Line-haul vehicles such as flatcars, container ships, and cargo planes must be specially adapted to carry containers. Also, expensive cranes and specialized lift trucks must be provided at all terminals where the containers are to be handled.

2. As with all line-haul vehicles, containers must be frequently hauled back to origin in an unloaded condition because no backhaul traffic is available for them.

3. Carriers must invest in thousands of containers to make them generally available, and are then faced with the problem of keeping track of their locations.

LINE-HAUL MOVEMENT

The term line-haul probably comes to us from rail transportation, where it referred to movement over the line after the train had cleared the terminal. It is also used in reference to shipment costs to indicate those costs that arise in moving the goods from origin to destination exclusive of terminal costs. With either meaning there are still some overlaps between terminal and line-haul activity.

Distinguishing between physical terminal and line-haul activity is sometimes difficult. For example, suppose that an over-the-road truck-trailer combination leaves a freight terminal in a large metropolitan area destined for a distant city. As the driver finds his way through congested streets to the main highway it could be said that he is still engaging in terminal activity. Another example is the transcontinental airliner that is forced to circle in a "stack" some time before there is room for it to land at a crowded airport.

Another kind of overlapping occurs because terminal activity for some shipments must affect the line-haul movement of others that are moving in the same vehicle or multi-vehicle. Previously, some reference has been made to the idea that the unit costs of transportation can be reduced if costs can be spread over a larger number of units. Thus, carriers typically offer lower rates per hundred pounds for large shipments than for small ones. Additionally, the costs per mile of transportation typically decrease as the total length of the journey increases and startup costs are amortized over more mileage units. Therefore, both carriers and shippers strive to consolidate shipments in any way that can reduce unit costs.

On the other hand, the ideal situation for both vehicles and shipments is for them to move directly from origin to destination as quickly as possible. This is not always compatible with the idea of consolidating goods into large lots to reduce unit costs. At least two alternative methods of such consolidation are possible; both affect the efficiency of line-haul service.

Holding for Volume

One method of building volume is to delay all shipments for a certain destination until sufficient volume has accumulated to justify a lower freight rate. Either a shipper or a carrier can do this, but it has a serious drawback: it cuts down schedule frequency. Usually customers at the other end of the line are not willing to postpone receipt of goods. Part of the service package that common carriers usually offer to the public is frequent, regular schedules. If carriers are to operate on the advertised timetable, the equipment must leave on schedule whether fully loaded or not.

Carriers overcome the difficulty of holding for volume by combining destinations. When volume is too little for frequent through-scheduling to a distant destination, they must include shipments for intermediate points along the way. Serving all the stops on one trip can produce enough revenue to justify the complete journey, but obviously it delays service to the most distant point. It also introduces the problem of progressive consolidation and break-bulk. At each stop along the line either equipment or cargo must be sorted out of the vehicle or consolidated into it.

Sorting En Route

With shipments that move in very small packages it is sometimes possible to incorporate some of the sorting that would ordinarily take place in the terminal into the line-haul. For many years in this country the Post Office and the Railway Express Agency had operations of this sort. Envelopes, parcels, and packages were pre-sorted at the origin terminal by route and direction only. Outbound shipments were then placed on railway Post Office cars or Railway Express cars staffed by traveling employees. These men then further sorted the mail or express so that the consignment for each station was ready when the train arrived there. Receipt of shipments at way points and further sorting for subsequent stations was, of course, also possible.

Trucks, airplanes, and ships carrying general cargo have similar sorting problems when loaded with cargo for each station along the route. They are so tightly stowed, however, that sorting en route is out of the question. Preplanning of stowage so that the first item that must come off is the last loaded is the most efficient solution. Truckloads and planeloads are often small enough so that operations are still conducted where the cargo is shuffled at each stop. This is time-consuming and causes excessive loss and damage. In traditional deep-sea transportation, the size of the vessel and the nature of the stowage makes preplanning mandatory. Changing the order of ports of call on an ocean voyage can have serious cost consequences, because the desired cargo cannot be reached until consignments for later ports are temporarily offloaded.

Here again, in the line-haul, the advantages of containerizing shipments become apparent. Containers holding individual shipments are stacked in the hold and on the deck of modern ocean-going vessels. When a container deep in the stack is needed for offloading, those around it can be moved quickly and stacked on another part of the ship. Containerization thus brings a characteristic of the railway train to the steamship—the ability to set out unit loads during the line-haul.

In the past, railroads did not always take advantage of this characteristic. Railroads are organized into geographical divisions of about a hundred miles, more or less, in length. When communications were not as good as at present, this was necessary so that a division superintendent could provide close control over what amounted to a small railroad company. Long-distance trains often left the origin terminal with cars for all way-points mixed helter-skelter in the train. On receiving the train, each division superintendent would order it into a classification yard, where the cars for his division would be sorted into delivery order and put onto the head end of the train. These were then switched off and delivered en route, and the next division would repeat the process. Today, when they cannot run a solid train straight through to destination, railroads engage in a practice known as "blocking." At origin, the cars are sorted by destination and the train is put together in destination blocks. Frequently, the cars for the first intermediate station are put nearest the engine so they may be switched off expeditiously.

Physical Constraints

In addition to the operational factors just discussed, there are inherent physical forces that affect the efficiency of line-haul movement. These are friction, gravity, and curvature; again, the different transport modes deal with them differently.

Friction. Friction is the resistance to relative motion of two surfaces in contact. It is most obvious in motor and rail transportation, where the wheel on the way is subject to rolling friction. A truck, however, has far more frictional resistance than a train; about 20 pounds of tractive effort per ton of weight are required to keep a motor truck rolling on a level surface. The required force for a railroad train is about 5 pounds per ton. The difference is due, of course, to the relative smoothness of the ways and to the large area of truck tire that touches the surface compared to the small surface of railroad wheel that does so.

The 5 pounds of force per ton required for the train compares favorably with the force required to keep an ocean vessel moving on calm, flat water. To increase the speed of a ship requires a greater increase in power than it does to speed up a train, however, because the pressure of the water builds up and holds the ship back. After a certain limit, each knot of increased speed demands so much more fuel that the cost becomes prohibitive. Speeds in excess of about 25 miles per hour for ocean freighters are presently considered uneconomic. Although the water an ocean liner operates upon is theoretically level, highways and railways never are, so trucks and locomotives need power resources to overcome the force of gravity as well as the resistance of the way.

Gravity. In air transportation, gravity is the major force the vehicle must overcome, and a very large proportion of its horsepower must be used for creating lift. In surface transportation, gravity appears in the form of grades. Gradient is expressed as the percentage that the rise from horizontal is of the length of the grade. Thus, a way that rises 2 feet in a run of 100 feet has a 2 percent grade. To climb a grade, a vehicle obviously requires more horsepower than to run on the level. Because of the relatively great friction between tire and road, a truck requires only a little more than twice as much tractive force to go up a 2 percent grade than to run on a horizontal surface. Because of lack of friction, a train requires five times as much.

So far, we have shown that both speeding up the vehicle and going up a grade require increased use of horsepower. Also, the typical highway, railway, or waterway is not level for very much of its length. Thus, an important effect of friction and gravity on the line-haul is that one cannot use both the entire pulling capacity and the entire speed capacity of a vehicle over the entire length of a journey. When a vehicle using all of its horsepower to haul a load on the level starts up a hill, it must reduce its speed. If the speed is to be maintained in spite of the increased resistance of gravity, horsepower must be increased. Because of this, railroad managers quickly learned that the most economical way to schedule trains is to construct the timetable so that they run as slowly as possible. In this way, the major proportion of the horsepower produced can be devoted to pulling tonnage rather than to creating speed.

Although oceans are theoretically flat, the effect of gravity appears in inland-water transportation in the form of current. Major rivers do not flow at the speed of mountain streams, but the force of the water is sufficient significantly to retard a tow-boat bound upstream. For instance, the typical transit time for a barge tow from Kansas City to New Orleans, a distance of 1,434 miles, is 11 days and 22 hours upstream and only 6 days downstream.

Even in inland water transportation, technology is solving the problem of gravity. With the exception of the lower Missis-sippi River and the Missouri River, our inland waterways are "slack-water routes." They have been improved for navigation by a system of dams and locks. The dams hold back the cur-rent and cause the river to "pool," perhaps as far back as the next dam upstream. Since there is very little current in the pool, the effect of gravity is overcome. At each dam there is a lock, which is, in effect, a marine elevator to raise or lower tows to the next level in the river.

Curvature.   Curves in the way also increase resistance to movement. Largely this is because centrifugal force tends to throw the vehicle to the outside of the curve, and speed must be reduced to prevent overturning. In rail transportation this lateral motion can produce substantial resistance because it makes the flanges of the outside wheels rub sharply against the inside of the rail.

In the early days of railway and highway construction, methods of moving earth were relatively primitive. This often necessitated the building of routes that were steep and circuitous. Because the technology of motive power was also crude, this meant that only comparatively small loads could be carried. Since the turn of the century, much progress has been made both in earth-moving equipment and in powerful transporta-tion engines. Modern highways and railways are being con-structed with minimum gradients and curvature at the same time that extremely powerful trucks and locomotives are ap-pearing to operate over them.

EFFECTS OF SPEED, VOLUME, AND DISTANCE

Usually, faster transportation is more expensive than slower methods. A ship needs 30 pounds of crude fuel oil to transport a ton of cargo across the Atlantic Ocean, whereas an airplane needs 4,000 pounds of aviation fuel to carry the same amount. Doubling the speed of a ship may cause it to burn four times as much fuel.

An indirect cost effect also arises when the design of a vehicle is changed to give it more speed. This requires a bigger power plant and room for more fuel, thus reducing payload capacity. Costs must then be shared over fewer revenue-earning units, which either reduces the profitability or requires a rate increase. Therefore, designers try to increase both speed and capacity when redesigning vehicles.

Technological improvement thus causes increases in the capacity, power, and speed of vehicles. If a greater increase can be made in capacity than in power and speed, more payload units can share in the total cost. Then the cost per unit to the user can be less, but only if the vehicle is filled to capacity. To encourage customers to fill transport vehicles to capacity, carriers set rates to attract large-volume shipments. As a general rule, the more weight that is shipped at one time, the less will be the rate per unit.

One can see that rates per unit decrease if costs can be shared among a greater number of payload units. A similar effect is seen in relation to distance and is called the "tapering principle of freight rates." Any journey requires a certain amount of effort to get it started and to terminate it. These are the activities of consolidation and break-bulk discussed above. On shipments of the same size, these startup costs and terminal costs are the same regardless of the length of the journey. Pickup, documentation, and loading costs are the same for a 500-pound shipment whether it goes a hundred miles or a thousand miles. However, on the longer distance, these costs can be spread over more mileage units. Thus, the cost per mile will be less on the long haul even though the cost per hundred pounds is more.

Summing up, one can see that the most efficient transportation is produced when terminal activities are made as simple as possible, when a reasonable volume of goods can be handled as a unit, and when there is as little interference or restriction in the line-haul as possible. It is still true that a straight line is the shortest distance between two points.

REFERENCES

Chandler, Alfred D., Jr. *The Railroads: The Nation's First Big Business*. New York: Harcourt Brace & World, 1965.

Grossman, William L. *Fundamentals of Transportation*. New York: Simmons-Boardman, 1959.

McDowell, Carl E., and Helen M. Gibbs. *Ocean Transportation*. New York: McGraw-Hill, 1954.

Oram, R. B. *Cargo Handling and the Modern Port*. London: Pergamon Press, 1965.

Roxbury, L. E. *Let's Operate a Railroad*. Warwick, Va.: High-Iron Publishers, 1957.

CHAPTER 3

The Development
of Transportation

The first chapter of this book described the five modes of transportation that make up the world's transportation system. These modes are familiar to everyone now, but 200 years ago most of them were unknown. Only in the last 70 years did the present complex system of carriers begin to develop. The purpose of this chapter is to describe this development, thus aiding in the understanding of route patterns and the evolution of carrier equipment.

STAGES OF TRANSPORTATION DEVELOPMENT

From the time of prehistoric man to the present, the improvement in means of transportation can be marked in stages. One classification describes these stages as human, animal, and machine. Primitive man's first vehicle was himself, or more probably his wife; when animals were domesticated they became the beasts of burden. Finally, with the Industrial Revolution, machines were invented which became our present vehicles.

A perhaps more sophisticated classification is to refer to the stages as primitive, transitional, and advanced. In the primitive stage, man uses a vehicle such as a horse or a floating log pretty much as he finds it in nature, and makes no effort to improve the way. In the transitional stage, he improves upon the vehicle—perhaps to a great extent as with a clipper ship— but still makes no improvement in the way. In the advanced stage, man improves both the vehicle and the way.

Whichever way one prefers to classify this development,

note should be taken that the different levels or stages of transport sophistication exist side by side in the world today. Also, frequently what appears to be a primitive form of transport may on closer inspection turn out to fit into the advanced category. The high development of the transportation of ancient Mexico is a case in point. In those days, the American continent, except for the llama of Peru, was devoid of animals suitable as beasts of burden. Mexico, however, was a successful commercial nation. Merchants traveled with trains of professional porters who belonged to a guild or association and also acted as soldiers when necessary. A network of improved foot-roads linked the parts of the empire. These were provided with bridges and kept in a good state of repair. According to our classifications, this high level of development makes this an example of the advanced stage of transport.

TRANSPORTATION ROUTES

Today, nearly all of our transportation facilities are in the advanced stage of development, with highly improved routes as well as vehicles. Through the years, our transport ways have been continually overhauled to reduce gradient and curvature, improve safety, and increase the speed and volume they can accommodate. Highways have been given limited access, railways have been equipped with continuous welded rail, and airways have been established through electronic traffic control. All these improvements cost money, but these additional costs are recovered from the increased traffic that can move.

Our highly sophisticated rights-of-way sometimes obscure the fact that main transportation routes tend to follow natural pathways over the earth's surface. The land is covered with barriers such as mountains, rivers, forests, and deserts which impede swift transportation. The history of route development has been a search for natural corridors that bypass these obstacles easily. Once found, the same natural routes are used by succeeding generations of modes and carriers. A case in point is the central route across the western United States. The easiest grades follow a path across the states of Nebraska, Wyoming, Utah, Nevada, and California. Attention was directed to this route before the Civil War as a possible way to tie California to the northern states of the union, and plans were made to build the Pacific Railroad along it. Development of the route was pioneered by the founders of the Pony Express, who set up a string of outposts across the country in 1861. Although their riders carried the mail for less than two years, they provided the fastest available communication and attracted people and traffic to the area. The Pony Express was soon supplanted by the telegraph, and, after the war, by the railroad in 1869. After the turn of the century, the same pathway became the "Columbia" route of the early airmail, eventually to be flown by United Airlines. Probably the last mode to adopt the route was the automobile, when in the 1920's the Lincoln Highway, now Interstate 80, was pushed through.

Ocean transportation and air transportation seem to present fewer obstacles to movement than do land routes. However, they have barriers of a different sort. In both modes, weather has been a serious handicap, although modern weather observation and forecasting have made it possible for sea and air carriers to be aware of difficult weather far enough in advance to avoid it.

A less obvious obstacle is the "hump" of the earth's curvature. To the casual observer of the world map, Tokyo, Japan, would seem to be due west of San Francisco. Yet ships and planes follow a "great-circle" route far to the north, nearly reaching the Aleutian Islands, in order to get to Japan. This is because the curving course they follow around the great circle is actually shorter than the hump of the earth on the line that runs straight west from California to Japan. Other great-circle routes, of course, can be plotted between other origins and destinations all around the globe.

Transportation and Cities

Cities thrive and develop for many reasons. Some were originally forts or military outposts, some are located near large mineral deposits, some become educational or religious centers, and some are political capitals. In most cases, however, the original site was probably selected, albeit unconsciously, for transportation reasons. Population and economic activity tend to develop where there is a break in transportation.

The most important urban developments tend to occur where a change of mode is necessary. Seaports are a good example of this. At a seaport, a complete transfer of goods must take place. Ships bring large cargoes, which must be sorted and consolidated into many new shipments to be sent out in various directions. Much commercial activity also develops because change of title to many of the goods becomes necessary.

Places where routes must concentrate or disperse also attract population. Examples are major river crossings and mountain passes. These features tend to funnel widespread cross-country routes together on one side and fan them out again on the other. An economic center tends to develop to exploit the concentration of traffic, provide service in preparation for crossing the river or mountain obstacle, and facilitate interchange between the converging routes.

Stopping places along routes can also cause towns to develop. Today this is most obvious in automobile transportation. Of auto drivers who cross the country on transcontinental highways there is a modal number who tend to drive about the same number of miles per day. Congregations of motel and restaurant facilities grow up at intervals along the routes to accommodate this traffic. An important factor in motel feasibility studies is the relationship of the projected location to the schedule pattern of automobiles using the route.

Of all the interruptions to transportation, a mere intersection of two routes is the least likely to produce urban growth unless one of the above factors is also present.

Significance of Route Location

Location on or near an important natural route can reduce shipping costs. This is because a route that is cheaper for a carrier to traverse should reflect lower costs to its customers. Small businesses often locate without regard to this principle, and then find they must pay for an additional feeder line-haul to obtain access to the major carriers serving the market in which they hope to deal.

Where one major mode of transport uses a natural pathway, other modes can be expected to be giving service also. In the past, this was perhaps not true of water transport on the high seas. Today, however, the airlines find it convenient to traverse essentially the same great-circle courses as ships.

The most direct routing and the fastest means of movement are possibly not the cheapest ways of getting from one point to another. Direct and speedy carriers may have had to invest much more in overcoming obstacles than have their competitors who follow the slow and meandering way. In fact, a practice in railroad rate-making allows the slow carrier between two given points to establish a differential rate. Such rates apply over inferior, circuitous routes and are made by deducting specific percentages or amounts from the rate applying over the standard, direct route. Although rare today, there are some in effect that apply over Canadian railroads between New England and the Midwest in competition with more direct American railroads.

Usually, highly advanced carriers who operate with complex vehicles over improved routes provide the cheapest transportation because they can allocate costs over the greater volume of units carried. This is not always true, however. Some advanced-stage carriers, such as modern airlines, are inherently low-volume modes. The technological means they have adopted of overcoming barriers results in a relatively low-capacity vehicular unit; therefore, the unit costs and prices of such carriers are higher than those of their slower competitors of greater volume. The adoption of larger aircraft such as the 747 is an effort to correct this situation. Although it is effective in passenger transport, it still, however, has major limitations in regard to cargo movement.

BEFORE THE INDUSTRIAL REVOLUTION

The change from primitive means of transportation to advanced forms required thousands of years. For perhaps 5,000 years prior to the Industrial Revolution, which occurred in Europe about 1800, man's transportation vehicles were mostly either of the primitive or the transitional type. Only two modes were used, road transport and water transport. The early historical development of these modes had important effects on the way the transportation industry later came to be organized.

Road Transport

The horse is probably one of the most useful vehicles man has ever adopted. It was used in almost completely primitive form from perhaps as early as 10,000 B.C. nearly up until the time mechanization of transport began. Auxiliary devices to improve the horse and make it a transitional vehicle were extremely slow to develop. The stirrup and the horseshoe appeared about the time of the fall of Rome (about 420 A.D.). A proper method of harnessing did not develop until use of the horse-collar spread through Europe between 900 and 1400 A.D.

Wheeled vehicles were also slow in development. Chariots were used as early as 3200 B.C., but even the Romans with their good roads were unable to master the problem of a steering axle for their stiff four-wheeled wagons. Better carriages awaited better technology; really good carriages and wagons did not develop until modern road-building methods were invented about 1800.

The first improved roads probably were those of the Persian Empire about 500 B.C. This system connected the capital city, the Persian Gulf, and the eastern end of the Mediterranean Sea. It accommodated a traffic of couriers on horseback, chariots, and camel caravans. The greatest early road system, of course, was that of the Romans. From about 30 B.C. to around 400 A.D. the Romans built 52 thousand miles of hard-surfaced highways around the Mediterranean and across Europe. They believed that a road needed plenty of foundation, so they started with a wide trench three or four feet deep, filled it with layers of masonry, and topped it with cobblestones. Such a road is reasonably durable, and some of them are still in existence today. However, during the Dark Ages they fell into disrepair and many were torn up. The significant thing about this is that by the time the Dark Ages were over, mankind had forgotten the art of building such roads, and there were no more good roads until after transportation became mechanized.

From 1500 to 1800 the roads of both Europe and eastern America were so bad that water transport was used wherever possible. Often the roads were continuous mudholes; they were so bad in England that from 1600 to 1650 wagons were banned from them altogether. When heavy iron steam vehicles came along in the late 1700's there were few roads for them to operate on. Railed ways laid on a series of pontoons or ties were an obvious method to keep iron wheels from burying themselves in soft ground. When steam vehicles were applied to railed ways, road transportation immediately moved into the advanced phase of transport development. Just before that, it had, at best, been in the transitional phase because of the lack of road-building expertise.

Water Transport

Although it was preferable to road travel, water transportation was not useful for long-distance movement until after 1400 because ships could not sail against the wind. Before 1450, Mediterranean and European ships were equipped with one mast on which was raised a single square sail. Such a sail could be turned slightly to one side or the other in order to take the wind from the side of the boat, but this simply made the craft move sideways through the water ahead of the wind. A long voyage of exploration could not be undertaken in such ships because there was no guarantee of getting back. Sailing ships were also useless as warships because of this lack of maneuverability.

The early Greeks used the galley to overcome these limitations of the sailing ship. Since it was propelled by oars, it could go anywhere, turn quickly, and outflank enemy ships. War galleys were usually equipped with a ram to puncture the sides of opposing vessels. Because of the slow development of sail, galleys were used on the Mediterranean as late as 1530. The Vikings, of course, had similar craft propelled by oars and made some long voyages of exploration in them. Oar-driven ships are, however, badly suited for long voyages or trade because the crews take up too much space and large amounts of supplies must be carried to feed them. A sailing ship has a much better horsepower-to-payload ratio, but it must be able to make one leg of the voyage against the wind if necessary.

About 1450 the Portuguese solved the wind problem with a ship called the caravel. These ships had three masts. When the sails were set to take wind from the side they balanced each other so that the ship kept running ahead rather than slipping off sideways. The ship could sail for some distance at a slight angle to a head wind and then swing the bow and sail for some distance into the wind again. Following such a zigzag course is known as "tacking." With this invention, ocean exploration and trade began on a far larger scale than ever before. However, there was no further significant improvement in the ship until the Industrial Revolution.

THE MECHANIZATION OF TRANSPORTATION

The year 1800 is a milestone in transportation history because it marks the middle of a period in which all modern transport modes became operational. They did not arrive full-blown at their present state of development, of course, but the inventions of that time made modern transport possible. In the early application of these inventions one can see the beginning of competition between the modes and carriers of modern transportation. Although much of the progress was due to the steam engine, many social and economic forces were at work that caused people to try to develop new methods of transportation. While the steam engine was finding its way to general use, many changes in transportation occurred, with one new invention and then another vying for supremacy. Some inventions had slight advantages of time or technology over others and promising new methods of transport failed to develop economically.

The Steam Engine

James Watt is usually given credit for inventing the first practical steam engine about the year 1789. His engine was not an original invention, however, but rather a significant improvement on an engine invented in 1698 by a man named Savery, modified by Newcomen in 1712, and much improved by others down through the years. The first transportation use of the steam engine was probably on a very crude version of the automobile. In 1769 Nicolas Cugnot built a lumbering road contraption he called a "fardier." Much more successful steam coaches were built in England, starting in 1801, by Richard Trevithick. Probably because the roads were so bad, little was done about the steam coach, and Trevithick turned his hand to railed-way locomotives, building the first operable one in 1807. In the meantime, the development of canals and railroads would delay the automobile for years; but roads were also being improved, which would eventually make it possible.

Canals. Before the steam engine became really useful, men devised another way radically to improve inland transportation. This was to dig canals across the country wherever possible. The canal movement had started in France in the 1600's, but gained real momentum in industrial England from circa 1759–1834. The canal age started a little later in the United States with the Erie Canal across upper New York State in 1817. Both England and the United States constructed very extensive systems of overland canals during this time. The canals usually had a depth of about 4 feet and a width of perhaps 20 to 30 feet; sizable vessels towed by horses carried large amounts of bulk cargo on them. Eventually the victims of railroad competition, today most of them are filled in.

Railroads. Many early steam engines in England were used to pump unwanted water out of coal mines. In the early 1800's George Stephenson was employed as a steam engineer in the mines. Coal was at that time hauled out of the mine in horse-drawn wagons operating on a tramway, which is a crude version of a railway. Stephenson undertook to pull the wagons by steam power, and in 1814 built a successful tramway locomotive. By 1825 he had masterminded the building of the Stockton and Darlington, the first railway in England. Railroads soon spread across England, and in 1830 the Baltimore and Ohio became the first line in the United States.

Roads. While others were inventing steam coaches and locomotives, a man named John Macadam was experimenting at making roads in Scotland. In 1827 he was made general surveyor of English roads and introduced a cheap but surprisingly efficient new method of road-building. Macadam's idea was that a road should be graded so that it is well drained and has a rounded crown. Then the surface should be covered with a layer of interlocking gravel bound together with a sprinkling of dust or earth. This type of construction, ensuring a dry, all-weather route, revolutionized the roads of England.

Regularly scheduled common carriers operating both horse-drawn and steam coaches appeared on these highways. The steam coaches reached a high level of sophistication, and by 1864 they traveled over 30 miles per hour. But it was too late for the steam coach: stagecoach lines, canals, and railways were already well established. Their promoters lobbied against the steamers, and the "Man and Flag Act" was passed, which limited steam coaches to 4 miles per hour and required a man with a red flag to go in front of them. This prevented the further development of the automobile in England until 1896, when the law was repealed.

Better roads began to appear in the United States also. The most significant was the National Pike. This road started at Cumberland, Maryland, the end of the Frederick Pike, and connected Washington and Baltimore with the West. (Later, Cumberland was also the western terminus of the Chesapeake and Ohio Canal, which originated at Georgetown.) The National Pike was built by the federal government, starting about 1815. Original specifications called for the road to be gravel spread over 15 inches of stone, but later sections were built to lower standards. By 1838 the road had reached Vandalia, Illinois. The main vehicles using the road were stage-coaches and Conestoga wagons. Traffic was exceptionally great, and some reported it to be as heavy as on the main street of a large town. Because of the growth of railroad transportation, the road fell into disuse in the last half of the nineteenth century. After the turn of the century it became part of U.S. Highway Number 40.

Steamships. Ships were another logical application for the steam engine, and about 1788 William Symington, another Scotsman, built the first one. An American visitor, Robert Fulton, later took a ride on Symington's second vessel and carried the idea to the United States, where he started a successful steamboat business in 1807.

Although iron was being extensively used on railroads and in other industries, shipbuilders did not use much of it until after 1840. Perhaps the greatest iron steamship builder was the most famous civil engineer of the early 1800's, Isambard Kingdom Brunel. Brunel built tunnels, railroads, bridges, and finally steamships. He built the *Great Western*, the first steamship designed for ocean crossings; she made the first legitimate ocean-liner crossing of the Atlantic in 1838. In 1843 he built the *Great Britain*, the first iron steamship and the first to use a propeller instead of paddle wheels. In 1858 he completed the *Great Eastern*, the largest ship in the world until the *Lusitania* was launched in 1906.

The adoption by the British of iron steamships had severe effects on the shipping industry of the United States. The golden age of American shipping was from 1800 to 1840, when the American-built clipper ship ruled the seas. The United States had hundreds of skilled craftsmen in small shipyards located close to excellent supplies of timber. These resources plus an excellent design made American ships the best in the world. However, the United States did not have men who could build iron ships, nor an iron industry, nor the money to start one. Thus, the American merchant marine lost out to the British and has never recovered.

Balloons and Airplanes

If the steam engine was almost too heavy for a road vehicle, it was certainly too great a load for an aircraft. Perhaps more than anything else, it was this lack of a suitable power plant that delayed the success of heavier-than-air flight for so long. However, there were noteworthy advances in aviation along with the great inventions in road, rail, and water transport.

Leonardo da Vinci, who lived about 1500, is sometimes called the father of modern flight. Although some people credit him with inventing the parachute and the helicopter, and perhaps the glider, Leonardo's main interest was in the ornithopter. Ornithopters are machines that imitate bird flight—and to the present, none has been made to work. For hundreds of years before Leonardo, men all over the world had been strapping various ornithopter contraptions on themselves and jumping off cliffs, towers, and buildings—with predictable results. After Leonardo, the experimentation became more scientific, but public attention to heavier-than-air flight was suddenly diverted by the intervention of the Balloon Age.

The first successful flight by man in an aircraft took place in 1783. In France, the Montgolfier brothers, who were papermakers, more or less accidentally discovered the hot-air balloon. The following year, two of their countrymen flew a hydrogen balloon. Much of the later experimentation with balloons took place in France, and during the 1800's many successful elongated balloons (similar to blimps) were flown. The rigid balloon, or dirigible, was invented in Austria in 1897. By 1914, Count von Zeppelin in Germany had built five dirigibles and had flown about 35 thousand passengers in a successful operation. Dirigibles were used by the Germans in World War I, and after the war the U.S. Navy built and operated dirigibles until three of them were lost in severe weather. Zeppelin operated two airships, the *Graf Zeppelin* and the *Hindenburg*, in transatlantic passenger service until the *Hindenburg* blew up in 1937. This accident marked the effective end of the Balloon Age. In 1974 some engineers recommended that the dirigible should be reconsidered. They pointed out that since 1937 development of transistors, computers, and light metals have made dirigible construction and operation practical. They also stated that helium could be used safely instead of hydrogen.

While balloons were providing a practical way to fly and even developing some commercial possibilities, experimentation with heavier-than-air flight continued rather quietly. It began when Sir George Cayley invented the airplane in 1804, 99 years before the Wright brothers would make it practical. Cayley, a scholarly English baronet, was relatively unknown until recently and was the first man to approach heavier-than-air flight in a truly scientific manner. He designed and flew model and full-size gliders in 1804, 1809, and 1853. Since he recorded the results of his experiments, they were used as the foundation for research by others. Cayley was followed by a number of scientific experimenters including Henson, Stringfellow, Hargrave, Lilienthal, Chanute, Langley, and, of course, the Wright brothers. After the Wright brothers, commercial aviation developed swiftly, and in the United States, only 15 years after their achievement of 1903, the airmail service of the U.S. Post Office began in 1918.

Pipelines

Although the Chinese supposedly transported natural gas through bamboo tubes as long as a thousand years ago, the history of pipelines is not as colorful as that of the other modes. The first successful commercial oil pipeline began operation in Pennsylvania in 1865 in response to the transport demands of the newly established petroleum industry. Part of the reason for the utilization of petroleum was the demand by the steam engines of the transportation industry for better lubricants.

In turn, the supply of these lubricants and related petroleum products created a demand for a new form of transportation. At first, petroleum was hauled away from the producing wells in barrels by mules and wagons at a very high transportation cost. In 1865, Samuel Van Syckel finally solved some tricky leakage and pumping problems and built a pipeline 2 inches in diameter which ran for 6 miles to bring oil from the field to a railhead. This was the start of the pipeline industry.

EFFECTS OF MECHANIZATION

With the advent of the pipeline in 1865, all of our modern modes of transport except one had come into being. The exception was automotive transportation; this and practical air transportation had to await the light-weight, internal-combustion engine. However, regardless of the potential competition of other mechanized modes, railroads became the dominant method of movement at this time.

REFERENCES

Burke, J. L. "Oil Pipelines' Place in the Transportation Industry." *I.C.C. Practitioners' Journal*, April 1964.

Cooley, Charles H. "The Theory of Transportation." *Publications of the American Economic Association*, vol. 9, no. 3 (May 1894).

Dugan, James. *The Great Iron Ship*. New York: Harper & Bros., 1963.

Fabre, Maurice. *A History of Land Transportation*. New York: Hawthorn Books, 1963.

Gibbs-Smith, Charles H. *The Aeroplane*. London: Her Majesty's Stationery Office, 1960.

Lee, Norman E. *Travel and Transport through the Ages*. Cambridge: Cambridge University Press, 1951.

Locklin, D. Philip. *Economics of Transportation*, 7th ed. Homewood, Ill.: Richard D. Irwin, 1972.

Sampson, Roy J., and Martin T. Farris. *Domestic Transportation*. Boston: Houghton Mifflin, 1971.

Taylor, George Rogers. *The Transportation Revolution*. New York: Rinehart, 1951.

CHAPTER 4

The Transportation Buyer

Previous chapters have introduced the terminology of commercial transportation and made the reader aware of some of the problems of providing it. The purpose of this chapter is to discuss from an overall viewpoint the personnel, activities, and relationships involved in buying and using transportation. Each subsequent chapter then gives the specific details of each aspect of this job.

WHO IS THE TRANSPORTATION BUYER?

Everyone who directly purchases commercial transportation is, of course, a transportation buyer. Many companies, mostly small ones but even some large ones, fail to recognize that they are buying transportation every time they order supplies, raw materials, parts, or products for resale. The vendors of many products arrange for delivery to the buyer, who pays just one lump-sum price for what he gets. Whether the buyer realizes it or not, the cost of transportation is included in the price. Therefore, many people are indirect transportation buyers without knowing it.

The activity of buying transport service is often referred to as *traffic management*. Whether the person who does this work is called a traffic manager or not is immaterial; traffic management is a handy term for referring to an activity that nearly every company must perform or have done for it. An efficient transportation buyer works toward the goal of obtaining the best possible transportation at the lowest price, consistent with his company's needs.

In a randomly selected company, the person who buys transportation might be found almost anywhere in the organization structure. In a small company it might be the boss; in another it might be the purchasing agent, shipping foreman, or sales manager. In any company there are certain activities that must interlock to produce a flow of goods through the firm. An illustration of how these activities work together provides a better understanding of the importance of the transportation function.

THE PLACE OF TRANSPORTATION IN THE BUYER'S ACTIVITIES

Every company produces something: a product, a service, or a service affecting a product. Companies producing only services use transportation somewhat differently from those producing products, so they are not considered here. Product companies range from manufacturers who create something from scratch to retailers who shelve products for sale without altering them. Three broad activities must take place in any product-oriented concern: procurement, some kind of processing, and distribution. Figure 1 shows the interrelated activities that are necessary to move goods through a hypothetical manufacturing organization. The same scheme could apply to a wholesaler or a retailer if one simply consolidated the receiving-and-stores, the production, and the finished-goods inventory activities into an "inventory-processing" activity. The activities shown in Figure 1 are more fully explained below:

Production control, a subsection of Production, schedules what will be produced and determines what materials will be needed. These are requisitioned from the purchasing activity.

Purchasing activity contacts vendors who can supply the needed materials and, when buying them, confers with traffic activity to determine proper shipping procedure.

Traffic activity selects best method of moving products procured by purchasing activity and arranges for proper receipt by receiving and stores.

Receiving and stores receives inbound goods, exercises necessary inventory control, and moves goods to where needed by production activity.

Production activity engages in fabrication, assembly, or other

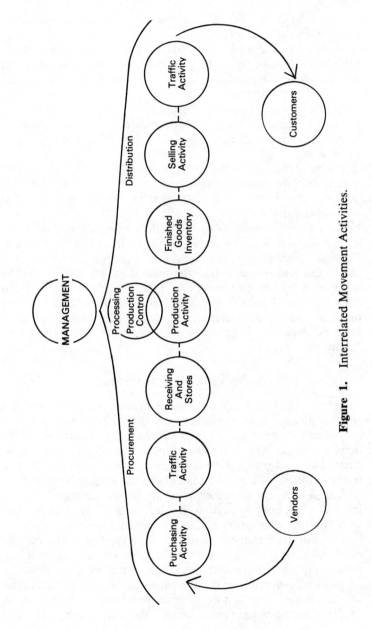

Figure 1. Interrelated Movement Activities.

45

processes to create the finished product, and then releases it to finished-goods inventory.

Finished-goods inventory holds the finished product pending sale to customers by selling activity, and performs physical activity of sending out shipments in response to orders from selling or traffic activity.

Selling activity assesses, stimulates, or creates demand for finished product and engages in transferring title to customers. It confers with traffic activity to determine proper shipping procedure.

Traffic activity determines the best method of movement and purchases or provides transportation and arranges with finished-goods inventory for release of goods and outloading on transport equipment.

Note that transportation as "traffic" activities appear twice in the material flow—both in procurement and in distribution. Depending upon how the company is organized and where the talent and interest for it lies, the transportation activity can be taken over by any of the other activities or departments listed above. Successful firms often find that this important function produces the most efficient result when it is centralized in a separate department, however. Usually this is called the traffic department.

THE TRAFFIC DEPARTMENT

Before going on to discuss the industrial traffic department, we should note here parenthetically that the term "traffic department" has several meanings. In the case of carriers, traffic departments are the sales departments of the transportation companies, and they handle not only sales but rate-making. The traffic manager of a railroad is akin to the sales manager of an industrial firm. On the other hand, the traffic manager of some trucklines has nothing to do with sales; he is the chief dispatcher who controls movement of the equipment over the road.

The industrial traffic department—the type of traffic department with which this chapter is concerned—is essentially a purchasing department that specializes in buying transportation. In principle, procurement of transportation for an industrial or commercial firm is the same as purchasing raw materials, supplies, products for resale, or anything else a company uses.

In practice, buying transportation may require a little more follow-up and control than buying goods. When goods are ordered and received they can be checked to see if the right thing has been provided. Transportation is less tangible, and much of what the buyer gets he never sees at all. The transportation carrier is serving not only its direct customer but the final receiver of the goods as well. The user of transport service must depend on the carrier to complete the production of whatever he himself offers to the public for sale. This leads to a consideration of the way traffic managers evaluate the performance of the carriers from whom they obtain service.

Evaluation of Performance

A well-run traffic department will evaluate the quality of the transportation service it buys on the basis of several criteria. The important ones are price, time, condition, and consistency. The ultimate in transportation control is for the department to set up a master control sheet for each carrier from whom it buys service. For each shipment a file of documents is set up containing papers such as a copy of the purchase order, the original bill of lading, tracing reports, receiving reports, and consignee's copy of the freight bill. Information from these is entered on the master control sheet, and in this way the carrier's overall performance can from time to time be evaluated objectively. Each element of the performance must also be evaluated independently of the others.

Price. In the United States, the freight rate tariffs of common carriers have the force of law: only the published rate is the legal rate. Since tariffs are complex, carriers make errors in finding the right rate to charge. Therefore, auditing of their freight bills is essential. This means traffic departments must have sets of freight rate tariffs or "farm the bills out" to an independent auditor who does. In "preauditing," bills are checked and corrected before payment. In "postauditing" they are checked afterward and overcharge claims are filed with the carrier.

Time. Most carriers advertise a certain time-in-transit between the points they serve. Frequently the advertised time is a bit optimistic and is based on the assumption that nothing will go wrong on the journey. Realistic transportation buyers recognize this discrepancy between advertised time and "delivered" time when setting up time-in-transit checks on shipments. An important factor is whether the delivered time-in-transit is reasonable considering the price that has been paid for transportation.

Condition.   When a shipment is lost or damaged, transportation is useless. Therefore, regardless of how high or low the freight rate, or how fast or slow the delivery time, the shipment must always arrive in good condition. Rough handling should be one of the strongest reasons to find a new carrier alternative.

Consistency.   A perhaps less obvious criterion is consistency. For instance, the traffic manager may deliberately select a slow carrier because the price is lower. Or he may select a fast, expensive mode because a warehouse can be eliminated and the expenses of inventory minimized. Whatever he does will probably affect the operation of the whole company. Because of this, he is extremely interested in having the same standard of service from the transportation carrier every day. Logically, one would not want service to get worse, but there are carefully planned situations in which a speedup of carrier service could be just as detrimental as a slowdown. Therefore, consistency is important.

Other factors.   Although the above factors are usually the most important, other considerations may come into play, such as the availability of the carriers in a certain geographic area. Type, size, and availability of equipment is important. The extra service the carrier can provide, such as heavy-lift crane service or Sunday and holiday delivery, may be another factor. The modern traffic manager makes his buying decision based on a combination of the factors important to him. He establishes priorities and trades off one factor against another.

Day-to-Day Duties of the Traffic Manager

In a small firm, the traffic manager may be a single clerk who types documents and makes telephone calls to carriers to order service and trace lost shipments. In a very large firm, the traffic department may be headed by a vice-president, have many employees, and be decentralized from coast to coast. In any case, certain day-to-day physical activities and procedures must be performed. A discussion of these serves as an introduction to the subsequent chapters of this book, each of which deals with a specific aspect of transportation service.

Making outside contacts. The traffic department has two major sets of outside contacts that fit it usefully into the material-flow pattern of the company. It must relate to other departments of the firm and it must interview carrier salesmen.

Contacts with other departments of the firm are for the purpose of finding out what is wanted in the way of transport service and for adjusting other operations of the firm to fit them to what can be provided. The first is reasonably easy because other departments will make their desires known. For the second to happen, interdepartmental relationships must be extremely good. This means that the traffic manager must be intelligent, thoroughly familiar with what the rest of the company is doing, and also accepted, trusted, and liked by the other executives.

Interviewing salesmen is not so high-level a managerial operation as relating to other departments, but it is important. Transportation salesmen are very much like the industrial salesmen who call upon the purchasing departments of business firms. As a group, however, they are probably not as well trained or as well informed as industrial salesmen generally. They can be an important point of contact between the shipper and the carrier. The traffic manager can make good use of carrier salesmen if he will take the initiative in directing them to get the information he desires. Freight salesmen often do not occupy a position of much prestige in the carrier organizations they work for. Because of this, the carrier operating departments frequently ignore requests the salesmen make for service to a customer. When this occurs, the industrial traffic manager can often improve the situation both for himself and the salesman by dealing with the salesman's supervisor in the carrier organization.

Selecting mode, carrier, and routing. Once the information as to what transportation is needed and what can be provided is at hand, the traffic department begins the shipping process. The first step is to decide which mode can best provide the needed service. Within the mode, the performance of the various competing carriers must be compared and one selected. In some means of transport, the shipper has one more choice even after the carrier is selected, and that is the choice of the exact physical route the shipment will follow. The rate charged may depend upon selection of a particular route.

Determining the rate.   Since shipping alternatives are evaluated on the basis of price, the transportation buyer must know what the rates are. In a small company shipping a few commodities, this probably can be done by telephoning the carriers' rate clerks and recording the results on a simple rate sheet. In complex operations, the best course frequently is for the traffic department to subscribe to the necessary freight rate tariffs and employ their own rate clerks to look up necessary rates. Because of the complexity of rate tariffs and the volume of shipments moving, rate errors by carriers are common. Therefore, after a shipment has moved, much can be saved by auditing the freight bill presented for payment to make sure the proper rate has been charged. As stated previously, some companies hire outside consultants and freight-bill auditors to aid them with rate checking.

Making the contract.   Shipments via common carrier are covered by a document called the *bill of lading*. This is a receipt, an indication of interest in title to the goods, and a contract between the shipper and carrier. Since the bill of lading stipulates what the carrier will be liable for in case of loss or damage, it is important for the transportation buyer to understand what he is signing when this document is executed.

Making the shipment.   Getting the goods actually on the way in carrier service involves physical activity, which usually is performed by the shipping department rather than the traffic department. This includes packing, loading, and ordering service. All must be done properly to ensure protection of the shipment and to avoid penalties for delay. Knowledgeable orientation and supervision can improve efficiency. Closely related is the matter of tracing and expediting shipments while they are in the hands of the carrier. Proper follow-up by the shipper while the goods are en route can prevent carrier routing mistakes and decrease time in transit.

Remedial activities. Corrective actions by the traffic department consist largely of filing claims against the carrier because he has violated the shipping contract in one way or another. The auditing of freight bills, previously discussed, may necessitate the preparation of overcharge claims. Claims for loss, damage, and delay are filed when the carrier is at fault. In addition, some freight rates may be in violation of the regulatory laws and call for action before regulatory agencies. Also there is the matter of seeking more favorable rates for the movement of the company's product.

Concern with regulation. For-hire transportation in the United States is regulated by both the state and federal governments. Where necessary, the government supports and encourages transportation, but in order to protect the public, carriers are also subject to safety regulations and stringent economic regulations. For instance, rate-making is carefully supervised, and the same services and privileges must be made available to all customers. Procedures have been set up by which shippers may officially complain about carriers who violate the law. Familiarity with these procedures is essential to the traffic man.

The government also imposes penalties for law violations on the part of the shipper. A customer who accepts a rate rebate or kickback from a carrier is liable for a heavy fine right along with the carrier. The leasing of trucks is carefully controlled to prevent illegal for-hire transportation. An industrial company that provides its own private transportation cannot sell transportation to others. Traffic managers must also understand these rulings in order to avoid breaking the law.

BUSINESS LOGISTICS AND PHYSICAL DISTRIBUTION

Logistics is a term borrowed from the army, who borrowed it from the French. It means "the science of supply." Business logistics, therefore, refers to the science of business supply. At first it could have been considered a little broader in meaning than "physical distribution" because business logistics included the activities of getting raw materials and supplies into the business as well as those connected with getting finished products out. But today, the meaning of "physical-distribution management" has been broadened to include the same things.

The term "physical distribution" originally referred to all of the activities necessary to distribute a product from point of manufacture to point of sale. It arose when traffic men and marketing men recognized that activities like selling, storing, shipping, and transporting are not isolated acts but are all part of a chain of related events that must occur to get a product into the hands of the consumer. This chain of events makes up a physical distribution system, and the best way to run a physical distribution system is so that it produces the best results at the lowest total cost.

Physical-distribution management and business logistics are popular topics of discussion in transportation and traffic circles. They are essentially the same thing. Both recognize the importance of the systems concept and the total-cost concept in the way a company solves its transportation and distribution problems.

The Systems Concept

The systems concept can be stated thus: if you set up a process to achieve a certain objective, the steps in that process are related and form a system. The activity of one step is directly related to and dependent upon the activities of the steps on both sides of it in the chain. In the past, managers of individual departments (like the traffic department) have tried to run their own operations without caring too much about their effect on other departments. The systems concept gets away from this and tries to get the different department managers to integrate their operations.

The Total-Cost Concept

The total-cost concept fits in with the systems concept because it appraises each step in a process according to the effect it has on the total cost of the whole process. No single step in a process should be cheapened if it increases the total cost of the process. On the other hand, maybe more can be spent on improving some step if that eliminates other costly steps altogether. For instance, the traffic department should not ship in volume lots to get a lower freight rate if the receiving-and-stores department has to rent additional warehouse space to store the material. But, the use of expensive air freight may be justified instead of rail movement if the faster movement will allow the elimination of warehouses and bring in more business through better service.

EFFECTIVE TRANSPORTATION BUYING

In many modern firms, transportation buyers and traffic managers work for a vice-president of physical distribution or are members of a logistics team or a logistics task-force. Transportation buying has become part of a group distribution effort that includes purchasing, warehousing and warehouse location, packaging, inventory management and control, perhaps marketing and sales personnel, and any other related activities that are pertinent in the given situation.

Regardless of whether the transport buyer is a clerk in a small firm or an executive in a large traffic department, effective purchasing of transportation requires initiative, imagination, and resourcefulness. Initiative involves taking the first step and not relying upon outside agencies to provide consistently perfect service. Much is to be gained by "getting on the ground" where the operation is taking place and noting where improvements can be made. Imagination and resourcefulness are often required to discover or create transportation alternatives to solve distribution problems. If the transportation buyer is to obtain the best-possible transportation at the lowest price consistent with his company's needs, he should adopt as his motto "there must be a better way."

The services of the five basic transport modes are well known, but some of the ways in which they can be used are not. In addition, innovations in using transportation services are frequently developed. The next several chapters set forth the standard shipping alternatives as well as some that are not so obvious to the public. They show that new ways of using transport services are always possible and that the professional transportation buyer should strive to develop them when appropriate.

REFERENCES

Bowersox, Donald J., Edward W. Smykay, and Bernard J. LaLonde. *Physical Distribution Management*. New York: Macmillan, 1968.

Colton, Richard C., and Edmund S. Ward. *Practical Handbook of Industrial Traffic Management*. Washington, D.C.: The Traffic Service Corp., 1965.

Heskett, J. L., Robert M. Ivie, and Nicholas A. Glaskowsky, Jr. *Business Logistics*. New York: Ronald Press, 1964.

McElhiney, Paul T., and Charles L. Hilton. *Introduction to Logistics and Traffic Management*. Dubuque: Wm. C. Brown, 1968.

McElhiney, Paul T., and Henry S. Ang. editors. *How Marketing Works: Practical Readings*. Dubuque: Kendall-Hunt, 1971.

CHAPTER 5

Railroads and
Related Services

The purpose of this chapter is to discuss briefly the development and scope of the American railway system. Railroad services that are available to the public are described, as well as related services that have developed from them.

HISTORICAL BACKGROUND

Railways became the mainstay of American transportation soon after the establishment of the Baltimore and Ohio Railroad in 1830. The first railroads were built to serve the local needs of seaports or inland cities that were trade centers. The merchants of leading cities encouraged the building of lines that would widen their own market areas but would not benefit neighboring trade centers. Therefore, each city along the Atlantic coast (and to some extent inland cities as well) deliberately selected a track gauge different from its neighbors to prevent rail cars from going to another port.

Track gauge is the distance between the inside of the rails. Today, most of the rail mileage is laid in "standard" or "English" gauge, which is 4 feet 8½ inches between the rails. Four feet 8½ inches has been the distance between wagon wheels since wheeled vehicles were invented before the time of Christ. It was the gauge of English coal wagons when Stephenson's first engine was built, and it became the gauge of the thousands of British locomotives that were exported to other countries. When Isambard Kingdom Brunel built the Great Western Railway he used a 7-foot gauge to give the equipment a better center of gravity. But because wide-gauge railroads are more expensive to build than narrow ones, other railroad developers appealed to Parliament, which passed a law that all British railways would have a 4 foot 8½ inch gauge. Some countries have established a different gauge, like Russia's 5-foot width, to make military invasion difficult. Others, like India, are hampered by having two or more gauges, so that all of their lines do not interconnect. The latter situation was what the United States faced until the Civil War. As late as 1861, a little under 18,000 miles of the American system, or 53 percent, was standard gauge. The rest was divided up among gauges of 4 feet 9¼ inches, 4 feet 10 inches, 5 feet, 5 feet 4 inches, 5 feet 6 inches, and 6 feet.

Building a Network

The Civil War changed the economic pattern of the United States from a pattern of partially isolated sub-economies into a national one in which whole regions interchanged products with one another. This demanded uniform long-distance transportation. Financiers moved to provide it because they could make fortunes in merging existing railroads and building new lines. The methods used were usually unethical. However, the railroads were America's first big business, and their owners and managers were the first businessmen to solve modern problems of management, accounting, finance, labor relations, and technology.

As railroad promoters merged lines, they changed them to standard gauge, and by 1886 most of the railroads of the North were standard. In that year the South changed the gauge of all its lines to 4 feet 9 inches, which made limited interchange of equipment possible. By 1900 all major lines were standard gauge, and total mileage had grown from the 23 miles of 1830 to 190,000 miles.

Many other developments were necessary to convert a collection of diverse railroads into the cooperative system of lines we have today. Among these were interline agreements and through bills of lading, uniform automatic couplers, uniform automatic air brakes. The meeting of schedules demanded uniform time, and so the railroads developed the system of standard time that we all use today.

World War I

The American railroad system reached a peak of 254,000 miles of line in 1916. Since then, route length has been contracted to the present 205,000 miles. The period of World War I represented a turning point in railroad development. Several factors were responsible, most importantly regulation and competition.

Regulation. Until the Civil War there was little reason for the federal government to regulate the business relations of the railroads and their customers. Rail lines were local in scope, and their novelty and superiority to other modes made them popular with the public. However, when financial promoters began to merge the lines into systems, railroad management began to show tendencies to make secret deals with big customers, to overcharge little ones, and to be generally indifferent to those injured either economically or physically by rail inefficiency and accidents. Because of the disregard of railroad promoters for the public interest, Congress finally placed railroads under economic regulation in 1887 by creating the Interstate Commerce Commission.

The original Act to Regulate Commerce required railroad rates to be reasonable, prohibited secret rebates to favored customers, made it illegal to charge more for a short haul than for a long haul, and required railroads to publish their rates and to actually use the published rates for all customers. Unfortunately, the Act gave very little power to the Commission, and so the railroads largely ignored it and the new law for some years. For the next 30 years the Interstate Commerce Act (and thereby the Commission) was strengthened by frequent amendments.

By 1910 the relationship of the railroad to its customers had changed substantially. The Interstate Commerce Commission had jurisdiction over not only railroads but express companies, sleeping-car companies, industrial railroads, private-car lines, pipelines, and, for a time, telephone and telegraph companies. Shippers had the power to specify over what combination of lines their goods would move. The railroads were required to issue bills of lading to customers and to be liable (with rare exceptions) for the full actual value of the cargo. Railroads were required to make physical connections with each other and with steamship lines and were prohibited from purchasing steamship companies to eliminate competition and also from operating ships through the Panama Canal. A 30-day public notification was required before rates could be changed. Carriers were emphatically prohibited from charging more for a short haul than for a long haul. The Commission could say what the maximum rate would be or determine if a rate were reasonable. The Commission could award reparations, which is a refunding of the unreasonable portion of a rate unlawfully charged in the past. It could investigate rates upon its own initiative without waiting for some customer to complain. The railroads were also required to keep uniform accounting records so that the Commission could see what was going on. Prices and costs were rising during the period preceeding the first World War, but the Commission tenaciously held rail rates down, which did not improve earnings. In addition, railroad investment ability was sharply reduced because large amounts of cash were siphoned off in the form of reparations to customers who had been overcharged. These economic events set the stage for government management of railroads during the war.

The outbreak of war in Europe in 1914 caused a tremendous increase in the movement of freight traffic in the United States. The railroads were eager to move this traffic, as the charges were paid as soon as the goods were loaded on the cars. The major movement was through a few East-Coast ports. Because of sinkings by submarines in the Atlantic, there were soon not enough ships to move all of the material that had been loaded upon freight cars. The result was that large parts of the eastern rail system became devoted to storage rather than to transportation.

To improve efficiency of movement, Congress authorized President Wilson to place the railroads under federal control in 1917. For 26 months, Director-General William G. McAdoo operated all the railways as one system. When the roads were returned to private ownership in 1920, Congress recognized the economic difficulty of the railroads and tailored subsequent regulation to help the carriers as well as to control them.

Competition.   Although railroads did not fully realize it until after the Second World War, competition was another factor forcing a turning point in their growth. Between 1900 and 1920, three fledgling competitors appeared. Although all transport modes were technically operational in the 1800's, the advantages of railroad transport had prevented wide commercial development of them. However, about 1910 the federal government decided to develop the inland rivers as waterways. An important reason for this was to provide another mode of transportation, which would give the railroads some competition and help to hold rail rates down. Then in 1916 the first federal-aid highway legislation was passed, which eventually provided a right-of-way for automotive transport. In 1918 the federal government, through the Post Office, started a government-owned airmail service which developed into the airline industry. The building of crude-oil pipelines began in the 1880's, and product lines for delivery of the light petroleum products leaving refineries began in 1930.

American railroad management has never adjusted fully to the impact of the competition from the four new modes that appeared between 1900 and 1950. This has been due to many factors. Until recently, managers of railway companies were well trained in railroading but not very conversant with modern ideas of accounting, marketing, or business economics. Thus, technical innovation to meet changing demand was not great in the rail industry. The attitude of the Interstate Commerce Commission has seldom been one that encouraged innovation, especially in the area of rate-making. This has resulted in practices that fail to exploit the advantages railways have to offer.

For instance, the principal advantage of rail over truck or airplane modes lies in the size and weight of the shipments railroads can carry. Yet, until recently, the rails have offered no greater incentive for heavy loading than have the truck lines. In addition, until recently the Interstate Commerce Commission has been reluctant to permit the establishment of rates that motivate the customer to load out a multi-car consignment or a trainload.

OUTLOOK UNDER COMPETITIVE CONDITIONS

The competitive situation presents a picture that seems paradoxical to some. The quality of railroad management has been improving greatly in recent years, and many innovations are being made. Many rail lines provide the customer with up-to-date equipment, sort cars in ultra-modern hump yards, and provide instantaneous, computerized car tracing. As can be expected in our growing economy, railroads carry more freight volume today than ever before—744 billion ton-miles in 1971 as against 454 billion in 1929. But, as might also be expected, with the increase in competitive modes, the rail share of the market has declined drastically—from 75 percent of all freight ton-miles in 1929 to only 39 percent in 1971.

Unfortunately, the 36-percent share of total traffic that the rails have lost since the 1920's represents substantial high-revenue business. Thus, the return on investment of United States railways as a group has declined drastically along with share of the market. In 1929, the relationship of net railway operating income to net investment in transportation property produced a rate of return of 5.3 percent, but in the years 1969, 1970, and 1971 return on investment averaged about 2.2 percent.

The paradox of course, is that even in the face of such a low return the railroad system represents many instances of innovation and improvement. The explanation includes at least two factors. First, the 2.2 return on investment figure is an average of the income figures of 71 Class I railroads, so that some had a better three-year average return than 2.2 and some had a worse one.

It should be noted parenthetically at this point that Class I railroads operate approximately 95 percent of the total railroad mileage of the United States, and earn about 96 percent of the operating revenues of all line-haul railroads. Operating railroads are classified by the Interstate Commerce Commission according to the amount of their annual operating revenues. Prior to January 1, 1956, the Interstate Commerce Commission classified railroad operating companies (including switching and terminal companies) into three groups for statistical purposes— Class I, annual operating revenue above $1,000,000; Class II, from $100,000 to $1,000,000; and Class III, annual operating revenues below $100,000. Effective January 1, 1956, railroads were reclassified into two groups—Class I, those having annual operating revenues of $3,000,000 or more; and Class II, those having operating revenues of less than $3,000,000 a year. Effective January 1, 1965, the point of distinction between Class I and Class II railroads was raised to $5,000,000. There were 71 Class I railroads at the close of 1970. Including Class II and Class III roads there are about 350 line-haul companies as well as many terminal railroads and non-operating railroad companies.

Secondly, the fact that some railroads are innovating is misleading. The modernization that is taking place is effective in producing better service, but it is not extensive because the entire railroad plant is shrinking. Low return upon investment makes railroad securities unattractive in the market, and therefore money for improvements must come from retained income. Obviously, with low income, not nearly enough can be retained to rejuvenate the entire system of a railroad. Therefore, management tends to rejuvenate those portions of the railroad that are producing a profit. Because there is no money to do it, no attempt is made to upgrade unprofitable parts of the system with a view to making them competitive and profitable. On the contrary, railroad managers usually seek to abandon branches that are marginal or operating at a loss. This is a major reason for the decline of rail mileage noted earlier. Some industry officials predict that tens of thousands of miles of track will be abandoned until we have a total system of only about 100,000 miles. This shrinkage is the inevitable result of continued low return on investment in the rail industry. It will work economic hardship upon localities where service is discontinued and upon consumers who must eventually pay the price of higher-cost transport forms.

Government ownership of railroads is not a popular transport investment alternative in the United States. Opponents of government rail ownership allege that the government could not operate the railroads profitably. Apparently, profitable operation is also difficult for private enterprise. The social cost of having the government operate the railroads, however, might be less than the social cost of shrinking the system by 50 percent as seems to be the current trend.

MODERN RAILROAD PASSENGER SERVICE

Since their beginning, railroads have been combination carriers. That is, they have carried both goods and passengers, although the common practice is for them to use separate trains of different types to do it. In recent years, the importance of good management of the physical distribution of goods has turned the attention of business and marketing students away from passenger transport and toward the movement of freight. Therefore, the main thrust of this book deals with freight traffic. Recent developments in rail passenger traffic deserve some comment, however.

As was shown in Table 1 of Chapter 1, 87 percent of the passenger-miles in the United States are generated by private automobile. Among commercial carriers alone, airlines account for 72 percent of the passenger-miles produced. Rail participation has slipped from 24 billion non-commuter passenger-miles in 1929 to only 2.5 billion non-commuter passenger-miles produced in 1971. (Commuter traffic has held steady at about 4.5 billion passenger-miles for 20 years.)

Under accounting rules prescribed by the Interstate Commerce Commission, railroad operating revenues and expenses are separated between freight and passenger service so as to develop a net railway operating income for each service. The result of the separation has been to show a deficit from passenger service every year since 1945. In 1970, the passenger deficit of the Class I roads reached $470 million.

In an effort to relieve the rails of this loss, Congress passed the Rail Passenger Service Act of 1970 which created the National Railroad Passenger Corporation, originally called *Rail Pax*. On May 1, 1971, given the new nickname *Amtrak*, it took over the operation of most of our intercity passenger trains, except for four railroads that elected not to participate, and except for commuter trains. ("Am" stands for American, "tr" for travel, "ak" for track.) NRPC is an independent but government-owned corporation that hires the railroads to run the passenger trains for it. The corporation has purchased 1,200 cars from the roads; has selected specific routes over which trains will run; and pays the affected railroads cost plus 5 percent for running them. Initial funding of the corporation was $337 million. Forty million came from government subsidy; $100 million was in guaranteed loans. Another $197 million was to be paid in over a span of 26 months by the railroads in consideration for the government relieving them of a $460-million-a-year loss. When Amtrak took over, it lopped off duplicate and "hopelessly uneconomic" routes, slicing the number of trains from more than 300 to 186 and running some less frequently—three times a week instead of daily. Now Amtrak has long-range plans for a number of things:

—A nationwide computerized reservation system.

—Revamped schedules to tighten connections with other trains and to arrive at terminal points at more convenient times.

—Elimination of uneconomical stops to speed up overall performance times.

—An advertising campaign to promote trains.

—Improved uniform food service that does not require intensive preparation. This may mean pre-prepared meals like those served by airlines.

—A training program for employees who meet the public similar to that used by airlines to assure courteous, polite service.

—A new fare structure including youth fares that would attract the young to trains.

Future railroad income statements are expected to show substantially reduced passenger deficits, but the government expects that its subsidy to Amtrak will be necessary for several years.

MODERN RAILROAD FREIGHT SERVICE

Because of their geographical coverage and the nature and volume of goods that they carry, railroads are essential to the smooth functioning of our economy. Over 200,000 miles of railroad line in the United States form one of the most comprehensive rail networks in the world and reach into every city and town of importance in the nation. As the companies are common carriers and are also required by law to form connecting routes, this complete network is open for use to everyone in the country. On it, about 29,000 locomotives pull 1.8 million freight cars and a few thousand passenger cars; employees number over 660,000.

Traditionally, American railroads have provided rate incentives for two basic shipment sizes. One set of rates applied on less-than-carload, or LCL, traffic. Another set of rates applied on carload, or CL, moves. Because of differences in the costs of performing the two services, there was a substantial spread between LCL and CL rates. For instance, let us suppose a shipment of iron or steel engine radiator caps in boxes was to move from a hypothetical factory in Illinois to the West Coast. A shipment of a few hundred pounds might be charged a rate in the neighborhood of $8.00 per hundred pounds. However, if the customer could move 30,000 pounds, the amount required for a carload rate, the charge would fall into the range of $4.50 per hundred pounds.

The Decline of LCL

A less-than-carload shipment was a consignment moving from one shipper, on one bill of lading, at one station, at one time, for one consignee and one destination, and weighing less than the minimum weight provided for carloads. Generally, shipments weighing between one pound and 10,000 pounds would have been of this type. Since shipments did not fill an entire freight car, the customer brought them to the freight station, where the railroad loaded them into the car along with other shipments to the same, or to an en-route, destination. At the other end of the line, the consignee was expected to pick up the shipment. From about 1935 to about 1955, when they were trying to compete with trucks for this business, some railroads provided pickup and delivery service for LCL.

In the beginning, LCL was a good service because it was so much better than horse and wagon. And when the railroads had all the LCL business, they could load solid cars to one destination. In earlier days, rail lines sometimes provided "trap" or "ferry" cars at origin, which were pulled around from business to business picking up LCL shipments every day. On line-haul freight trains they often provided "way-freight" or "peddler" cars. A special brakeman rode in the way-freight car and unloaded LCL shipments as the train stopped at small towns along the way.

When the trucking industry got its start in the 1920's, rail LCL became a much less attractive way to ship. Trucks went from store door to store door, not from station to station, and they often charged a little less than the railroad. They cut into the rail LCL business so that the railroads started to consolidate freight for more towns into one LCL car, thus making their service deteriorate. Another factor was that the rails had maintained open freight stations with agents on duty to handle LCL freight at most all of the towns they served. These became a large element in the losses on small-shipment business.

Finally, about 1965, most of the railways began to phase out less-than-carload traffic. They did this unobtrusively by simply amending their freight rate tariff books. The main change was to set a weight limit for LCL shipments. Some lines required a shipper to pay charges on at least 4,000 pounds; some required 5,000 or 6,000 pounds. Handling in the freight house was to be eliminated; unprofitable stations in small towns could be closed. This left a very restricted LCL service available. The general requirements of most western railroads provide an example:

1. (a) Rates will apply on less-than-carload shipments loaded in the same car with a carload shipment when such shipments are loaded by and received from the same consignor and destined to and unloaded by the same consignee as the carload shipment.

   (b) Rates will apply on less-than-carload shipments loaded in the same trailer with a trailerload shipment when such shipments are received from the same consignor and destined to the same consignee as the trailerload shipment.

2. Rates will apply on less-than-carload shipments of automobile parts moving in cars containing shipping devices for automobile parts which are in assigned service, when returning from destination to original shipping point via the reverse route of the inbound carload shipment.

3. Rates will apply on less-than-carload shipments tendered as 4000 pounds or more (depending on the railroad) loaded in or on one car when from one consignor at one point of origin on one bill of lading to one consignee at one destination, provided that shipment is loaded by consignor and unloaded by consignee on public team tracks or private industry tracks served by the railroad direct and does not require the railroad to perform break-bulk or freight house handling.

Less-than-carload rates still appear in the rate tariffs, but they only apply in instances such as the above. These, of course, vary somewhat from railroad to railroad. Since LCL is no longer available as an alternative for moving truly small shipments, the businessman has a problem in finding new alternatives to fill this service gap. New developments in rail as well as other modes provide some answers.

Carload Freight Service

The most important criterion for identifying a carload shipment is whether it meets the required minimum weight that the railroads establish. This varies from product to product and provides a way for considering the density of the product. A light and bulky commodity, for instance, might take a carload minimum as low as 10,000 pounds but be charged a relatively high rate. Heavier products would be given relatively heavier minimums ranging up to 40,000 pounds or more and take progressively lower rates. Considering the fact that the standard freight car has a capacity of 100,000 pounds, such minimums are not strong incentives for full car utilization. Also, as stated previously, the railways have been criticized because minimums in the range of 10,000 to 40,000 pounds are approximately the same weights as competitive trucklines can carry in truckload service. The railroads have artificially and unnecessarily held themselves down to the shipment size of the competitive market. To a large extent this was forced upon them by the Interstate Commerce Commission. The Interstate Commerce Act forbids discrimination against any customer. If the railroads published very low rates for very large minimum weight shipments they could only be used by very large business firms who did a very large volume of business. This would constitute discrimination against the small businessman who could not ship that much and who therefore would not get the advantage of the low rate. In recent years, the growth of our economy and progress in the education of management have forced a change in this sort of thinking. A slow breakthrough has occurred in railroad rate-making—one that creates important new shipping alternatives.

Higher carload minimums.   In recent decades, the more-or-less standard equipment of the railroads has been the 40-foot, 50-ton freight car in either the box, flat, or gondola design. One of their greatest competitive moves in recent years has been the willingness of railways to provide special types of equipment in order to attract traffic. The trend has been toward specialized supersize cars. Multilevel auto-rack cars with a capacity of 15 automobiles have recaptured substantial tonnage which had been lost to truckaway motor carriers. Boxcars, tank cars, and hopper cars approaching 90 feet in length and 150 tons in capacity have been placed in service by some lines. Today, when new rates are established to attract traffic for these cars, rail rate experts carefully assess the ability of the customer to load heavy, both in terms of product density and plant productive capacity. In some cases attractive carload rates that require carload minimums as high as 300,000 pounds have been published. Minimum weight requirements at this level, of course, contemplate the use of the new supersize cars. Additional incentives are available for shippers who can make a multi-car shipment at one time.

Multi-car rates. In a few instances, rail carriers have recently published rates to encourage customers to move a part trainload or even a whole trainload at one time. These can apply on groups of cars from 2 or 3 to 20 or more in number. Usually a minimum of cars and a minimum weight for each car is required to qualify for the reduced rate. For instance, a reduced rate on cement moving from California points to Texas points was recently published which requires a minimum tender of 20 cars containing at least 140,000 pounds each. Technically, these qualify as single-shipment rates, since the goods move on one bill of lading from one shipper to one consignee. However, other variations are also possible.

Annual tender rates. Some incentive rates are based on an annual tender of an aggregate minimum tonnage. In other words, the customer agrees that he will try to ship a certain amount of the product during a 12-month period. Each shipment he makes is then billed out at the reduced rate. A third-party organization then keeps an inventory of the amount of weight he accumulates—in the case of western railroads this is done by the Trans-Continental Freight Bureau. At the end of the year, if the customer has not shipped out the necessary aggregate tonnage, the railroad re-rates each of the shipments using the minimum weight that would apply on the amount actually shipped. For example, in one instance, rates have been established so that if the customer ships 700,000 tons annually he is billed $6 per ton, but if he ships between 500,000 and 700,000 tons, the rate increases to $7 per ton. As an added incentive, any tonnage over the 700,000-ton mark is billed at

$5 per ton. Annual tender rates can be written for shippers to accumulate weight through making individual shipments, but probably they are more commonly applied to unit train service.

Unit train service. Chapter 2 emphasized the point that excessive switching and sorting of freight cars causes inefficiency in railroad service. In recent years, United States railroads have begun to run unit trains which not only take advantage of the unit load concept, but nearly eliminate terminal activity altogether. A unit train consists of a set of like railway cars, usually gondolas, which are kept coupled together and dedicated to the service of one shipper and one consignee. They are usually loaded and unloaded mechanically or by gravity while moving slowly. Once loaded, the train is hauled directly to destination without being broken up, having power units changed, or passing through switching yards. When unloaded, it returns to origin empty. Sometimes the customer instead of the railroad invests in the equipment. Unit trains have been used for carrying coal, ore, grain, and steel. Obviously, the unit train is part of the present railroad trend toward heavy-loading incentives.

PIGGYBACK SERVICE

The discussion of containerization in Chapter 2 showed that the use of containers gives single-vehicle carriers such as ships the same ability to "set out" individual shipments that the railroads enjoy in train handling. Piggyback is the main form of railroad containerization and gives the rail lines some operating advantages that other transport modes have. The ability to pick up and deliver trailers from and to the customer's door gives the railroads the same service flexibility as the trucklines. Also, since the average trailer will carry less than half the load of a rail freight car, piggyback partly closes the small shipment gap left by the discontinuing of LCL service.

Officially, piggyback is known as TOFC, or trailer on flatcar service. In TOFC service, two fully roadable truck trailers are placed upon each specially designed flatcar. Loading is done by driving on over a ramp, overhead traveling cranes, or by "piggypacker" lift trucks. Special support posts on the flatcar make the trailers secure. Early shipment differed from road to road, but modern piggyback technique is reasonably uniform throughout the country. Some lines, however, prefer to transport the highway vehicle without the running gear attached—this variation is known as COFC, or container on flatcar service. Although the trailer bodies and containers in use look alike, they differ from mode to mode. Trucklines are interested primarily in high payload capacity with low tare (vehicle) weight. Therefore, the sides and tops of truck trailers are relatively flimsy. Rail carriers have tended to acquire slightly more rugged vehicles, although recent acquisitions follow truck practice. Steamship containers, however, must be very durable as they are stacked on top of each other and must not distort with the motion of the ship.

In the 1950's, when TOFC was first seriously considered, the ICC had doubts as to whether railroads had the right to engage in such a service. Fortunately for the carriers, the decision was affirmative. However, the commission designated five plans under which contract arrangements with customers and other carriers could be made.

Piggyback plans. The five piggyback plans, and their subsequent modifications, do not appear *pro forma* in the freight tariffs. Rate provisions, however, must not be such as to make other types of arrangements possible. Also, not all plans are offered by all carriers.

Plan 1: Highway trucklines publish the tariff, solicit the traffic, deal with the customers, and pay the railroad to carry the truckline trailer on a railroad-owned flatcar.

Plan 2: The railroad publishes the rate tariff, solicits the traffic, deals with the customer, and carries its own trailer on its own flatcar. Variations are possible depending upon who picks up or delivers the trailer.

Plan 3: The railroad accepts shipper-owned trailers directly from shippers and moves them on railroad-owned flatcars. Rates encourage mixing of different commodities in the loads, and no commodity can make up more than 60 percent of the weight.

Plan 4: The railroad pulls shipper-owned trailers on

shipper-owned flatcars. Under this plan, the trailers may be loaded or empty, but, when loaded, certain restrictions apply. Typical limitations would be that the two trailers must contain a minimum of 60,000 pounds but that no single commodity in them can total over 36,000 pounds. Thus, mixed loads are again encouraged.

Plan 5: Coordinated rail-truck service with joint rail-truck rates, rail or truck ownership of equipment, and either mode soliciting the traffic.

The restrictions on single-commodity loading in Plans 3 and 4 are illustrative of the uneconomic inconsistencies that crop up in the complexities of railroad rate-making. Plan 3 and 4 rates tend to be of the sort where the railroad just charges for pulling the equipment; for some products the piggyback rates come out cheaper than the regular boxcar carload rates. So in order to keep boxcar shippers from switching entirely to piggyback, the customer is forced to mix other merchandise in the load. This has inevitably forced the creation of third-party consolidating operators who profit from this situation. Technically, these consolidators are mutual, nonprofit, non-advertising "membership" organizations. These organizations function by combining a trailerload of one product from one member with a trailerload of another member's different product on one flatcar. Thus, neither trailer exceeds the 60-percent-or-36,000 pounds limit for a single commodity, and the reduced piggyback rate applies. A simple change in the tariffs and a slight increase in rates could shift this revenue from the piggyback associations to the rail carriers.

The landbridge concept. Although TOFC service is the mainstay of rail containerization, important international developments in COFC (container on flatcar) service have occurred. These are the landbridge and the minibridge concepts.

Landbridge was originally visualized as a competitive alternative to ocean steamship service between Europe and the Far East. American railroads would solicit and divert the traffic of steamship lines going around South America or through the Panama Canal. Because of cost and, especially, time savings, they could convince foreign customers to send containerized cargo across either ocean to a U.S. port. There, the container would be loaded on a flatcar, speeded across the country to the other ocean, and transferred to another container ship for the remaining ocean voyage. Containers would move "in bond" across the United States not subject to customs interference. So far, landbridge has not developed; but a domestic counterpart, minibridge, has.

Minibridge is a through container movement between Europe and U.S. West Coast points, or between the East Coast and the Orient. Combined rail-water costs are competitive with all-water costs. In addition, there is a substantial time and turnaround cost saving if the container ship can make one drop instead of visiting two or more U.S. ports—especially on different coasts. The volume of this traffic may increase until unit trains can be justified, thus increasing time savings even more.

Railroad Traffic Services

In addition to the variety of load sizes discussed above, the American railroads probably offer more special traffic services to the customer than any other form of transport. Some of the most important of these are related to the railroads' ability to keep track of the location of individual freight cars.

American (including Canadian) railroads exchange freight cars freely under a *Code of Per Diem Rules* established by the Association of American Railroads. This makes possible through shipments over the lines of two or more carriers. The term *per diem* means "by the day" and refers to the system by which carriers assess each other daily charges for the use of cars. Proper accounting requires keeping track of car location. Traditionally, this was done by manually entering car numbers in a "jumbo book" at interchange points and classification yards. Today, on many railroads it is done electronically. A trackside scanner "reads" car data from a rectangular arrangement of rows of reflective code strips near the center of each freight car's side. This data is then fed into a computer memory bank.

Passing reports and tracing. Because car location can be instantaneously retrieved from the computer, railroads are able to provide customers with meaningful information on the location of their in-transit shipments. Passing reports are simply statements as to the time at which a particular car passes a checkpoint. Tracing is the activity of obtaining such a report to find out where the car is. Such information is vital to other traffic services.

Diversion and reconsignment. For an extra fee, the railroad will change the destination of a carload after it has left the origin point. Technically, "diversion" is the change to a new destination while the car is still en route. "Reconsignment" refers to assignment of the shipment to a new consignee after it arrives at destination. These services are used in the sale of agricultural products. The shipper may originally consign the car to himself at a distant city. While the car is in transit, the goods are sold to another party, and then they are diverted to his place of business. This would be useful, for instance, in the case of certain fruits almost ripe enough for market which cannot be held longer awaiting a sale.

Transit privileges. Railroads frequently publish special rates that allow the shipper to stop his freight at some place between origin and destination for milling, fabrication, wrapping, bottling, etc., and then to forward the goods on to destination and allow the through rate to apply. Without this privilege, a combination of local rates would apply on a shipment stopped at an intermediate point, unloaded, reloaded and sent on to destination. In other words, the total charge would be the rate from the origin to the intermediate point plus the rate from the intermediate point to the destination. Because of the tapering principle, the total of these two rates would be higher than the through rate. Thus, transit privileges create the fiction that the shipment is still moving while it is stopped for processing, and for a extra charge allow the through rate to apply anyway. Transit privileges are discussed further in Chapter 12.

Other services. Because of their extensive holdings of land and diversified business interests, modern railroads can aid the customer in many ways. The real-estate departments or subsidiaries of many carriers will build and lease out plants to the specifications of the customer. Motor-carrier affiliates provide trucking service to fill out the rail package. Some lines own warehouses that shippers can use at distribution centers. Pipeline service is available from some railways. The export department or marine subsidiary of the rail carrier can provide expedited service in international trade.

INDIRECT CARRIERS

Common carriers charge reduced rates for volume shipments. The traditional spread between rail less-than-carload and carload rates, discussed previously, is a good example. Volume shipments also tend to move more expeditiously than small lots, which the carrier must handle in and out of the equipment. The indirect carrier can operate profitably on the spread between small-lot rates and volume rates. He solicits small shipments from the public and buys volume transportation from common carriers. Frequently, he can offer the public a lower small-lot rate than the common carrier, and he gives the benefit of expedited volume-lot service. Thus, the indirect carrier owns no line-haul equipment but buys transportation from an underlying carrier.

Domestic Surface Freight Forwarders

Domestic freight forwarders are, perhaps, the best example of the indirect carrier. These organizations are also sometimes called "carloading" companies. Both the terms "forwarder" and "carloading" are misleading, however, as these firms are essentially consolidators.

Domestic freight forwarding originated shortly after the turn of the century when some shippers in New York and Chicago discovered they could pool their LCL shipments, buy transportation on a carload basis, and move their freight more cheaply and quickly than the railroads alone could. Congress placed the forwarders under the control of the Interstate Commerce Commission in 1942, and in 1950 declared them to be common carriers. Today, through the use of piggyback they provide a transit time competitive to rail carload service and publish rates that are competitive with long-distance motor trucking.

Shippers' Cooperative Associations

A shippers' cooperative association or mutual freight forwarder is a nonprofit organization made up of shippers (and

consignees) for the purpose of consolidating small shipments
into carload lots. Because of their status as "private" carriers,
they are not subject to economic regulation by the Interstate
Commerce Commission. However, for the same reason, they
cannot hold themselves out to serve the general public. Users
of the service must be members who pay a fee to join the
group.

Usually the association is operated by a professional manager,
who obtains the necessary service from for-hire carriers to pick
up the freight, assemble it into carload lots, line-haul it to
destination, and deliver it to the consignee. Billing is on a
cost-plus basis; any profit or loss is prorated back to the
members at the end of the fiscal period.

Mutual freight forwarding is becoming very popular, with
hundreds of such organizations reported to be doing business.
The Interstate Commerce Commission watches these associations closely to ensure that they are not acting as common
carriers through subterfuge. One large shippers' association
specializes in "marrying" piggyback trailers from different
members to make flatcar loads eligible for the rail carload rate.
This was discussed above in relation to piggyback.

PRIVATE CAR COMPANIES

Another feature of American railroad transportation is that
shippers are permitted to own their own railway cars. This can
be a great convenience when specialized equipment is needed.
It is also helpful in times of freight-car shortage. Private car
ownership can also reduce the company's total transportation
bill if managed properly. The private car user pays the railroad
the regular freight rate just as if he were using a railroad-owned
car. The carrier then pays the shipper a certain fee per mile
for the use of the car. There are also no demurrage penalties
for holding cars overtime when private cars are on the tracks
of their owners. Demurrage is discussed in Chapter 11.

About 300,000 cars are owned by private car companies,
who specialize in building or buying freight cars and selling
or leasing them to shippers. A shipper who does not wish to
buy cars can lease them from a private car company.

Many of the private car companies were once indirect
carriers known as "fast freight lines." These carriers came into

being about 1856 because of the many different track gauges used on American railroads. The fast freight lines owned equipment that could be adjusted for different sizes of track. They undertook to provide a through movement for long-distance shippers across the lines of carriers with non-compatible gauges. Thus, they bought service from the underlying rail carrier and resold it to the public. Many such companies were operated by railroad officials as a means of siphoning profits from their railroad operations. The need for such carriers decreased when the railways nearly all adopted the uniform standard gauge of 4 feet 8½ inches between 1880 and 1900.

REFERENCES

Baker, Harry, and Richard J. Riddick. "The Role of the Forwarder in Efficient Transportation." *Transportation and Tomorrow.* Stanford, Cal.: Stanford University Press, 1966. Reprinted in *Modern Transportation: Selected Readings,* 2d ed., edited by Martin T. Farris and Paul T. McElhiney. Boston: Houghton Mifflin, 1973.

Dean, Joel. "Competitive Pricing in Railroad Freight Rates." *Transportation Journal,* Spring 1962. Reprinted in *Modern Transportation: Selected Readings,* 2d ed., edited by Martin T. Farris and Paul T. McElhiney. Boston: Houghton Mifflin, 1973.

Hunter, Holland. *Soviet Transportation Experience: Its Lessons for Other Countries,* Washintogn, D.C.: The Brookings Institution, 1968.

Johnson, Emory R. *American Railway Transportation.* New York: D. Appleton, 1905.

O'Connor, Richard. *Gould's Millions.* New York: Doubleday, 1962.

Srivastava, S. K. *Transport Development in India.* Delhi: S. Chand, 1964.

Stover, John F. *American Railroads.* Chicago: University of Chicago Press, 1961.

Taylor, George Rogers, and Irene D. Neu. *The American Railroad Network, 1861–1890.* Cambridge, Mass.: Harvard University Press, 1956.

Westwood, J. N. *Soviet Railways Today.* New York: Citadel Press, 1964.

CHAPTER 6

Motor Freight Transportation

The purpose of this chapter is to sketch the history of American highway transportation and to describe the motor-vehicle carrier services that are available to the businessman today.

HIGHWAY DEVELOPMENT

Although the federally financed National Pike carried a heavy traffic during the early 1800's, it was turned over to the states through which it passed during the administration of President Andrew Jackson. Jackson, an advocate of "states' rights," did not believe the federal government had the constitutional power to spend money on internal improvements within individual states. Although the country had a road system of sorts, for the next 80 years it was to consist mostly of disjointed, unpaved county roads. Long-distance transportation was taken over by canal boats and railroads. By 1880 the canal age also had come to a close.

Until World War I, highway transportation lacked a suitable vehicle to make it anywhere near as attractive as rail transport. In Germany, Daimler had invented the automobile in 1884 and it was slowly developing around the world, but it was not the automobile which first aroused public opinion to demand better roads. It was the farmers and, oddly enough, the bicyclists that did it. Although cities generally had paved streets, farmers trying to bring food to the markets of those cities found the connecting roads very poor. So, a good deal of pressure was exerted to "get the farmers out of the mud." However, the efforts of the League of American Wheelmen were probably more persuasive. This was a club of bicycle enthusiasts who formed a national organization to lobby for good roads. They even published a magazine called *Good Roads*. In the 50 years following its invention circa 1830, the bicycle had become a popular vehicle for recreational rides out into the country. The pressure of bicycle groups resulted in the establishment of the Federal Office of Public Road Inquiry in 1893. Later this became the Bureau of Public Roads, which today is part of the Department of Transportation.

After the turn of the century, the automobile and truck had also reached a high degree of development, and the need for better roads became obvious. In 1916, Congress passed the Federal Aid Road Act. This law called for a system of interconnected state highways designed in consultation with officials of the War Department and the Post Office. The basic idea of the federal aid system was that the states would put up 50 percent of the necessary money to build the roads and the federal government would put up 50 percent. States were eligible if they had centralized state highway departments and would cooperate in the networks and build to Bureau-of-Public-Roads standards. This program resulted in what has been called our ABC system of highways—primary interstate highways, secondary feeder routes, and urban streets. Federal-aid highway acts have been passed consistently by subsequent Congresses. The Federal Aid Highway Act of 1956 set the stage for our modern rural freeway system by authorizing the National System of Interstate and Defense Highways. For this network, the federal government supplies 90 percent of the funds and the states provide 10 percent.

DEVELOPMENT OF MOTOR CARRIERS

Probably the first users of trucks to carry freight were the cartage and transfer companies who operated in cities, where the streets were reasonably passable. Long-distance truck transportation suddenly became a reality during World War I. The principal reason for this was the extreme congestion of the railways during this period. Several instances of long-line truck hauling as a substitute for rail service are often cited. As part of the war effort, the government designed the U.S. Liberty truck. This was an extremely rugged, hard-rubber-tired vehicle designed for military use. Along with minesweeper watercraft and observation airplanes, it utilized the ubiquitous Liberty engine of World War I fame. The government purchased several thousand of these trucks in Detroit, but rail transportation was not available to take them to eastern seaports. The officer in charge carefully reconnoitered a road route to the East Coast, making sure that all bridges were safe. The trucks were then successfully driven across country for shipment to France. One of the leading railway locomotive builders is also credited with starting a trucking operation to deliver subassemblies for the manufacture of army tanks when rail transportation was unable to do so. After the war, the interstate highway system began to grow, and many freight-trucking operations were started by returning veterans as well as other entrepreneurs.

By the late 1920's, motor transportation was so important that the majority of the states regulated it in some way. Most states were mainly concerned with protecting their new highways and with safety regulations. Some, however, regulated the economic activities of motor carriers. These states dealt mostly with common carriers who operated regular schedules over regular routes. The competitive threat of itinerant and sporadic carriers was not recognized. Trucks were considered to be essentially short-haul carriers, and at first even the railroads welcomed them as possible feeder lines that would bring the rails more business.

Attitudes changed, however, during the Great Depression. From 1929 to 1939, the United States, as well as much of the rest of the world, suffered the worst decline in business conditions that has ever been known. Transportation volume fell off by about half, and millions of people were unemployed. Many unemployed men acquired old trucks on credit and went into the trucking business at that time. Some of them even lived on the trucks with their families. They would haul nearly anything for enough money to pay for gas and oil and have a little left over. Such activities further disrupted the transportation market and hurt the railroads as well as the established trucking companies. This was at least a partial reason for Congress to extend federal regulation to the motor-carrier industry in 1935.

Regulation

The Motor Carrier Act of 1935, which brought interstate truck and bus companies under regulation, was incorporated into the Interstate Commerce Act and is now known as Part II of that law. It extends to motor carriers approximately the same regulatory requirements that cover railroads. Motor carriers are to publish their rates and observe them, establish reasonable rates and practices, and avoid discrimination. There are several differences from rail regulations, however. Among these are the fact that some types of carriers are exempt from regulation (these are discussed subsequently). Moreover, the long- and short-haul clause does not apply to motor carriers; also the motor-carrier law introduces the concept of the contract carrier.

In the first days of federal motor-carrier regulation, the Interstate Commerce Commission granted operating authorities to more than 20,000 interstate motor carriers. As both highways and vehicles have improved, small carriers have been merged into larger ones in a trend similar to that of early-day railroads. This trend became pronounced in the two decades following World War II, when transcontinental trucklines began to appear. The development of a national system of high-speed freeways has made it obvious that trucks and buses are not limited to short-haul operation. Today, there are a few more than 15,000 interstate motor carriers of property reporting to the ICC. As with the railroads, the Commission classifies them by gross revenue. Class I carriers take in more than $1 million per year; Class II receive between $300,000 and $1 million; and Class III have annual revenues of less than $300,000. Over 11,000 of the truck lines fall into Class III.

Modern Industry Structure

Motor carriers are regulated in a number of respects. First, they are restricted as to the territory and type of route they may cover. Operating authorities granted by regulatory agencies specify the cities motor carriers can serve and the highways they can follow. The average length of haul for intercity trucklines in the last few years has been 260 miles. Certificates or permits issued to trucklines by the ICC designate several types of route authority: regular-route scheduled service, regular-route non-scheduled service, irregular-route radial service, irregular-route non-radial service, or local cartage. Most general-freight common carriers possess regular-route regular scheduled operating authorities. Most of them have also obtained other types of route authority in portions of the territory in which they operate.

Second, trucking companies are restricted by regulation as to the commodities they may carry. In a proceeding known as *Ex parte MC 10*, the Interstate Commerce Commission set forth a listing of 17 commodity groups for which motor carriers would be granted operating rights. The operating authorities that the Commission issues to motor carriers may specify one or a combination of commodity rights.

Third, not all motor carriers are common carriers who hold themselves out to the whole public. Much tonnage is carried by contract carriers who are allowed to serve under long-term contracts, only a few customers each. These carriers were discussed in Chapter 1. Occasionally a carrier will hold rights to operate both as a common carrier and a contract carrier. This is known as "dual operations" and is contrary to the Interstate Commerce law unless specifically approved by the Commission. Generally, such approval is not given except when the operations are clearly non-competitive or in different geographic territories.

Statistics about interstate carriers do not reveal the whole picture about trucking. Most states have hundreds and even thousands of trucking companies who operate entirely on an intrastate basis and, of course, do not report to the Interstate Commerce Commission. Intrastate carriers are regulated by the public utility, railroad, or transportation commissions of the states in which they operate. In some states, regulation closely resembles federal regulatory practice; in others, it differs greatly.

Figure 2 shows a chart prepared by the Interstate Commerce Commission schematically depicting the contractual, route, and commodity rights that can be granted to interstate motor carriers. Note that the classifications of private and exempt carriers are included only to include them as possibilities, since neither of these is subject to any regulation by the ICC, nor do they need to obtain operating authority.

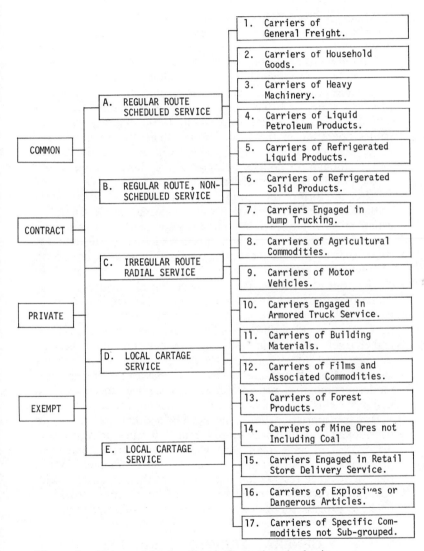

Figure 2. Types of Motor Truck Operating Authority.
Source: Interstate Commerce Commission.

MOTOR-CARRIER PASSENGER TRANSPORT

Although stagecoaches have been known for more than 200 years, the modern passenger bus takes its name from the horse-drawn omnibus, which appeared in London as a mass transportation vehicle in the middle 1800's. One of the earliest over-the-road bus operations in the United States used a 15-passenger Hupmobile touring car which ran from Hibbing to Alice, Minnesota, in 1914. This line eventually grew into the Greyhound system. Today there are about 1,200 intercity bus companies operating in the United States. These companies carry 63 percent of the for-hire passengers who move in the United States (though, of course, because of the short average length of the bus haul, airlines generate far more passenger miles).

After the turn of the century, population centers, particularly in the East and Midwest, were well connected by electric interurban railway lines. These companies formed a sort of second American railway system and specialized in carrying intercity passengers as well as short-haul freight shipments. The growth of highways and automobile travel forced most of these carriers out of business. Buses were a logical substitute for the traffic that remained. In the early days, some bus lines tried to be combination carriers, that is carry both freight and passengers. Some utilized vehicles that were a bus in front and a truck in the rear, but this configuration never became popular, and today motor carriers of property and motor carriers of passengers are separate companies. Although most modern companies provide short-haul service, there are two major systems that provide transcontinental service.

Bus transportation has some advantages that are sometimes overlooked. For distances up to about 200 miles, it is probably just as fast as an airplane trip when travel time to and from the airport is considered. The major bus companies do not require advance reservation but guarantee the passenger a seat. Also, bus travel is inexpensive. The bus companies provide a package express service, which is discussed subsequently.

GENERAL FREIGHT CARRIERS

The motor freight carrier probably most often used by the average businessman is the common, regular-route, scheduled-service carrier of general freight. These companies serve all the public and accept each shipment on a bill of lading as do the railroads. The Interstate Commerce Act does not require them to form through routes and to publish joint rates as the rail lines are required to do. Technically, this means that the shipper does not have the right to choose the exact combination of carriers over whose lines his shipment will pass. In practice, however, general freight carriers do interline with connecting carriers and so form a national network open to anyone for use. Usually trucklines do not exchange equipment at junctions with other lines but must physically unload the goods. In a few instances, cooperating lines have permanent arrangements for trailer interchange for through movement over two or more lines without unloading.

Services and Innovations

Services. Services offered by railroads, such as special equipment, protective service, diversion and reconsignment, and processing in transit, are not usually a feature of the general freight truck operation, although if one searched carefully through motor carrier tariffs one could find them. General freight trucklines are reluctant to provide these extras because their average shipment size is smaller and the average haul shorter than is the case with railroads. For volume customers, activities tailored to meet their special needs are most often provided by specialized common carriers, contract carriers, or private truck operations (these are discussed later).

Motor carriers do, however, have a flexibility unequaled by railroads in the matter of pickup and delivery service. In order to make a stop-in-transit to complete loading or to partially unload a volume shipment, a railroad must usually switch the freight car containing the customer's shipment in and out of the train along the line. A truckline can load the various parts of a volume shipment destined for different stops along the way into different trucks along with loads from other customers destined for the same stop. Motor transporters can in the same way arrange for pickup of parts of a volume load along the way. Therefore, while railroads limit their stop-in-transit service to two stops in addition to the origin and destination (either allowing three origins and then moving through to one destination, or allowing one origin and two stops for partial unloading before reaching destination), some trucklines allow stops-in-transit for both completion of loading and for partial unloading, and some even allow unlimited stops.

The basic flexibility of the motor truck is also seen in two other services. Since the semi-tractor with its detachable trailer has come into wide use, some carriers have found it possible to leave trailers with the customer for loading at his convenience or as goods come off the production line. When the vehicles are loaded, the tractors pull them out and leave others. Under such circumstances, freight rates can be lowered because the shipper does the loading, and the carrier may use its driver labor more efficiently.

Another motor freight service is the "split" pickup or the "split" delivery. This type of collection or distribution is limited to the prescribed delivery limits of the origin or destination city. For a small additional charge per hundredweight, the carrier makes additional pickups or deliveries on the same shipment as specified by the shipper on the bill of lading. Usually the "split" is allowed only at one end of the haul. This is useful for a shipper who makes one truckload shipment to serve many outlets in another city.

Innovations.   Recently, innovation by general freight carriers has been more along the lines of improving basic services than inventing new ones. Time-in-transit and tracing are examples.

As airlines introduce larger and faster planes, the number of products for which they are cost-competitive with trucks increases. This puts pressure on trucklines to reduce journey time in an attempt, perhaps futile, to be service-competitive with air freight carriers. At least one transcontinental motor line has introduced nonstop, two-man sleeper service to reduce transit time. Coast-to-coast line-haul time is 69 hours, with third-morning delivery of truckload and fifth-morning delivery of less-than-truckload freight. Because trucks must operate in a heterogeneous traffic stream, and because they must make some pretense of observing the legal speed limit, line-haul speeds probably cannot be substantially increased further.

Operating efficiency is also improved through centralized computer memory storage of data about truck and shipment location. Large general freight carriers invest in these machines to keep track of tractors, trailers, and other equipment as well as cargo consignments. Instantaneous shipment tracing becomes possible, and tracing personnel can give customers nearly precise information on the current location of their shipments.

Shipment Size

General freight carriers provide service for two ranges of shipment size. Less-than-truckload, or LTL, service is usually a door-to-door service for shipments from one to about 10,000 pounds. The LTL rate includes an allowance for pickup and delivery, and the shipment ordinarily must be sorted and reloaded at the origin and destination terminals. Truckload, or TL, service is provided for full loads of single or mixed commodities. It may or may not include a free pickup and delivery service. Carriers prefer to handle truckload shipments on a "loaded-to-go" basis without terminal handling. Because of lower unit costs and greater volume, truckload rates are substantially lower than less-than-truckload rates; in order to qualify for the lower rate the shipment must meet a set minimum truckload weight. A typical general freight truckline will handle about 50 percent loaded-to-go and 50 percent dock-handled shipments.

When trucking started in the 1920's, most carriers were effectively single-truck operators who went around from customer to customer assembling shipments destined for another town. When the truck was full, they went to the other town and delivered the shipments. These operators did not know much about costs or accounting or rate-making. Sometimes they just took the railroad-rate tariff and cut 2 cents off every rate. In the Midwest, for instance, they spelled the doom of interurban electric-car lines by taking away the food-and-produce traffic that moved into Chicago every day. Because they provided pickup and delivery and the rail carrier did not, the truckers aided in the gathering function of outlying produce wholesalers. As truck traffic grew, trucklines had to establish terminals where the freight could be sorted, because small shipments went so many different places they could no longer be loaded to go on the pickup truck by the pickup driver. Loaded-to-go operation could only be used for large shipments where the road truck could be sent out for loading.

The Small-Shipment Problem

If all less-than-truckload shipments were reasonably large and the shippers were located close together, the spread between the LTL and the TL rates would probably be sufficient to more than cover the cost of handling so-called small shipments. Many less-than-truckload consignments consist of one or a few packages, however, whose total weight may be only 100–200 pounds. A truckline may find that on some of its pickup routes the driver is receiving nothing but package shipments from widely spaced customers. Since one stop can take from a quarter to half an hour or more of expensive driver and truck time, a load of small shipments can easily cost more to handle than it brings in.

To prevent loss on small shipments, transportation companies traditionally have established minimum charges designed to cover the startup cost that applies to any shipment regardless of size. The regular rate for moving hardware from one town to another, for instance, might be 94 cents per hundred pounds. A 1,000-pound shipment of hardware would pay $9.40. However, if the carrier had a $5 minimum, it would cost $5 instead of 94 cents to move 100 pounds. In fact, for any shipment size under about 535 pounds the charge would be $5. In spite of such rate relationships, some trucklines feel that they lose money on shipments of less than 450 pounds.

One solution might seem to be to raise minimum charges even more in spite of the fact that they have been raised about 600 percent in the last 25 years. In some cases, minimums are more than the value of the goods being shipped. In economic reality, goods that cannot afford to pay a compensatory rate do not deserve to move in transportation, but a very high minimum charge is open to challenge on the grounds of not being reasonable. And then there is always the possibility that the minimum shipper may give the carrier a more profitable volume of traffic later on.

Because of this situation, the LTL service of some carriers is deteriorating. Pickup trucks stay away from customers who send out only small orders, and requests for service on small consignments going to out-of-the-way towns are politely ignored. On the other hand, a few carriers have decided to concentrate upon small shipments because a large volume of minimum-charge shipments can be extremely profitable if they can be picked up and delivered quickly or in concentrated groups.

The irony of the situation is that the general-freight type of motor carrier who introduced the concept of door-to-door movement for small shipments is no longer an eager specialist in this trade. Motor freight carriers, however, remain the largest carriers of shipments under 10,000 pounds. Of a total of 100 million tons in this category, they move 86 million tons annually. Even so, the marketing man and businessman must continually search for new ways to fill the small-shipment gap. Other alternatives are discussed subsequently.

The Backhaul Problem

Every transportation carrier who sets out enthusiastically to haul things from here to there sooner or later must face up to the problem of what he is going to haul from there to here. This is the backhaul problem. There are several alternative ways in which it may be solved. One way is to double (or almost double) the charge made for the outhaul in order to cover the cost of coming back empty. Situations in which this can be applied are very rare, because such apparently inflated rates attract competitors, and the customers may even choose to provide their own transportation. Another way is to double the amount carried on the outbound trip, thus making twice as much on the outhaul and justifying the empty return. Some say this is the reason old-time motor truckers started pulling trailers behind their conventional trucks. Again, this solution works only until the competitors do likewise and cut the rates in half because they, too, are carrying twice as much. A third way, of course, is to develop some backhaul business. In order to do this, motor carriers often publish attractive rates. Sometimes these do not cover the full cost of performing the backhaul service. This is justified by the argument that the company is ahead as long as the rate brings in more than would be spent if the truck went back empty.

The small-shipment problem and the backhaul problem lead many truck operators to avoid the general-freight type of operation entirely. This is why a large volume of traffic moves by specialized common carriers, contract carriers, exempt carriers, and private carriers.

SPECIALIZED MOTOR CARRIAGE

Frequently a business firm will develop a potential bulk traffic of a new product, perhaps between two relatively out-of-the-way points. A check of the freight rates of regular-route general freight carriers either reveals that no incentive rates are published for this commodity or that the rates are too high to move it profitably. Often the specialized common carrier is called upon in such instances. Such carriers hold irregular route and schedule rights for one or a few of the ICC commodity groups presented in Figure 2 above. The specialized carrier bases his attractive rates on the facts that he is interested only in volume and he has no terminal costs. He may also be seeking backhaul traffic to match big movements of specialized commodities for other shippers. Specialized carriers often will apply for the operating authority to handle a commodity if the shipper assures them of a constant volume; most of the common-carrier rights issued by the ICC in recent years have been of this variety. Another attribute of the specialized carrier is that he will often invest in specialized equipment such as refrigerated vans with special bulkheads, tank trucks for gases transported at subzero temperatures, or self-unloading dry-bulk trailers. The specialized operator also will frequently fit his operation into the production cycle of the customer.

CONTRACT CARRIERS

Under the individual enterprise system, the right of a businessman to haul his own goods in his own vehicle is clearly established. Under common law he could even employ an individual who owned a vehicle to do it for him on a continuing basis. Since the right to contract with employees is protected from government interference, contract carriage of this sort was considered to be the same as private carriage. When the United States decided to regulate motor carriers in 1935, many operators were calling themselves contract carriers but actually soliciting traffic and hauling for almost anyone. Therefore, to protect regulated common carriers, it became necessary to classify contract carriers as for-hire carriers and to regulate them also.

Contract motor carriers in interstate commerce must obtain permits to operate from the ICC. They must file with the Commission, publish, and keep open for public inspection the actual rates that they charge. They are not, however, required to maintain the same rates, rules, and regulations for the same service for all shippers served. A contract carrier is not allowed to hold itself out to the general public: it must negotiate long-term (generally 30- or 60-day) contracts with only a few customers. Although the ICC refuses to be bound by an absolute limiting number, a general rule has developed that such a carrier should not have more than 7 customers. In an extreme case, however, an armored-car operator was allowed to have 300.

Another ICC requirement is that the contract between the shipper and the carrier shall specify a minimum volume of traffic that shall move under it each year. This requirement protects the carrier and helps insure the volume upon which attractive rates can be based. The ICC does not approve of shippers using contract carriers just to get lower rates, however. Therefore, low rates must be justified by lower costs, such as the elimination of terminal expense, and usually the operation is specially tailored to the customer's needs in some way.

Since contract carriers are not allowed to hold themselves out to the public, it may be necessary for a shipper to advertise that he wishes to employ a contract carrier. Sometimes competitive bids are solicited from a group of carriers.

EXEMPT CARRIERS

Some for-hire motor carriers are not subject to economic regulation by the Interstate Commerce Commission. This means that they can begin or end operation without permission and negotiate any rate or contract provisions the customer will accept. Of course, if they hold themselves out to the public, they are apt to be held by the courts to be common carriers and liable as such under the common law.

The specific categories of carriers that are exempt from ICC regulation are as follows: (1) motor vehicles employed solely in transporting school children and teachers to or from school; (2) taxicabs, or other motor vehicles performing a bona fide taxicab service, having a capacity of not more than six passengers and not operated on a regular route or between fixed termini; (3) motor vehicles owned or operated by or on behalf of hotels and used exclusively for the transportation of hotel patrons between hotels and local railroad or other common-carrier stations; (4) motor vehicles operated under the authorization, regulation, and control of the Secretary of the Interior principally for the purpose of transporting persons in and about the national parks and national monuments; (5) motor vehicles controlled and operated by any farmer when used in the transportation of his agricultural commodities and products thereof, or in the transportation of supplies to his farm; (6) motor vehicles controlled and operated by a cooperative association as defined in the Agricultural Marketing Act; (7) motor vehicles used in carrying property consisting of ordinary livestock, fish (including shellfish), or agricultural commodities (not including manufactured products thereof), if such motor vehicles are not used in carrying any other property, or passengers, for compensation; (8) motor vehicles used exclusively in the distribution of newspapers; (9) the transportation of persons or property by motor vehicle when incidental to transportation by aircraft; (10) the transportation of passengers or property in interstate or foreign commerce wholly within a municipality or between contiguous municipalities; (11) the casual, occasional, or reciprocal transportation of passengers or property by motor vehicles in interstate or foreign commerce for compensation by any person not engaged in transportation by motor vehicle as a regular occupation or business; (12) the emergency transportation of any accidentally wrecked or disabled vehicle in interstate or foreign commerce by towing. In the interest of simplicity, some special qualifications that the law puts on some of these categories have been left out.

One exemption that has caused controversy is the one allowing the hauling of non-manufactured agricultural products. Anyone can go into the interstate, for-hire trucking of farm products without government permission or rate control. An agricultural trucker can bid for a load on the spot, but a railroad must charge a legally published rate. Probably Congress did not intend to create this type of carrier when it passed the Motor Carrier Act of 1935; the purpose of this exemption seems to be to allow a farmer to carry his own goods and those of his neighbors.

Regulated common and contract for-hire carriers can also haul exempt agricultural commodities as long as they don't put them in the same vehicle with regulated commodities. Exempt commodities become non-exempt when hauled in a mixed load with commodities subject to regulations. Private carriers can also haul agricultural commodities on a for-hire basis.

PRIVATE TRUCKING

When a business firm is trying to save money on its transportation bill, one alternative is private trucking. Anyone can carry his own goods in his own vehicle in interstate commerce as long as he follows state and federal safety laws. When for-hire carriers are uncooperative, even a fairly small shipper can introduce a note of competition by getting his own truck.

A private carrier does not need to make a profit from transportation since his gain comes from the commodity he sells or the service he performs. He does not need a heavy volume of traffic because trucks are relatively inexpensive and he can buy one or a dozen according to his need. Unlike the for-hire carrier, there is not a heavy terminal cost. Although good management is essential in order to realize these benefits, the convenience and dependability of private transportation may also be worthwhile.

The significance of private trucking is seen in national vehicle-registration statistics. About 19 million trucks of all sizes (including some station wagons) are registered in the United States. Of these, about 1.7 million are over-the-road freight trucks, and only about 300,000 of these are operated by for-hire carriers; the balance are operated privately.

The firm that contemplates starting a private truck operation should make a careful analysis first. One aspect of this should be a forecast of "revenue" and expenses to determine how competitive private trucking will be with for-hire transport. Modern trucks cost from 50 to 60 cents per mile to operate over the highway. The prospective private carrier should forecast the volume he will handle and the mileage he will travel. He can then convert per-mile costs into per-hundredweight costs and compare these to the freight rates that for-hire carriers are charging him.

Backhaul

If the private carrier cannot fill his vehicle in both directions of travel he must double the cost-per-mile estimate that he has made for his operation. Some industrial firms are successful in loading their own products in both directions. Other companies act as exempt for-hire carriers on the return trip, carrying fruits and vegetables from growing areas to market. The backhaul problem often creates a strong temptation. Suppliers or his customers may consider it a favor if the private carrier will haul their goods on a for-hire basis at less than the going rate; with the exception of agricultural products, however, this constitutes illegal carriage and must be avoided entirely.

Leasing

Because they are reluctant to invest in trucking equipment, some companies lease trucks instead. Leasing rules in interstate commerce are very strict, as the Interstate Commerce Commission tries to prevent leasing companies from acting as illegal common or contract carriers without having the required government operating authority. The leasing rules can be stated as follows:

1. The leased truck can carry only the goods of the lessee.
2. The truck cannot be subleased or rented to others in an attempt to utilize it fully.
3. It cannot be leased on a single-trip basis to a for-hire carrier to utilize it on the backhaul.
4. It cannot be leased to another company who will use it in the opposite direction.
5. The truck must be in the exclusive possession of the lessee.
6. It must be operated by his own employees under his direction and control.

Leasing rules of the individual states may differ substantially from the above, so different arrangements may be possible when leasing vehicles solely for use in intrastate commerce.

SMALL-SHIPMENT CARRIERS

There are two motor carriers—bus express and United Parcel Service—that are moving an increasing volume of small shipments. They carry only a fraction of the amount of the traffic hauled by common carriers of general freight, but they are specifically interested in very small shipments.

Bus Express

Bus express was originated by motor carriers of passengers in order to utilize unused baggage space in their vehicles. The best-known of these services is probably Greyhound Package Express. Altogether the lines have increased their annual volume from 168,000 tons in 1951 to over 250,000 tons in 1972.

Bus-express shipments are limited to 5 packages per shipment, but packages can be up to 5 feet in length and weigh 100 pounds each. Although pickup and delivery service is not provided, most bus depots are open day and night, so sending or receiving hours are long. Greyhound advertises same-day delivery up to 350 miles and overnight delivery up to 700 miles. Buslines blanket the United States and stop at some places not served by other types of carriers. Because the company covers its costs by moving passengers, bus-express rates are said to be surprisingly low.

United Parcel Service

United Parcel Service started in Seattle in 1907 as a messenger service using bicycles. Soon it started specializing in delivering parcels of merchandise from department stores to customers' homes, and it spread to principal West Coast cities. Consolidation of parcels into larger shipments followed, and after World War II the company extended its services to wholesalers, manufacturers, and other businesses.

Today, United Parcel's main volume is in intercity parcel service. It is very competitive to parcel post, although it is still not quite national in scope. Also, local services vary from place to place depending upon the operating rights the carrier holds in each state.

UPS has a novel pickup service in which the customer pays a small weekly fee. For this charge the UPS driver calls automatically each day whether or not there are packages to be sent out. Packages up to 50 pounds weight and 108 inches length and girth are accepted, but not more than 100 pounds may be sent from one consignor to one consignee on one day.

United Parcel has both a motor-carrier and an air service. On the ground, consolidated shipments are moved from origin city to destination in UPS line-haul trucks. In the air service, shipments are consolidated into jet freight containers. Land services are essentially regional rather than national in nature. Air service is available between major West Coast cities and between the West Coast and 28 eastern states. The company increased its volume from 27,000 intercity tons handled in 1951 to 2.6 million tons in 1969.

REFERENCES

American Trucking Associations, Inc. *Highways: the Years Beyond 1972*. Current Report No. 5. Washington, D.C.: 1965.

Broehl, Wayne G., Jr. *Trucks, Trouble, and Triumph*. Englewood Cliffs, N.J.: Prentice-Hall, 1954.

Hudson, William J., and James A. Constantin. *Motor Transportation*. New York: Ronald Press, 1958.

Rae, John B. "The Evolution of the Motor Bus as a Transport Mode." *High Speed Ground Transportation Journal*, vol. 5, Summer 1971.

Transportation Facts and Trends. Washington, D.C.: Transportation Association of America. Revised quarterly.

United States, Interstate Commerce Commission, *85th Annual Report, Fiscal Year Ended June 30, 1971,* Washington, D.C.: Government Printing Office.

Westmeyer, Russell E. *Economics of Transportation*. Englewood Cliffs, N.J.: Prentice-Hall, 1952.

CHAPTER 7

Water, Air, and Pipeline Transport

The purpose of this chapter is to complete our treatment of the shipping alternatives available to the businessman. Previous chapters presented information about transport modes on land; consideration of the water and air modes remains. Although they are not an alternative that everyone can use, pipelines are discussed briefly at the end of this chapter.

MARINE TRANSPORTATION

Early America was largely a maritime nation. Before the Civil War, most of the population was located along the Atlantic Coast, and railroads and highways were only just beginning to appear. Interior points were linked together and to the seaboard by an extensive system of canals. Most intercity commerce was conducted through coastal navigation or river and canal transport. On the high seas, American clipper ships were supreme.

Technology and war changed the situation drastically. The English iron steamship made the clipper ship obsolete. Railroads became more popular than canals, many of which were filled in. The Civil War disrupted river commerce, and the riverboat did not again become important until the 1920's.

One of the greatest advantages of water transportation is that it is inexpensive. Table 1 in Chapter 1 revealed that the average cost of using inland-water barge service is only 28/100 of a cent per ton-mile. The line-haul cost of moving bulk cargo by ocean vessel is even less.

Therefore, it is somewhat surprising that the water-carrier share of the market is so low and that the American merchant marine must struggle to survive in face of foreign competition. Part of the answer lies in the fact that until containerization was introduced, all water vessels were essentially large single-unit vehicles. When they carry general cargoes of mixed commodities they must be stowed by hand. The continuing pressure of labor for better wages and working conditions has made such handling costs prohibitively expensive. Therefore, water transport is usually best suited for bulk cargoes or for containers, so that ships can be loaded and unloaded through mechanization.

COMPLEXITY OF WATER TRADES

Because it must adapt to differences in geography and political subdivisions, the water-transportation business takes several dissimilar forms. Colloquially, these different forms within the same mode are called "trades." (The word "trade" is also used to designate any particular traffic a water carrier may regularly engage in or any geographical route or area it customarily operates over.) Our principal water-transport trades can be set forth in two basic categories—United States international merchant shipping and United States domestic water transportation. These two trades are sometimes differentiated by calling them "offshore" and "domestic," or "ocean" and "domestic."

Another way of categorizing the water trades is by whether they are "deep-sea" or "shallow-draft." Obviously, there must be physical differences in vessels that cross the oceans as opposed to those that operate on inland lakes, rivers, and canals. However, it should be noted that some shallow-draft ships operate in international shipping and that some deep-draft ships operate in the domestic trade.

One might suspect that international shipping and domestic shipping would also be regulated by separate government agencies, and this is true; but here, again, there is no parallelism in the categories. The Federal Maritime Commission has jurisdiction over American international carriers and over the so-called "non-contiguous" carriers. Non-contiguous carriers operate between the continental and offshore portions of the country such as Alaska and Hawaii; technically, they are engaging in interstate rather than foreign commerce. Domestic water operations along the coasts and on the inland waterways are under the jurisdiction of the Interstate Commerce Commission.

Because of the differences between the water trades, the history, characteristics, services, and regulation of each are discussed in separate sections of this chapter. First, however, an explanation of two principles of American maritime policy is in order.

AMERICAN REGISTRY AND PROTECTION FROM FOREIGN COMPETITION

The first Congress in 1789 established a rule that only ships built in the United States can be registered as United States vessels. Such vessels must also be owned by American citizens and staffed with American crews. Similar laws are enacted by other merchant nations. The principal benefit of such programs is to create a merchant fleet that can be requisitioned or controlled for logistical support during a war. The benefit to the ship operator is that only American-registered vessels are eligible for government subsidy programs. One objective of American martime policy has been to create a large American international merchant fleet under American registry. This objective has been poorly achieved.

In 1817, Congress established another rule, sometimes called "cabotage," which prohibits foreign-registered ships from engaging in United States domestic trade. Thus, any cargo moving between United States ports must move in an American-registered vessel. The purpose of this rule, again, is to encourage the building of a large merchant fleet by guaranteeing domestic traffic to American operators. There is no restriction against an American steamship company operating both in the international and the domestic trade. Unfortunately, our domestic traffic moves most efficiently by rail, truck, barge, and air transport, so *cabotage* has not contributed heavily to the building of a large merchant fleet.

THE UNITED STATES INTERNATIONAL MERCHANT MARINE

The health of the American merchant marine can be measured by the percentage of the country's imports and exports that it carries. The story of the merchant marine is largely one of decline since the golden age of American shipping, which occurred circa 1800–1840. Although our fleet was decimated during the Revolution, the country had an excellent shipbuilding industry. During this period, American builders contributed as much to sailing-ship design as other countries had in the past 300 years. The extremely fast clipper ships and flexible schooners that American shipbuilders produced were in demand all over the world. During this era American ships carried 90 percent of our foreign trade.

Although Great Britain had long exhausted its supply of shipbuilding timber, by the 1800's it had a good iron-making industry. This soon led to the development of an engineering profession, and men like Isambard Kingdom Brunel built iron steamships like the *Great Britain*, the *Great Western*, and the *Great Eastern*. The decline of the American merchant marine dates from about 1850, when such steamships began to appear. At first, the lack of capital and the nonexistence of an iron industry were responsible. Later, the opportunity to profit by internally oriented, land-based investments directed the attention of entrepreneurs away from foreign commerce. More recently, higher labor costs have made American shipping unable to compete with foreign operators in a free-price market.

The government has repeatedly tried subsidy programs to encourage the development of an American merchant fleet. Indirect subsidies through lucrative ocean mail contracts were tried for short periods after 1845, after 1864, and from 1891 to 1936. Since 1936, direct subsidies in the form of construction-differential and operating-differential payments have stopped the shrinking of the United States merchant fleet. During World War I and World War II, the government built and owned huge fleets of mass-produced, utilitarian vessels. After both wars it was faced with the problem of disposing of large numbers of ships that were pretty much unsuited to highly competitive for-hire ocean transportation.

In 1939, just before World War II, most American foreign trade moved in Scandinavian ships, and the Scandinavian countries employed over 1000 vessels in this trade alone. In 1956, 20 percent of all United States export-import commerce moved in American bottoms. Today, only about 6 percent of our foreign trade moves in American ships. The percentage carried by regular-route cargo liners has not decreased at so fast a rate because such vessels are subsidized and must be registered under the American flag. The greatest traffic decline has come in the percentages carried by American tankers and tramp ships. The reason is that although United States companies own or lease many of these types of vessels, they do not register them as American ships but enroll them under the "flag of convenience" of certain foreign nations.

Vessels and Services

The vehicle of ocean shipping is the steamship (or sometimes its modern counterpart, the motor ship). Conventional steamships are self-sufficient vessels loaded by their own booms or derricks through hatch openings in the decks. The goods are carefully stowed and virtually built into the vessel so that the vessel and cargo will react as a unit to the force of the sea. Today, many such vessels are being replaced by container ships, which greatly reduce the amount of time and labor needed for loading and discharging cargo. Modern freighters are frequently over 500 feet in length and have carrying capacities ranging upward from 10,000 tons. The largest super-tankers recently placed in service have previously unheard-of capacities of about 250,000 deadweight tons. Modern cargo vessels are truly deep-sea craft, as they may draw from 25 to over 50 feet of water.

Currently, the privately owned, active American merchant fleet consists of about 660 vessels of over 1,000 gross tons in size. More than 400 are dry-cargo vessels, most of which are operated in foreign trade. Some 200-odd are tankers, most of which carry petroleum between United States ports and which therefore are classified in the domestic trade. There are about 250 American steamship companies operating all these vessels. The government owns about 600 additional vessels, which lie inactive in the reserve fleet.

Common and contract carriers. Most of the dry-cargo vessels in the American fleet are operated as common carriers on regularly scheduled voyages between regular ports of call. In the shipping industry this is called "berth" or "liner" service.

We have been able to keep American ships in this trade because their construction cost and their operating cost is subsidized by the government. Today this fleet is rapidly being renewed through the introduction of container ships. There is optimism about the possible growth of this segment of the industry.

An important part of world shipping has always been conducted by "tramp" ships. A tramp ship is a for-hire contract carrier that specializes in the movement of shipload lots, particularly of bulk cargo. Unlike the liner, which issues bills of lading on individual consignments of cargo, the tramp frequently operates under a longer-term contract called a "charter." Tramps tend to follow the flow of world trade in search of cargo and may be forced to bid against other ships when large volumes of products such as grain suddenly appear in the market to be moved. The operating costs of American vessels of this type were not subsidized until recently, and we have not been able to keep more than a very few ships in this trade.

Tanker vessels are probably best considered as a class apart from dry-cargo vessels. Usually, tankers are owned by petroleum companies or are leased by them on contracts known as "time charters" or "bareboat charters." Since this effectively makes them private carriers, they are not eligible for subsidy. Thus virtually all American-flag tankers are found in the domestic trade, where American registry is required by law.

Flags of Convenience

The statistics reported for the American-flag merchant marine do not reveal the size of the effective fleet that American businesses use. Forty percent of the total bulk imports into the United States move in some 550 foreign-flag vessels owned by American companies or their foreign affiliates. American companies also charter an unknown number of vessels from foreign owners. Most of the American-owned foreign-flag vessels are registered in Liberia, Panama, and the United Kingdom.

Usually the "convenience" of foreign registration is explained by cost savings in three areas. First, American shipyard wages are higher than other countries, so it is cheaper to buy a ship from a foreign yard. Such ships cannot be placed under American registry. Second, a foreign-flag vessel may be crewed with men of any nation, and usually foreign wage-scales apply. Third,

Panama and Liberia specialize in providing registry for ships regardless of where they are owned and assess very low fees and yearly taxes against the vessels in their so-called fleets.

There is another reason that United States companies own foreign-flag ships, however, and it is not usually well publicized. Our Internal Revenue Code provides that the earnings from ships registered under the laws of a foreign country are exempt from taxation if the foreign country grants an equivalent exemption to American companies. Such earnings are tax-free if the foreign subsidiary does not return them to the U.S. parent company in the form of dividends.

MARINE CONTAINERS

Today, with about 125 container ships, the United States-flag fleet carries about 50 percent of the container cargo on our trade routes. Traffic is heavy on the North Atlantic and Far Eastern runs.

The first containers were used in the 1960's in the United States domestic trade, where labor costs had risen to prohibitive levels. The Matson Navigation Company is credited with building the world's first container ship. It was built for the Hawaii traffic in 1960. Van containers similar to truck-trailer bodies were stacked six-high in vertical slots or racks below-decks in converted freighters. Later, Matson developed the first specialized gantry crane of the type used in major container terminals today. Matson was also instrumental in establishing new longshore union agreements permitting mechanized loading.

Although containers allow combined movement by rail or truck and water from the interior of one country to the interior of another, not every van body that looks like a container is suitable for ocean shipment. Motor trucklines use trailers that are light in weight with high cubic capacity. Such trailers, of course, are also used as rail piggyback containers. The main strength of such vehicles is in the floor or underframe; the sides and top are relatively flimsy. Ocean containers, however, must be stackable and strong enough to support the cargo against the lateral movement of the vessel.

Large container operators such as Sea-Land Service, Inc., with 50,000 containers, and Seatrain Lines, Inc., with 30,000, use computers to keep track of container movement. Such control over a large number of containers aids intermodal flow and overcomes the lack of container standardization between modes.

Container-Ship Variations

The success of container ships with interior racks for stackable vans led to experiments with other devices. One of these is the roll-on/roll-off, or RORO, ship. Such a vessel is fitted with stern and/or side-port ramps so that vehicles can be driven on or off. A few RORO ships have been built, chiefly for military cargo. Such ships have also been used in the non-contiguous trade to the Virgin Islands. The first RORO ship to be used in United States foreign trade is expected to be completed by 1975, and will be a combined lighter-aboard-ship and RORO vessel.

Lighter-aboard-ship, or LASH, is a useful concept for carriers who call upon ports where the ship must tie up by several wharves in the same area. The LASH vessel carries small barges, or lighters, instead of or in combination with standard containers. Ordinarily, the ship does not dock but sends out barges to the shore terminals. A traveling crane on deck lifts them on and off over the stern and stacks and sorts them as needed. Such a vessel carries a good deal of non-payload weight, but savings in terminal costs allegedly compensate for this.

Intermodal Shipping

The physical difficulty of making a through shipment by land and water carriers is intensified by the regulatory situation. Land carriers are regulated by the Interstate Commerce Commission; United States international and non-contiguous shiplines come under the Federal Maritime Commission. These two agencies have had difficulty in agreeing on a way that land and water carriers can publish a single-factor through rate and share the revenue. With the obvious intermodal possibilities of container transport, some intermodal services have been established to overcome this.

Non-vessel-operating common carriers. In 1961, the Federal Maritime Board, as the regulatory body was called at that time, introduced a new concept in water carriers. These were non-vessel-operating common carriers. These companies, which are also referred to as non-vessel-operating steamship companies, have been permitted to establish a through land-water service between inland points and overseas destinations. Essentially super-ocean-forwarders, they arrange for containerized transport over the lines of the various underlying carriers. They pay the individual freight and handling charges, prepare documentation, and then bill the customer a single rate on a single bill of lading for the through service. One shortcoming of this concept, apparently, is that the non-vessel carriers do not need to establish financial reliability as a qualification for entry into business. Therefore, there is danger of a company becoming bankrupt before it has paid the charges of the underlying carriers, with consequent double billing against the goods and the stranding of the cargo en route.

The NVO type of carriage becomes more reliable when it is provided by the marine transport subsidiary of a major railroad. The railroads are financially reliable and, of course, handle the shipment as much as possible with their own equipment. The services of a typical railroad marine-transport subsidiary include:

Overland transportation to port area.

All necessary container yard or container freight-station and terminal services.

Customshouse documentation.

Marine insurance.

Overseas transportation by ocean vessel.

Customs clearance (except payment of import duty) at port of entry.

Delivery of containers to receiver in port area, or transfer to land carrier.

Overland transportation to destination for final delivery.

Single-carrier liability throughout.

Intermodal carriers. At the time of this writing, the Federal Maritime Commission had a proposal before Congress for the establishment of a new category of common carrier to be designated "intermodal carrier." Such operators would be licensed by the F.M.C. and be required to demonstrate the necessary financial responsibility to carry on an intermodal container operation. These carriers would have authority to negotiate single-factor rates with land carriers and would represent an improvement over the NVO carrier concept.

UNITED STATES DOMESTIC WATER TRANSPORTATION

In addition to the international trade, there are three trades in the domestic commerce of the United States that utilize deep-draft vessels. These are the non-contiguous operations, the inter-coastal service, and the coastwise trade. The remaining two areas of domestic water commerce, which require specialized vessels, are the Great Lakes and the inland waterways.

Domestic Deep-Sea Fleet

Ocean-going vessels are used in the non-contiguous, the inter-coastal, and the coastwise trades. In these trades, only United States-built and -documented vessels may be used. The same ships can also be used in foreign trade by non-subsidized American operators. Before World War II this fleet was so strong it provided substantial military support until a wartime fleet could be built. Today it is insignificant. In 1968, there were about 60 vessels in the domestic offshore trades. About half of these were container ships, the bulk of which were in the non-contiguous service. The reasons for the severe declines in inter-coastal and coastwise shipping are discussed subsequently.

Non-contiguous trade.   The non-contiguous services connect the mainland of the United States with offshore parts of the country. Specifically, these are Alaska, Hawaii, Puerto Rico, Guam, American Samoa, and the U.S. Virgin Islands. Because territories of the United States were treated somewhat like foreign countries, service to these areas was traditionally regulated by the Federal Maritime Commission and its predecessors. When Alaska and Hawaii became states, transportation to the mainland technically became interstate in nature. Provisions in the articles of statehood of these states, however, provide for continued regulation by the FMC.

Seatrain Lines, Sea-Land Service, and Matson Navigation Company, the pioneers of marine containerization, all operate in the non-contiguous trade. Thus, this traffic is heavily and efficiently containerized and represents the healthiest sector of

American domestic water transport. The fact that there is no foreign or land-transportation competition makes a strong contribution to this health.

Intercoastal and coastwise transport.   Intercoastal steamship service is that connecting the East and West coasts through the Panama Canal (or around South America). Service along either the Pacific coast or the Atlantic coast or between Atlantic and Gulf ports is called coastwise service.

Before World War II there were nineteen companies offering package and volume freight services between East Coast ports and West Coast ports. Voyages began at cities including Boston, New York, Philadelphia, Baltimore, Norfolk, and Charleston and served Los Angeles, San Francisco, Portland, and Seattle. Calls were made at cities such as Tampa, Mobile, and New Orleans. During the past few years, only one or two companies have served the route, depending on business conditions; ports of call have been somewhat limited. At least one container-ship operator offers service between the Port of New York and California points. Coastwise service is practically nonexistent.

There are several reasons for the decline of the coastal domestic trades. Around the turn of the century, the rail/water-rate relationship was such that a shipment could be made from an inland point such as Pittsburgh to a western point such as Salt Lake City as cheaply by intercoastal shipping as by rail. In order to offset this water competition, railroads steadily over the years engaged in a policy of selectively increasing rates to the coasts and of reducing transcontinental rates. At the same time, maritime labor unions pressured shipowners into continual pay raises and decreasing productivity until loading and unloading costs represented 60 to 70 percent of the total for line-haul water movement. Probably the greatest detriment to the coastal trade, however, is distance. The journey from Boston to Seattle is some 6,000 miles; some coastwise trips may exceed the length of a transocean voyage. As truck and rail services have become faster, ships have been unable to offer quick enough service to compete with them.

Inland Waterways

In the early 1900's the federal government was seeking a way to create alternate means of transport competitive to the railroads. The decision was made to improve the inland waterways and encourage the development of barge traffic. Since that time, the Army Corps of Engineers has had the responsibility for improving and operating the navigable waterways.

A system of over 25,000 miles of improved rivers and other channels has been developed. Most of it is in the eastern part of the country, where nearly all of the channels are interconnected. Considered alphabetically, the parts of this system are:

1. Atlantic Intracoastal Waterway: a system of dredged channels and rivers extending from New Jersey to Florida along the coast and suitable for barge and small-boat traffic.

2. Great Lakes and St. Lawrence Seaway: opens the Great Lakes to ocean-going vessels but is limited to a maximum draft of 25 feet.

3. Gulf Intracoastal Waterway: a protected channel dredged along the Gulf coast from Brownsville, Texas, to northern Florida; suitable for barge traffic.

4. Inland river systems: includes the Arkansas, Mississippi, Missouri, Ohio, and Tennessee rivers; various depths with the minimum being 6 feet.

5. New York State Barge Canal: originally the Erie Canal.

6. Pacific Coast waterways: include Puget Sound, Columbia and Snake rivers, and the Sacramento River.

Great Lakes.   For many years mine ores and grain have been the dominant steamship traffic on the Great Lakes. There is also substantial movement of ferries, which act as highway and rail links. Intercity volume on the Lakes amounts to about 5 percent of all ton-miles carried annually in the United States. In addition, cities such as Cleveland, Toledo, Detroit, and Chicago are classed as seaports, because ocean vessels can reach them through the St. Lawrence Seaway. Since the governing depth of the Seaway and other Lake canals is 25 feet, many ocean liners cannot enter or leave the Lakes when fully loaded. Local-use vessels such as ore-carriers are usually tied up during the winter months because the Lakes freeze.

Barge transport.   The river and canal portion of our inland waterways is served by bargelines. Well over 1,000 companies operate as regulated common carriers, regulated contract carriers, or exempt common carriers. They utilize the barge as their vehicle. Called "tows," these are moved in groups of up to 20 or more. The motive power is provided by a vessel called a towboat. Research reports indicate that there are over 4,000 towboats and more than 16,000 barges in use in the United States. Some of these are the towboats and scows of the typical harbor scene, but a very large percentage are used in the trade on the inland rivers and the intracoastal waterways. Over 150 billion ton-miles of cargo are moved over this system each year.

Nearly any commodity can be shipped by barge. About 100 or more bargelines are regular-route common carriers who combine general commodities in a single tow. Over 1,000 of the companies are "exempt" carriers not subject to ICC regulation. The latter specialize in tows combining not more than three bulk commodities. A general tow can be operated in much the same manner as a freight train, picking up and delivering individual barges all along its journey up or down the river.

A unique feature of the bargelines operating on the inland rivers is that the so-called "towboats" actually push rather than tow the barges. As many as 40 barges may be securely fastened together, giving the tow a possible capacity of as much as 100,000 tons. Such tows are propelled by 4,000- to 9,000-horsepower towboats lashed securely to the rear of the assembled barges. The speed of the tows is between 6 and 15 miles per hour, depending upon the amount of current in the river as well as the horsepower of the towboat in relation to the weight it is pushing.

Regulation of Domestic Water Transport

Responsibility for the economic regulation of intercoastal, coastwise, and inland water transportation was given to the Interstate Commerce Commission by the Transportation Act of 1940. This is also referred to as Part III of the Interstate Commerce Act. The law provides for the control of entry into business of domestic water carriers through the issuance of documents called certificates of public convenience and necessity to common and permits to contract carriers. It also provides for exemptions from regulation. These are so broad that about 90 percent of for-hire barge operators are not regulated as to entry or rates and service. The law does not apply to any vessels (or two or more vessels as a unit) that carry not more than three commodities in bulk, nor does it apply to the transportation of liquid cargoes by water in tank vessels. Since substantial amounts of the traffic are of this kind, domestic water transport is largely unregulated.

COMMERCIAL AIR TRANSPORT

Two attributes of air transportation make it more the "ideal" form of transportation than any other mode. First, it is extremely fast, which minimizes the lost time elapsed in transportation. Second, it can follow a straight line as the shortest distance between two points. As the most expensive mode, it demonstrates the economic costs of achieving these objectives. The airline industry also illustrates other principles of transportation development in that government support was essential to its maturation and it followed the paths mapped out by other modes of transport.

Although the Wright brothers made heavier-than-air flight a practical reality in the United States, both technological and commercial development were faster in Europe. Between 1903 and 1914, the main aeronautical activity in the United States was provided by subsidiaries of aircraft companies such as the Wright Exhibition Company. These companies hired "birdmen" who went around the country giving flying exhibitions at county fairs. The birdmen flew planes still very much like the original "flyer" the Wrights flew at Kitty Hawk. European planes had begun to resemble the machines of World War I.

During World War I, American industry was eager to demonstrate that mass production could provide a large supply of planes for the war. The government appropriated huge sums of money for aircraft, and industrialists, mainly from the automobile industry, hastened to set up airplane assembly lines. The industry decided upon the Liberty 12-cylinder, liquid-cooled engine as its standard power plant. The De Havilland 4, a British observation design, was one of the few airframes capable of carrying so large an engine. So American industry undertook to build 4,000 DH-4's under lucrative government contracts. Since the plane was virtually useless in battle, only about 300 were ever sent to Europe. Many were stored in kit form to await a more peaceful fate.

In 1918, the Post Office Department decided to begin an experimental airmail service. At first, Army Signal Corps pilots and planes were borrowed. Soon, however, the Post Office hired its own pilots and tapped the huge reserve of DH-4's. In the next eight years, airmail routes were developed until they extended from coast to coast and were beaconlighted for night operation. In Europe, commercial airlines were beginning to use large passenger biplanes flying mail, express, passengers, and baggage between continental cities and between Europe and Africa. The greatest civilian activity in America was provided by "barnstormers" in surplus aircraft. Like the birdmen, these pilots went around the country giving exhibitions and selling airplane rides. Soon, pressure developed for civilian participation in the airmail.

In 1925, the Kelly Act authorized the Postmaster General to contract for the airmail service with private operators. Airmail payments were generous in order to carry out the Post Office's policy of encouraging this new transport form. Several of the early contract airmail lines became the domestic trunk airlines of today. Since payment was only for carrying mail, most lines did not show much interest in carrying passengers until the Watres Act was passed in 1930. This law made it possible for the Postmaster General to pay incentives to lines that used larger, multi-motored cabin planes, two-way radio, and navigational aids. Controversy about airmail pay and airline regulation culminated in the Civil Aeronautics Act of 1938. This established the Civil Aeronautics Board and the present regulatory structure of the industry. Under C.A.B. guidance since 1938, domestic airline routes have expanded to about 300,000 miles, consistently better aircraft have been adopted, and airline safety has improved until air travel now ties with rail as the safest means of passenger movement.

MODERN INDUSTRY STRUCTURE

Most airlines are "combination" carriers, who move both passengers and cargo, usually in the same vehicle. The Air Transport Association of America, the trade association of the scheduled-airline industry, deals with several generally recognized categories of air carriers.

Domestic Trunk Airlines

These carriers are permanently certificated by the Civil Aeronautics Board to operate regular schedules over long-distance routes between major cities. Domestic operations of the following lines are included in this group: American Airlines, Braniff International Airways, Continental Airlines, Delta Air Lines, Eastern Airlines, National Airlines, Northwest Orient Airlines, Trans World Airlines, United Air Lines, and Western Airlines.

Local-Service Carriers

Local-service airlines are certificated to operate in specific regions of the country to provide service for smaller cities linking them to the total airline network. This class of carrier was created following C.A.B. investigations in 1943; current examples of local-service airlines are: Allegheny Airlines, Frontier Airlines, Hughes Air West, North Central Airlines, Ozark Air Lines, Piedmont Airlines, Southern Airways, Texas International Airlines.

Intra-Hawaiian and Intra-Alaskan Carriers

As the names imply, airlines in these classes operate entirely within the state of Hawaii and the state of Alaska.

All-Cargo Airlines

These carriers are certificated to deal exclusively in air cargo. Although they possess regional operating authorities, they tend to operate only over high-density routes including international service. Current examples are the Flying Tiger Line and Seaboard World Airlines.

Helicopter Carriers

Helicopter lines are authorized to operate over definite routes within urban areas such as New York, Chicago, Los Angeles, and San Francisco.

International and Territorial Carriers

This class of carrier holds certificates to operate between the United States and foreign countries and between the United States and its territories. Most of them were originally certificated in other categories and hold both types of rights. The exception is Pan American World Airways, which pioneered in the days of the contract airmail and holds no route privileges in the continental United States. For many years, as the "chosen instrument" of the government in international aviation, Pan American was the only subsidized American carrier in foreign commerce.

Other Air Carriers

Several of the states of the Union are large and populous enough to support airline operations wholly within their borders. Intrastate carriers usually provide service very similar to that of the interstate carriers. If intrastate carriers elect not to interline with C.A.B.-controlled carriers and not to engage in interstate commerce in any way, they may be completely exempt from economic regulation by the C.A.B.

Supplemental air carriers may also be useful to the businessman. In the past, supplemental carriers have been known variously as "non-scheduled carriers," "fixed-base operators," and "irregular air carriers." Today, they are certificated by the C.A.B. to engage exclusively in charter operations. Supplementals use modern jet equipment, and although they are not permitted regular schedules, some go to the same destinations with reasonable frequency. These carriers offer attractive charter rates to the shipper who can use the cargo space available on passenger charter flights.

Third-Level Airlines

So-called because they are a type of scheduled carrier in addition to domestic trunk and domestic local-service airlines, third-level airlines are not regulated and are free to establish regular route service and to set appropriate rates. They generally have short hauls between large cities or from cities to outlying small towns. Fares are usually higher than those of the regulated carriers. These airlines can serve towns where no other air service is available. Also referred to as "air-taxi operators" or "commuter air carriers," they are exempt from C.A.B. economic regulation as long as they fly planes grossing less than 12,500 pounds takeoff weight. Sometimes, however, in special cases they are allowed to fly larger aircraft.

AIR CARGO SERVICE

Airmail and air parcel post are a useful method of shipping, particularly for small parcels. These services are essentially Post Office services and are similar to postal services discussed in relation to rail transport. In their continuing search for additional business, air carriers have established other categories of air cargo service also.

Air Freight

The first national air cargo service was provided in the years following 1927, when the major airlines contracted with the Railway Express Agency to perform pickup and delivery and to supervise the through air movement of small cargo shipments. For years, Air Express provided a premium, but expensive, parcel-freight service. Air Express shipments enjoyed a space priority next to that of airmail. With the decline of the express business, REA, as it is now called, is being converted to a regular air freight forwarder.

Concurrent with the rise of Air Express, each airline also developed its own air freight service. Thus, air freight service in several different forms is available from nearly all scheduled air carriers, in addition to that provided by the all cargo airlines. Table 1 in Chapter 1 indicates that air freight has the highest ton-mile cost of any transport mode. With the advent of containerization, however, attractive volume rates are becoming available. This has led to an expansion of services by the indirect carriers, the air freight forwarders.

Air Freight Forwarders

Like the surface modes, air transportation has indirect carriers known as forwarders. These companies began to appear after World War II. There was great enthusiasm for the rapid growth of air freight volume, and a natural assumption was that money could be made by consolidating small shipments to take advantage of the spread between less-than-planeload and planeload rates. Because of C.A.B. regulatory policy and because the total air freight market remained small, airlines did not publish volume discount rates until relatively recently. At first, therefore, air freight forwarders were mainly expediters. They could offer a reliable pickup and delivery service and get the shipment on the first plane out regardless of what airline handled it. They charged for ground handling and expertise in addition to the line-haul rate.

Entry into the air freight forwarder field is presently unrestricted. Although these forwarders must register with the C.A.B., effective operating authority is nationwide, there are no commodity restrictions, and justification of rate levels is not required.

Today, many domestic air freight forwarders are true consolidators who take advantage of volume discount rates. (The usual weight-break is about 5,000 pounds.) By using containerization, these indirect carriers may provide the solution to a problem that airlines seem ill-equipped to deal with—that of ground handling.

Since air freight, so far, has been pretty much a package service, ground handling of the packages has been a messy operation. Customers or pickup trucks brought packages to a ground-level freight room at the airport. There, parcels of different shapes were placed in heterogeneous piles and eventually shuffled onto trains of carts. They were pulled, unprotected, across the airfield and stuffed by hand into the waiting airplane. If airlines moved as much cargo as trucklines, the resulting congestion would make airports unusable. Fortunately, the forwarder and the container make decentralization possible. Some distance from the airfield the forwarder can maintain a freight dock very similar to a motor freight terminal. As pickup trucks come in, shipments can be sorted by destination and placed in containers. The containers can be hauled to the airport and quickly placed aboard the plane.

Note should be made that air containers do not resemble surface containers. They are smaller, they are built of lightweight materials, and they are shaped to fit the airplane. Jumbo jets, such as the Boeing 747, the Douglas DC-10, and the Lockheed L-1011 have great capacity for containers on the lower, cargo deck. Fuselage-shaped containers of 3,000 to 6,000 pounds maximum capacity are designed for each particular aircraft. In order to fill this container space, some combination carriers are introducing rates that consist of a flat charge for carrying the loaded container from origin to destination. These rates are as low as 5 cents to 10 cents per pound for journeys up to about 2,000 miles. This is lower than some truck LTL rates for similar distances, and much lower than previous air freight rates. Of course, these rates do not include pickup or delivery of the container.

PIPELINE TRANSPORTATION

The United States has about 400,000 miles of pipeline that are used to transport petroleum products, natural gas, and, to a limited extent, other products such as chemicals or coal mixed into a slurry with water. About 200,000 miles are petroleum pipelines; about 200,000 miles are natural-gas lines. Natural-gas lines are under the regulatory jurisdiction of the Federal Power Commission. Of all the lines carrying all products, only petroleum lines are legally classed as common carriers; they are under the economic regulatory power of the Interstate Commerce Commission. They were made subject to this regulation by the Hepburn Act of 1906 because the Standard Oil Company was monopolizing all oil pipeline transportation in order to gain or complete monopoly of the petroleum business in the United States. Pipelines are not required to obtain certificates of public convenience and necessity in order to start in business or build new lines. Today there are about 90 companies in this business; most of them are controlled by the major oil companies. They of course have only one group of customers, the petroleum industry.

PIPELINE CHARACTERISTICS

Obviously, the average businessman is not able to use pipeline transportation. If piplines could be adapted to the movement of capsules, however, general freight might be moved in this manner. This would be difficult with present technology because the system is made up of lines of different sizes. The different lines range from 2 inches to 31 inches in diameter. Some fundamental characteristics of pipelines would make them an interesting general-transportation device:

1. Pipeline is the only mode in which only the cargo moves while the vehicle stands still.
2. Pipelines tend to be laid out in straight lines across country, which substantially reduces line-haul distance.

3. The line is buried in the ground; therefore it is unseen, quiet, and causes no traffic congestion or accidents.
4. Theft is difficult, and damage or even contamination of cargo is rare.

The shipping document in the pipeline industry is called a pipeage contract and is sometimes referred to as a "tender." This is because pipelines require customers to tender a minimum amount of product for shipment at one time. This minimum tender ranges from 10,000 to 100,000 gallons. One reason for requiring a minimum tender is that different products are not separated in the line; they follow one another in sequence. The point at which the products meet in the line is called the "commingled face." Some mixing occurs, but as long as pumping pressure keeps the liquid turbulent, it is not serious. Compatible products are moved together, and the comingled face of the higher-quality liquid can be blended into the lower-quality one at destination without harm. Since 100,000 gallons of product stretches out for many miles in a pipeline, the point at which two consignments meet in the line involves a very small percentage of the total volume.

SUMMARY

This chapter and the two previous ones have considered most of the modern methods of shipping things. The businessman should never adopt the attitude that he is limited only to the transportation methods that are immediately visible to him. The many arrangements that exist were developed because someone was not satisfied with existing service and sought a better way to do it. This attitude can produce new transport alternatives in the future.

REFERENCES

Air Transport 1971: The Annual Report of the U.S. Scheduled Airline Industry. Washington, D.C.: Air Transport Association of America, 1971.

Big Load Afloat. Washington, D.C.: American Waterways Operators, Inc., 1965.

The Labor-Management Maritime Committee. *The U.S. Merchant Marine Today.* Washington, D.C., 1970.

"Launching: U.S. Lines Increasing Share of Global Distribution." *Handling and Shipping*, vol. 13, no. 9 (September 1972).

Marshall, Kenneth. "Containerization: The Long Revolution." *Transportation and Distribution Management*, November 1970.

McDowell, Carl E., and Helen M. Gibbs. *Ocean Transportation*. New York: McGraw-Hill, 1954.

Mesirow, Harold E. "Ocean Carrier." *I.C.C. Practitioners' Journal*, vol. 39, no. 6 (September-October 1972).

Schreiner, Eugene H. *Understanding Air Freight*. Los Angeles: Air Freight Training Service, 1971.

Smith, Henry Ladd. *Airways*. New York: Russell & Russell, 1965.

United States, Federal Maritime Commission, *Ninth Annual Report, 1970*, Washington, D.C.: Government Printing Office, 1971.

Wagner, R. L. "Petroleum Products Pipeline Transportation." *Petroleum Marketing & Transportation*. Houston: Gulf Publishing, 1964.

CHAPTER 8

Government Control and Regulation of Transportation

The purpose of this chapter is to set forth a brief description of the role of government in promoting, controlling, and regulating transportation in the United States. The material presented is not an in-depth discussion of the philosophy of regulation or of national transportation policy. It is, instead, an exposition for the business student of the existing state of regulation and some of its background so that he will realize how governmental activity affects the transportation choices available to the businessman.

INTRODUCTION

Transportation facilities are so important to the proper functioning of a nation and its economy that governments typically establish some sort of control over them. This control may be direct, as in the case of government ownership and operation, or indirect, as when laws are passed to control the transportation provided by private enterprise.

Those who rule nations are interested in good transportation for several reasons. Traditionally important have been the communication of directives quickly to all parts of the realm and the movement of armed forces for national defense. Even more important is the encouragement of production and trade, so that the people will have the things they want and need and be satisfied with the government. Thus, the end object of all laws concerning transportation is, in some way, to aid those who use it, to make it available, to keep it safe, or to ensure that it will be reasonably priced.

Government control affects different types of transportation companies differently. It can provide for greater or less availability, responsibility, or flexibility in rate-making in comparison to alternative means of transport. Certain regulations also provide for penalties for the shipper as well as the carrier who breaks the law. Therefore, at least a rudimentary understanding of government regulation and control of transportation is important to the businessman. Such knowledge can aid him in recognizing all the carrier alternatives open to him; it can help him correct the situation when they do not perform as expected; and it can restrain him from breaking the law himself.

PROMOTION, POLICE POWER, AND ECONOMIC REGULATION

Government control of transportation usually involves three kinds of activity: promotion, police power, and economic regulation. Promotional activity includes all actions that encourage the development and maintenance of transport facilities. Police power ensures that the facilities will be operated with as little harm as possible to human health and welfare. Economic regulation stresses the provision of a continuing supply of transportation available to all on some rational basis.

In the United States all three of these activities are provided by both the state and the federal governments. The states are concerned only with intrastate commerce, which moves entirely within their borders, and generally the federal government controls only that which moves in interstate commerce, crossing state lines. There are exceptions to this, however. The Coast Guard regulates watercraft safety in most of the states, The Federal Aviation Administration controls aircraft safety nationally, and the Interstate Commerce Commission has some power over railroad lines and rates within the individual states.

Another generalization that has exceptions is that promotional-activity and police-power regulation are a function of the executive branch of the government, while economic regulation is performed by the legislative branch. This is because promotion usually involves spending money that Congress has appropriated, and police power involves enforcement of laws that it has passed. Both of these are administrative functions. Economic regulation, however, often includes deciding who may go where, what he may carry, and how much a carrier may charge. Since making such rules is akin to making laws, it is a duty of the legislative arm of government.

PROMOTION OF TRANSPORTATION

The most obvious way a country can support a transportation system is to buy it or build it and to operate it under government ownership. Most nations own their railroad systems, and some own their international air carriers. Another type of aid is direct payment of subsidies to make up operating losses and ensure profitable operation. In the United States, most often the methods used have been indirect ones—encouraging private business to establish transportation service.

Some of the earliest legislation was the least direct in its effect. For instance, an early act of Congress was to bar foreign vessels from competing in American domestic water transportation. A few years later, Congress gave indirect support to railroads by removing the import duty on iron, from which rails were to be made.

Direct aid to railroads came in the land-grant program which began with the Illinois Central lines in 1850 and ended with the Texas and Pacific Railway in 1871. Land-grant lines received a right-of-way flanked by alternate sections of land that they could sell or develop to obtain revenues and financing.

Possibly the most popular form of subsidy that has been used down through the years is that of mail payments. Lucrative mail rates that more than cover the cost of service have acted as incentives to our shipping, railroad, and airline industries, although they have often been open to charges of favoritism and unfair treatment. Ocean mail contracts were tried in the 1840's and again in the 1860's, and mail payments under the Ocean Mail Contract Act of 1891 were an important incentive to our ocean shipping industry until 1936. The railroads, too, benefited for many years from mail pay, and some people credit the disappearance of rail passenger service to the reduction of railroad mail rates and contracts.

Perhaps the most impressive effect of mail subsidy can be seen in our airline industry. Using surplus World War I aircraft, the Post Office began to operate an airmail service in 1918. By 1925, 1,900 miles of beaconlighted airways and some radio communication had been developed. In that year, Congress passed the Kelly Act, which empowered the Post Office to contract the airmail routes out to private operators. Many of our modern airlines have grown from companies who were successful bidders at that time. In the following year, the Air Commerce Act committed the federal government to a policy of providing airways and navigation aids and controlling air safety, thus relieving the private lines from providing many facilities.

Today, there are still many ways transportation operators are supported and encouraged. There is at least one substantial promotional program for each means of transport.

Water-Transport Subsidies

In ocean shipping, the ocean mail contract system was replaced by direct subsidy under the Merchant Marine Act of 1936. Construction-differential subsidies are paid to American deep-sea steamship operators so that they may acquire American-built ships as cheaply as if they had purchased them from a foreign shipbuilding firm. Under the 1936 Act, operating-differential subsidies were paid to American companies who contracted to operate over predetermined Essential Trade Routes. These subsidies equalized the cost of operating an American vessel with that of foreign competitors traversing the same area.

The Merchant Marine Act of 1970 eliminated the Essential Trade Route restriction and extended construction-differential and operating-differential benefits to American carriers who do not operate over fixed routes. Consequently, bulk carriers as well as general carriers are now eligible for these payments. Currently administered by the Maritime Administration, these subsidies amount to about $277 million per year.

Another way the government supports water transport is by providing the waterway for our bargelines and other inland-water carriers. The Northwest Ordinance passed by the Continental Congress in 1787 provided that certain rivers should always be usable free of charge. This principle has been maintained, and today no tolls are charged on any of our inland waterways except the St. Lawrence Seaway. Since 1902, improvement and supervision of the inland waterways has been the responsibility of the U.S. Army Corps of Engineers. Congress makes substantial appropriations for river and harbor improvement nearly every year.

Air-Transport Subsidies

The contract airmail system begun in 1925 was altered by the Civil Aeronautics Act of 1938, when economic regulation was imposed upon the domestic trunk-line air carriers through the establishment of the Civil Aeronautics Board. This board is an independent regulatory commission or agency and has a role in determining the amount of subsidy an airline shall receive. Until 1953 the Board determined the rate of airmail pay each carrier was to receive, and the Post Office paid it. In 1953 the subsidy element of the pay was separated from the service element, so that the Post Office paid only for value received; the C.A.B. then administered the subsidy. Since about 1960, the domestic trunk-line carriers have been only lightly and infrequently subsidized. The local-service carriers are still fully subsidized, however.

Substantial additional subsidy benefits also accrue to the airlines. The Federal Aviation Administration develops and operates the airways over which the lines operate. This includes provision of radio and electronic navigational facilities and a huge complex of air-traffic controllers who direct the planes in flight. Airports have traditionally been provided by municipalities, and the federal government was restricted by the Air Commerce Act of 1926 from aiding airports until 1938. The Federal Airport Act of 1946 provided the groundwork for heavy federal assistance to urban airports. Something over a billion dollars has been spent under this program. The Airport-Airways Modernization Act of 1970 created a federal trust fund that will make additional billions of dollars available to improve these facilities in the future.

Aid to Highways

The most expensive transportation promotional program has been a joint undertaking of the federal government and the states. Although there had long been political pressure from bicyclists and farmers for improvement of the roads, railroads dominated the transport scene until automobiles became efficiently operational. The Federal Aid Road Act of 1916 and the Federal Highway Act of 1921 authorized the federal government to pay 50 percent of the cost of constructing state highways. States were eligible who established state highway departments and who would build part of a connected national network. This program provided over 500 thousand miles of federal-aid highways within about 30 years. The Federal Aid Highway Acts of 1944 and 1956 introduced a new concept. This was the National System of Interstate and Defense Highways to be financed 90 percent by the federal government and 10 percent by the states. It is essentially a multi-lane, grade-separated freeway system that connects all cities in the United States. Since 1921, over 250 billion dollars have been spent on building our highways, and the shape of transportation has been profoundly altered by them in the short space of 50 years.

Aid to Railroads

Since the last land grant was made over 100 years ago, there has been little subsidization of American railroads. To some extent this is agreeable to the railroads because government subsidy might mean even more stringent government control. Also, the rail lines fear government ownership, and have not forgotten the experience of government ownership during World War I. Lack of popular enthusiasm for rail subsidies also may be due to the extremely poor public image the railways acquired in the heyday of monopoly during the last century. Recently, however two attempts have been made at direct aid to the rail lines.

The Transportation Act of 1958 authorized the Interstate Commerce Commission to arrange government guarantees for loans from public or private lending agencies to railroads. Loans could be utilized for capital expenditures or maintenance work. In spite of this support, rail managements were reluctant to borrow privately because of their weak financial position. The loan program known as Part V of the Interstate Commerce Act was permitted to expire in 1963.

Convinced that passenger service is basically an unprofitable operation, especially in view of competition from airplanes and automobiles, many railroads have sought for several decades to abandon passenger service altogether. Perhaps in response to public opinion, the government position seems to be that some railroad passenger service is essential. The result has been the establishment of Amtrak, a government-subsidized passenger service, which has been discussed previously.

Future of Transport Promotion

Our federal promotional program for transportation since 1789 has been extremely effective. On the average, all means of transport in the United States except ocean shipping are more extensive and usually more productive than those of other countries. However, the program has been discontinuous, inconsistent, and unequal in application. This is because Congress really has no master plan for transportation, so that each problem is solved more or less independently when public opinion indicates that the situation can be tolerated no longer. Perhaps this is as it should be in a country that professes the free-enterprise system and a democratic approach to government.

POLICE-POWER REGULATION

The term "police power" refers to the inherent powers of a government to maintain the general welfare, safety, and security of social and political life. As exercised in the United States, it includes programs that deal with health and sanitary laws, the import and export of various goods, and different types of safety regulations. Since careless operation of any transportation vehicle can be very detrimental to health and welfare, most police-power regulation in transport concerns vehicle operation and maintenance. An ideal of modern political science is that police power should be exercised by as local a governmental jurisdiction as possible. Most local governments do have some transportation safety regulations, but with the exception of highway transport, the most effective regulation is exercised at the national level. Important agencies that regulate transport safety are located in the Department of Transportation, which of course is in the executive branch of the government.

United States Coast Guard

The oldest of these agencies, the Coast Guard was established in 1790 as part of the Treasury to aid in the collection of customs revenues. Other early agencies such as the Revenue Cutter Service, the Life Saving Service, and the Bureau of Marine Inspection and Navigation were later included in it.

Today the Coast Guard enforces federal maritime safety in general.

Federal Aviation Administration

Originally known as the Civil Aeronautics Administration, the Federal Aviation Administration was renamed and reorganized in 1958. It deals with the advancement of safety in flight, such as the determination of qualifications of airmen and the issuance of certificates of airworthiness to aircraft. It develops and controls the federal airways through the operation of flight-control centers and other facilities that monitor aircraft in flight. It also administers the federal aid program for the construction of airports.

Land-Transport Agencies

The titles of the Bureau of Motor Carrier Safety and the Bureau of Railroad Safety are more or less self-explanatory. These offices deal with for-hire carriers of these two transport modes. The National Highway Traffic Safety Administration deals with automotive safety in general, but the specific regulation of highway safety is mostly a matter for state, county, and municipal control.

National Transportation Safety Board

The cabinet-level Department of Transportation to which the above agencies are attached was created in 1966. At the same time, an independent safety board that reports directly to Congress was established. This is the National Transportation Safety Board. The board is largely investigative in nature and determines and reports causes, facts, and circumstances relating to transportation accidents. It reviews appeals of certificate revocations by the Department of Transportation and performs all functions in the investigation of aircraft accidents.

Future of Police-Power Regulation

Inefficient operation and maintenance of transport vehicles can be as detrimental to ecology as it is to safety. The preservation of ecological balance is a matter of general welfare, safety, and security. Concern with ecological matters has only begun to appear at both the state and federal levels of regulation. As people become more aware and concerned with the quality of life on our planet, undoubtedly more control over it will be exercised through the means of police power.

ECONOMIC REGULATION OF TRANSPORTATION

For nearly 100 years, the economic operation of the American transportation industry has been rather strictly regulated. The purpose of economic regulation is the same as that of police-power regulation: to protect the public. This protection takes the form of ensuring that there will be adequate, reliable, safe transport facilities available for everyone; that the prices charged will be reasonable; and that no user will be unduly favored over another. To accomplish this, the state and federal governments control at least three aspects of the way a transportation company does business. These are: (1) control of entry into the industry, (2) control of service standards, and (3) control of prices.

At the federal level, the agencies that provide economic regulation of interstate transportation are the Interstate Commerce Commission for railroads, oil pipelines, trucklines, buslines, domestic interstate water carriers, and domestic freight forwarders; the Civil Aeronautics Board for air carriers; and the Federal Maritime Commission for steamship lines in the ocean and non-contiguous trades. These are independent regulatory agencies that report to Congress. Most of the states have similar organizations, usually called Railroad Commissions, Public Utility Commissions, or Public Service Commissions, to regulate intrastate commerce.

One alternative to economic regulation is unrestricted free competition. There was free competition in American transportation until 1887, when the Interstate Commerce Act was passed. Under free competition, entry into the market supposedly is controlled by demand for the service; as demand increases, more carriers will start up a business. Standards of service are controlled by what the public demands and what they are willing to pay for. Prices are determined by the bidding of the various carriers for the business of the various customers. When tried in the early days of railroading, this system did not seem to work very well.

Another alternative is government ownership and operation of transportation facilities. This idea has never been popular in the United States, possibly because the institution of private property and thus free enterprise (or at least individual enterprise) is fundamental to our way of government. However, government ownership of the railroads was tried from 1917 to 1920 in connection with World War I. Although the railroad managers understandably did not like it, it seemed to work quite well and succeeded in doing a job that regular railroad management either could not or would not do. Government ownership of railroads and some other transport facilities is common in other countries and also seems to work reasonably well.

The system of regulation that has been developed in the United States limits the number of carriers of each type that serve each route or region of the country. Thus each carrier has at least a partial monopoly on some traffic and is more or less guaranteed enough revenue to make operation worthwhile. At the same time, regulatory control of services and practices allegedly preserves the benefits of competition for the public. Due to the nature of the modes of transportation that they control, the powers of the Civil Aeronautics Board and of the Federal Maritime Commission are not as complex and comprehensive as those of the Interstate Commerce Commission. The tenor and spirit of regulation by these bodies is, however, the same as that of I.C.C. regulation, although the techniques of application and enforcement are different.

Control of Entry

The document that is used to bestow a grant of operating authority upon a common carrier is usually called a *certificate of pubic convenience and necessity*. Any person proposing to start a new common-carrier service by railroad, truck, bus, or aircraft, or inland, coastwise, or intercoastal water must obtain such a certificate. The certificate specifies what route or territory a carrier may cover, and, with truck lines, the type of schedule and commodity to be carried. Railroads must obtain a certificate to abandon an old line as well as to start a new one. Since we have a large supply of transportation, the issuance of extensive certificated rights is extremely rare today.

The granting of a new certificate of public convenience and necessity usually requires that the regulatory body hold a public hearing to determine if the proposed service is or will be required by the present or future public convenience and necessity. This is not necessary in the case of common carriers who were operating a bona fide service before the regulatory law applying to them was passed. Such carriers are said to hold "grandfather rights." For some types of transportation companies, the operating-rights document is something other than a certificate. Freight brokers are given "licenses"; contract carriers and domestic freight forwarders receive "permits."

In spite of the limiting influence of the certificate system, the regulatory agencies have probably created too many rather than too few carriers. This can have the advantage of causing service competition even though rates are closely controlled. One cannot say that this policy has been entirely deliberate, because services have been developed on a route-by-route rather than a master-plan basis. Only in air transportation was there ever anything approaching an integrated overview of a complete transport system. When local-service (or feeder) airlines were created about 1947, the C.A.B. set up for them a regional route structure that did not conflict with the route structures of the domestic trunk carriers. The domestic trunk routes were also reasonably non-conflicting. This situation has become more complex, and it is safe to say that route awards and changes for all modes of transport are made with greater regard for competition on the particular route than for the total transport picture.

Control of Service Standards

The requirement that a common carrier shall provide a minimum standard of service comes down to us from the English common law. The duties imposed upon a common carrier probably date back to before William of Normandy conquered England in 1066. This shows that people have long considered it very important that transportation be easily available to everyone. Under common law a common carrier must provide service to anyone who reasonably asks for it, must treat everyone alike and not discriminate between customers, must charge reasonable rates, and must be liable to deliver the goods (or people) at the end of the journey in the same condition in which he received them. Service standards and price standards thus become intermixed and overlapping. For purposes of clarity, price standards and regulation are discussed separately in the next section.

Once a certificate or permit of operating authority has been granted, the regulatory body must see to it that the carrier uses the operating rights to provide the service he said he would. Therefore, regulatory laws usually make a general statement of the minimum services that are expected. The provisions of Section 1, paragraph 4 of the Interstate Commerce Act, which applies to railroads, pipelines, express companies, and sleeping-car companies, are illustrative:

> It shall be the duty of every common carrier subject to this part to provide and furnish transportation upon reasonable request therefor, and to establish reasonable through routes with other such carriers, and just and reasonable rates, fares, charges, and classifications applicable thereto; and it shall be the duty of common carriers by railroad subject to this part to establish reasonable through routes with common carriers by water. . . .
> It shall be the duty of every such common carrier . . . to provide reasonable facilities for operating such routes and to make reasonable rules and regulations with respect to their operation. . . .

Similar statements appear in the laws pertaining to motor carriers, domestic water carriers, domestic freight forwarders, and air carriers. In the case of buslines, trucklines, and airlines, the laws require them to provide *safe* and adequate service, equipment, and facilities. When the quotation above was written to apply to railroads, the major concern was with preventing discrimination and not with safety; concern with safety came later.

Also worthy of note is that the law not only expects carriers to provide safe and adequate service, it also expects them to form into networks. Thus, the requirement that they establish through routes and joint rates is made of railroads (as above), buslines, domestic water carriers, and airlines. Trucklines have no mandate to do so, but may form through routes with joint rates if they choose.

Many specific provisions that can be interpreted as service standards also appear in the regulatory laws. Examples are: carriers are required to issue bills of lading, and cannot set a time shorter than nine months for the filing of loss and damage claims; motor carriers can be required to provide surety bonds, policies of insurance, and so forth. Consideration of these many points is outside the scope of this discussion; the purpose here is to emphasize the extensiveness of service standards that may be imposed.

One way to ensure that transportation companies comply with the law is to give the regulatory commissions the power to revoke certificates and permits that it has issued. Certificates of railroads and domestic common carriers by water are not revokable. The I.C.C., however, has the power to revoke certificates of motor carriers who willfully fail to comply with the Interstate Commerce Act. The C.A.B. has similar power over airlines. Such harsh measures are seldom used, as the laws also provide other penalties for violators. Nevertheless, there is probably no way for the regulatory commissions to enforce the aspect of service standards the shipper is interested in. The transportation user is usually chiefly concerned with the quality of the service he gets. Revocation of certificates deals with the question of whether the carrier provides some service or no service at all. If a shipper can prove that a carrier has refused him service when it was reasonaby requested, then that shipper has a case to take before the regulatory body. If the carrier is only guilty of giving a poor and unsatisfactory service, the customer's remedy is in the marketplace: he can find another way to ship or travel.

Control of Rates

A common misconception is that freight rates are set by the government. While it is true that the regulatory agencies do have extensive power over transportation prices, most freight rates are set by negotiation between carriers and shippers. Because most freight moves on carriers supervised by the I.C.C., most freight rates are subject to approval by the Interstate Commerce Commission. The I.C.C. is empowered to investigate rates upon receiving a complaint or on its own initiative. It can conduct a public hearing and determine what rate or rates will be lawful in the future. Since it has the power to set minimum rates and maximum rates, it can, in effect, set freight rates. This power does not apply, however, until after an existing rate has been declared unreasonable or otherwise unlawful. Freight rates are being changed continuously, and by far the majority of them are set by the carriers and simply approved by the I.C.C. All proposed changes must be filed with the Commission 30 days before they became effective (with some exceptions). The I.C.C. checks the new tariff pages and if they are in the right form approves them. Only when official protests are made to a new rate, or when an unorthodox change causes the Commission to investigate on its own motion, is a newly published rate suspended.

Rate requirements. The general provisions of all of our economic regulation of transportation is perhaps best exemplified in the first six sections of the Interstate Commerce Act. These were designed to prevent abuses by railroads, about which there was a great deal of concern a hundred years ago. They are still valid guidelines and have since been extended in about the same form to all modes of transport. Here again, the regulations extend to practices as well as prices.

Section 1 of the Interstate Commerce Act, among many other things, requires that all charges be just and reasonable, and that every unjust and unreasonable charge be prohibited and declared to be unlawful. This section also prohibits the granting of free passes except in certain specific instances.

Section 2 of the Act prohibits a common carrier from giving rebates or drawbacks, or charging one person a greater or less amount than another for the same service. Penalties for such "kickbacks" are exacted upon both carriers who give them and shippers who receive them.

Section 3 of the Act reaffirms the first two sections in that it is a broad prohibition of preference or prejudice. Sometimes it is referred to as dealing with "place discriminations," because it forbids any common carrier to give undue or unreasonable preference or advantage, or prejudice or disadvantage, to any particular person, company, firm, corporation, association, locality, port, port district, gateway, transit point, region, district, territory, or any particular description of traffic. This section of the law also provides that goods shall not be delivered until all charges have been paid, except as prescribed by the Commission.

Section 4 prohibits railroads (and domestic water carriers) from charging more for a short haul than for a long haul. This, of course, applies to movement of passengers or goods of the same kind, in the same direction, over the same line. In the 1870's long- and short-haul discriminations were a matter of serious public concern. Today, exceptions are permitted in particular competitive situations. This section also forbids a carrier to charge more as a through rate between distant towns than what the total of the rates between the intermediate towns would be. The type of regulation found in Section 4 does not apply to buslines and trucklines, domestic freight forwarders, or air carriers.

Section 5 of the Interstate Commerce Act leads with combinations and consolidations of carriers. Section 5 was originally designed to prevent railroads from pooling freight or pooling revenue to restrain competition. Now this section gives the I.C.C. power over railroad and railroad-truck mergers. This sort of restriction is found in all of our economic regulation. It carries out a rather firm policy that ownership of the modes of trans-portation shall be kept clearly separated.

Section 6 of the Act also expresses a type of regulation that applies to all of our modes of public transportation. It requires that common carriers must file with the Commission all rates and fares that are to be charged, must publish them, and must make them readily available to public inspection. No rate may be changed on less than 30 days notice unless by special permission from the Commission. In addition, the published rates are to be strictly observed. The latter is generally enforced even where the published rate has been put in the rate book in error and mistakenly violates some other part of the law. In general, this requirement that rates be published and observed applies to all types of carriers in the United States, and in fact gives all published rates the force of law.

Reasons for Regulation: The Early Railroad Industry

Unless one understands the reasons why the regulations just discussed came about, their restriction upon the transportation businessman may seem rather severe. The behavior of the railroad industry before they were enacted made them seem very necessary at the time. There is some argument for easing restrictions today, but certainly many of the rules are reasonable requirements which protect the ordinary businessman.

If you wanted to ship something in the United States before 1830, you could send it on a stagecoach, a Conestoga wagon, a canal boat, a flatboat down river, or a coasting schooner. If you didn't like the prices or the services of the for-hire carriers, it was relatively easy to get your own wagon or boat and do it yourself.

Partly because of this limited transportation, the economy of America was really not national in scope until after the Civil War. It was a series or network of small, local economies; each was centered around a seaport or trade center from which merchant proprietors did business with craftsmen and farmers in the immediate hinterland.

When the railroad came in 1830, local merchants quickly recognized that it was a better way than boat or horse and wagon to get things to and from the hinterland. However, they did not want it to become a tool that would siphon off any of their business to neighboring trade centers or seaports. Consequently, the early railroads were built with a different track gauge in each local economic region of the country so that they could not interconnect or provide through service. This situation was not completely corrected until almost 1900.

When trade and travel were local, the difference in gauge did not seem to be a handicap. Railroads did not compete with each other, they were far superior to horse and wagon, and people did not feel discriminated against. The Civil War, however, changed the economy of the United States into a national one. Local sources of food and manufacturing were disrupted. The Midwest became the breadbasket of the nation and the Northeast became a manufacturing district. A strong demand developed for long-distance rail transport.

At the same time, the modern corporate method of financing business enterprise began to develop. America was rich in natural resources, but no one, not even the government, had enough money to develop them on the scale considered necessary. Therefore, a method was found in the corporation for pooling the savings of many to raise large amounts of capital. This attracted men who realized intuitively that the great need for long-distance railroads would make people eager to invest in them. These men were not dedicated railroaders interested in providing a public service. They were robber barons who were interested in exploiting the corporate method of financing in order to become rich. They accomplished this in several ways. One way was to sell the public far more stock than what the assets of the railroad were worth and to pocket as much of the proceeds as possible. The siphoning off of cash was often done by establishing another company that sold services or supplies to the railroad at exorbitant prices. Fortunes were also made by manipulating railroad securities on the stock market by selling short in "bear and bull" raids, Also, the merger was, then as now, a useful device for raiding a company that had a large cash surplus and draining it off.

From 1850 to the early 1900's men like Cornelius Vanderbilt, Jay Gould, Jim Fisk, Daniel Drew, Thomas Scott, Edward Harriman, and J. P. Morgan merged the country's railroads into large regional or transcontinental competing systems. To them, owning railroads was a game; the object of the game was to maximize profits so that the stock would sell well on the market. The best way to maximize profits was to eliminate your competitor and to get a monopoly on all of the traffic. Service was not a primary consideration in doing this because the public had to use the railroad; there was no other way to go. But the monopoly game had serious consequences for the public who needed to use the railroads on a day-to-day basis.

When railroads compete on a long-distance basis, the heaviest traffic, of course, is between the largest cities. However, two competing railroads do not necessarily go through all the same intermediate small cities en route to the big ones. This quickly gave rise to long- and short-haul discrimination. Competing lines would cut rates on desirable traffic between heavy traffic points, and then raise rates to intermediate points where there was no competition.

Rate wars also were common. The object of a rate war is to bankrupt your competitior so that you can buy him out. Prices are cut far below cost on the assumption that you have a larger capital backlog than the competitor and can outlast him. When both lines are under one management and the monopoly is secure, rates can be raised to an unreasonably high level. Doing business on a cut-rate basis causes maintenance to be deferred, and safety then deteriorates drastically. Around the turn of century the railroads were killing about 12,000 people per year. On a fatalities-per-mile basis this is a far higher rate than on our highways today.

Many other devices were used by railroads to lure traffic away from competitors. Free passes were granted generously (these also were especially given to public officials). Very large shippers were given secret rebates of part of the money they had paid for transportation, or sometimes of part of the money their competitors had paid. Secret, unpublished rates were applied for some customers but not available for everyone. Rates were often suddenly lowered for a day or two and then raised, with only favored customers finding out about this. Other irritants were that it was hard to collect loss and damage claims from the railroads, and railway managers and employees were not particularly gracious in their treatment of the public.

Development of the Interstate Commerce Commission. By 1870 the public, and particularly the midwestern farmers, who constituted a powerful voting force, were very dissatisfied with the rail lines. The farmers formed an association known as the Patrons of Husbandry and popularly called the Grange. The Grange succeeded in having the states of Illinois, Iowa, Minnesota, and Wisconsin pass strict laws regulating railroads. Called the Granger laws, these regulations set maximum rates, forbade long- and short-haul discrimination, discouraged pooling and mergers, and prohibited free passes to public officials both for intrastate and interstate commerce. The laws gave way to state regulatory commissions; then in the Wabash Case in 1886 the United States Supreme Court decided that the states do not have constitutional power to regulate interstate commerce. The pressure of public opinion upon federal legislators at this time resulted in the passage of the Act to Regulate Commerce in 1887. Now called the Interstate Commerce Act, this law has been amended about 150 times to the present.

The Interstate Commerce Commission created by the Act did not have much power during its first twenty years. At first the railroads seemed cooperative, but when they discovered that the Commission could not enforce its orders, they were reluctant to obey them. In addition, they challenged the constitutionality of many parts of the Act; adverse decisions reduced the Commission's power further.

Thus, for almost the first twenty years of its existence, the Interstate Commerce Commission was not a particularly powerful body. Some writers have referred to this era as "the doldrums." At the turn of the century, however, the United States entered a period of "trust busting" in which the government attempted to bring big business corporations under control and to prevent price-fixing monopolies in basic industries such as petroleum, steel, and transportation.

Shortly after 1900, Congress passed a series of amendments to the Interstate Commerce Act. As a result of these, the Interstate Commerce Commission emerged at the time of World War I as perhaps the most powerful arm of the United States government. The most important of these amendments were the Elkins Act, the Hepburn Act, and the Mann-Elkins Act.

The Elkins Act of 1903 established stiff penalties for shippers who consented to accept rebates from railroads; these were in addition to penalties for carriers who gave rebates to customers. In addition, the law made it a misdemeanor for a carrier to charge any rate except that legally published in his freight tariff.

The Hepburn Act of 1906 brought sleeping-car companies, express companies, and petroleum pipelines under the jurisdiction of the Interstate Commerce Commission. It also gave the Commission the power to prescribe maximum rates. This did not give the I.C.C. power to set rates as an original action, but only to act after a rate had been found unreasonable. The amendment also gave the Commission the power to force railroads to establish through routes and joint rates. A very important provision was that the orders of the Commission were made binding upon carriers without the need for court action, and a $5,000 fine was provided for each day that disobedience to an order continued.

The Mann-Elkins Act of 1910 gave the I.C.C. power to suspend rates. Thus, when a carrier published a new rate that was protested or about which the Commission held some doubt, the rate could be postponed until an investigation was made. This Act also restored powers over long- and short-haul rate situations, which the Commission had previously lost due to court interpretations of the law.

Government ownership. The new powers that the Interstate Commerce Commission gained from these and other turn-of-the-century amendments were rather stringently applied. The result was that railroad rates were held down during a period when railroad costs were rising. Because of this, the rail system was not in a strong condition at the beginning of World

War I; the sudden growth of wartime traffic caused serious congestion on its lines. Thus, in 1917 the federal government took control of the lines and operated them as a single system until March, 1920.

Changes in regulatory policy. The Transportation Act of 1920, which became another amendment to the Act to Regulate Commerce, was passed by Congress to aid the transition of railroads from government control back to private ownership. In doing so, it made a shift from a generally restrictive policy of rail regulation to one that recognized that the carriers must have reasonable earnings in order to survive.

Although the Act of 1920 further increased the power of the I.C.C., it also contained provisions that aided the railroads. On the one hand, this law gave the Commission power to prescribe minimum as well as maximum rates, and required railroads to obtain certificates of public convenience and necessity before building new lines. On the other, it provided financial aid to them for the transfer to civilian control. Among numerous provisions designed to aid the roads, the most lasting has been the concept of the "rule of rate-making." Although modified more than once by subsequent legislation, this rule recognizes the principle that in adjusting freight rates the Commission should consider the effect of the rate changes upon the movement of the traffic, the need of the public for service, and the need of the carriers for revenue.

Economic Regulation Affecting Other Modes of Transport

Subsequent to the passage of the Transportation Act of 1920 and the change of regulatory policy that it represented, the impact of economic regulation has also been felt by carriers in the other modes of transport.

Water transportation. At the outbreak of World War I, the United States was depending on foreign ships to carry about 90 percent of its import-export trade. Foreign vessels became unavailable because of the war. Congress then passed the Shipping Act of 1916, which established the United States Shipping Board. The primary purpose of the Board was to establish a U.S. merchant fleet for use in the war.

The Shipping Board had some economic regulatory powers as well. The principal purpose of these was to exempt shipping conferences from the antitrust acts. Conferences are similar to land-carrier freight rate bureaus and engage in the publication of freight rate tariffs used by groups of steamship lines. Since this is "collusive" rate-making, it could be contrary to antitrust regulation if used in restraint of trade. In addition, the Shipping Act required carriers to refrain from preferential or prejudicial rates, refrain from deferred rebates, observe published tariff rates, and not engage in other unfair practices. The Board did not have control of entry into the business or control over the establishment of freight rates.

In 1936, the duties of the Shipping Board were taken over by the newly established United States Maritime Commission. Subsequent legislation and reorganization has changed the name of the body from time to time. The current organization is known as the Federal Maritime Commission, and it has jurisdiction over American steamship lines in foreign commerce and those operating in the non-contiguous trade between the mainland and our offshore states and possessions. Responsibility for the economic regulation of interstate water transport was given to the Interstate Commerce Commission by the Transportation Act of 1940. Thus, water transportation companies operating on the inland waterways, Great Lakes, coastwise, and inter-coastally are covered by Part III of the Interstate Commerce Act.

Motor transportation.   Prior to the 1930's, the state of the American highway system prevented the transcontinental expansion of the truck and bus industry. Many well-established for-hire motor carriers existed in different regions of the country. Because of their limited scope, they were regulated in economic as well as safety matters principally by the individual states.

During the Depression, many unemployed men secured trucks cheaply or on credit and began trucking on an itinerant basis. A similar "jitney" approach to bus transport also prevailed over some routes. By 1935 both the organized motor-carrier industry and the railroads were favoring some control of rampant competition. Congress therefore placed interstate motor carriers under control of the Interstate Commerce Commission in 1935.

The law is known as Part II of the Interstate Commerce Act and is very similar in its provisions of Part I, which applies to railroads and related carriers.

Air transportation.   The airline industry of the United States grew out of the airmail service started by the Post Office Department in 1918. Although the service was contracted to independent businessmen after the Kelly Act of 1925 was passed, the government's approach toward airlines was one of promotion rather than economic regulation of the industry. Until 1934, the administration of airmail contracts, routes, rates, and services was entirely in the hands of the Post Office.

After the transition from the Republican Hoover administration to the Democratic Roosevelt administration in 1932, there were charges that the airlines had been excessively subsidized. Investigations resulted in the Air Mail Act of 1934. This required the Post Office to establish airmail routes and schedules and to grant the contracts for them. The Interstate Commerce Commission was to set the airmail rates to be paid the carriers, and the Bureau of Air Commerce of the Department of Commerce was to continue its airway and safety regulation.

This three-way division of authority did not work well, but by 1938 the airlines had enough independence to be regulated as for-hire carriers rather than as servants of the Post Office Department. The Civil Aeronautics Act of 1938 established economic regulation of interstate air carriers for the first time. After a reorganization in 1940, this law established two agencies. One, the Civil Aeronautics Administration (this became the Federal Aviation Administration in 1958), was responsible for promoting aviation, enforcing safety regulations, and developing and operating the airways. The other agency, still known as the Civil Aeronautics Board, was an economic regulatory agency very similar to the Interstate Commerce Commission in function. Much of the Civil Aeronautics Act (rewritten to become the Federal Aviation Act in 1958) was patterned directly from the Interstate Commerce Act. It provides for very similar control of entry through certificates of public convenience and necessity, control of rates by the C.A.B., and the usual prohibitions of unreasonableness, undue preference or prejudice, and discrimination.

Freight-forwarder regulation. Since their inception shortly after the turn of the century, domestic surface-freight forwarders have grown to be relatively important carriers of small shipments. Since they "buy" service from the railroads on a carload-rated basis, they appear to the railroad to be shippers. However, they "sell" service to the public on a less-than-carload basis at a substantially higher rate. To the public they appear to be carriers. Thus, some confusion arose as to whether they could participate in establishing through rates and other divisions of revenue with regulated carriers or whether they were to be treated like customers. The Freight Forwarder Act of 1942 and an amendment to it in 1950 placed these companies under federal economic regulation and declared them to be common carriers. Today they are regulated in much the same manner as railroads, trucklines, and water carriers by the Interstate Commerce Commission under the provisions of Part IV of the Interstate Commerce Act.

MODERN REGULATORY AGENCIES

The preceding discussion has mentioned many of the federal promotional, enforcement, and economic regulatory agencies that deal with transportation. Transportation is such a pervasive activity that many departments of the government are concerned with it. The reader should be aware that general promotional activity and safety regulation are done by the executive branch of the government, and that the economic regulatory agencies report to the legislative branch. At the federal level, these agencies deal with interstate commerce, with some exceptions. The individual states also have various offices to deal with transport regulation; these, of course, are limited to intrastate commerce.

Modern federal economic regulatory agencies include the Interstate Commerce Commission, which has jurisdiction over railroads, petroleum pipelines, express companies, sleeping-car companies, trucklines, buslines, domestic water carriers (except those to offshore states and possessions), and domestic surface-freight forwarders. The Civil Aeronautics Board regulates the economic activities of interstate airlines. Although the emphasis of the Federal Maritime Commission was originally on foreign commerce, it also regulates interstate commerce because of its jurisdiction over water carriers to Alaska and Hawaii.

The exhibits that appear as Figures 3, 4, and 5 on the following pages present detailed information about the many transportation offices and organizations found in the structure of our federal government.

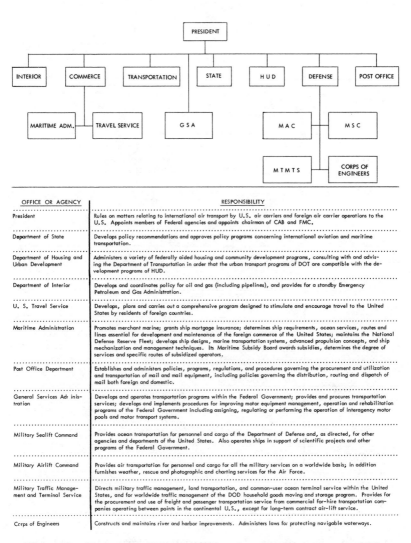

OFFICE OR AGENCY	RESPONSIBILITY
President	Rules on matters relating to international air transport by U.S. air carriers and foreign air carrier operations to the U.S. Appoints members of Federal agencies and appoints chairman of CAB and FMC.
Department of State	Develops policy recommendations and approves policy programs concerning international aviation and maritime transportation.
Department of Housing and Urban Development	Administers a variety of federally aided housing and community development programs, consulting with and advising the Department of Transportation in order that the urban transport programs of DOT are compatible with the development programs of HUD.
Department of Interior	Develops and coordinates policy for oil and gas (including pipelines), and provides for a standby Emergency Petroleum and Gas Administration.
U. S. Travel Service	Develops, plans and carries out a comprehensive program designed to stimulate and encourage travel to the United States by residents of foreign countries.
Maritime Administration	Promotes merchant marine; grants ship mortgage insurance; determines ship requirements, ocean services, routes and lines essential for development and maintenance of the foreign commerce of the United States; maintains the National Defense Reserve Fleet; develops ship designs, marine transportation systems, advanced propulsion concepts, and ship mechanization and management techniques. Its Maritime Subsidy Board awards subsidies, determines the degree of services and specific routes of subsidized operators.
Post Office Department	Establishes and administers policies, programs, regulations, and procedures governing the procurement and utilization and transportation of mail and mail equipment, including policies governing the distribution, routing and dispatch of mail both foreign and domestic.
General Services Administration	Develops and operates transportation programs within the Federal Government; provides and procures transportation services; develops and implements procedures for improving motor equipment management, operation and rehabilitation programs of the Federal Government including assigning, regulating or performing the operation of interagency motor pools and motor transport systems.
Military Sealift Command	Provides ocean transportation for personnel and cargo of the Department of Defense and, as directed, for other agencies and departments of the United States. Also operates ships in support of scientific projects and other programs of the Federal Government.
Military Airlift Command	Provides air transportation for personnel and cargo for all the military services on a worldwide basis; in addition furnishes weather, rescue and photographic and charting services for the Air Force.
Military Traffic Management and Terminal Service	Directs military traffic management, land transportation, and common-user ocean terminal service within the United States, and for worldwide traffic management of the DOD household goods moving and storage program. Provides for the procurement and use of freight and passenger transportation service from commercial for-hire transportation companies operating between points in the continental U.S., except for long-term contract air-lift service.
Corps of Engineers	Constructs and maintains river and harbor improvements. Administers laws for protecting navigable waterways.

Figure 3. Transport Responsibilities in the Executive Branch. Source: Transportation Association of America, *Transportation Facts and Trends*, 9th ed., July 1972.

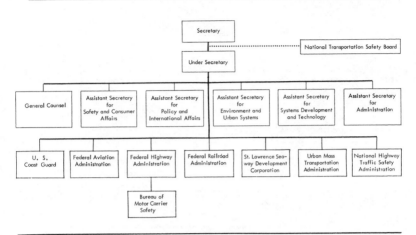

OFFICE OR AGENCY	RESPONSIBILITY
Secretary of Transportation	Under direction of the President, exercises and provides leadership in transportation matters, develops national transportation policies and programs, including compliance with safety laws pertaining to all modes of transport.
National Transportation Safety Board	Determines and reports causes, facts and circumstances relating to transportation accidents; reviews on appeal the revocation, suspension or denial of any certificate or license issued by the Department; and exercises all functions relating to aircraft accident investigations.
General Counsel	Legal services, including the legal aspects and drafting of legislation.
Asst. Secy. for Safety and Consumer Affairs	Safety coordination; regulation of movement of hazardous materials; gas pipeline safety regulations; and representation of the public viewpoint, in the Department, with regard to transportation matters.
Asst. Secy. for Policy and International Affairs	Economic and systems analysis; policy review; transport data; international transport facilitation; and, technical assistance.
Asst. Secy. for Environment and Urban Systems	Coordinate policies, programs, and resources of DOT transport program with public and private efforts to solve environmental problems having an impact on transportation.
Asst. Secy. for Systems Development and Technology	Scientific and technologic research and development relating to the speed, safety and economy of transportation; noise abatement; and, transportation information planning. .
Asst. Secy. for Administration	Organization, budgeting, staffing, personnel management, logistics and procurement policy, management systems and other administrative support for the Department.
U. S. Coast Guard	Provides navigational aids to inland and offshore water and trans-oceanic air commerce; enforces federal maritime safety, including approval of plans for vessel construction and repair. Administers Great Lakes Pilotage Act of 1960. Has responsibility for water vessel anchorages, drawbridge operation, and locations and clearances of bridges over navigable water (Previously under the Corps of Engineers).
Federal Aviation Administration	Promotes civil aviation generally, including research and promulgation and enforcement of safety regulations. Develops and operates the airways, including facilities. Administers the federal airport program.
Federal Highway Administration	Responsible for implementation of the Federal-Aid Highway Program; National Traffic and Motor Vehicle Safety Act of 1966; and the Highway Safety Act of 1966. Responsibility for reasonableness of tolls on bridges over navigable waters (previously under the Corps of Engineers). Administers federal highway construction, research planning, safety programs, and Federal-Aid highway funds (formerly under Bureau of Public Roads).
Federal Railroad Administration	Responsible for the operation of the Alaska Railroad; administration of the High-Speed Ground Transportation Program; implementation of railroad safety laws; oil pipeline safety; and advises the Secretary on matters pertaining to national railroad policy developments.
St. Lawrence Seaway Dev. Corp.	Administers operation and maintenance of the U. S. portion of the St. Lawrence Seaway, including toll rates.
Urban Mass Transportation Administration	Responsible for developing comprehensive coordinated mass transport systems for metropolitan and urban areas, including R & D and demonstration projects; aid for technical studies, planning, engineering, and designing; financial aid and grants to public bodies for modernization, equipment, and training of personnel.
National Highway Traffic Safety Administration	Formulation and promulgation of programs for use by the States in driver performance; development of uniform standards for keeping accident records and investigation of accident causes; vehicle registration and inspection and the safety aspects of highway design and maintenance. Planning, development and enforcement of federal motor vehicle safety standards relating to the manufacturing of motor vehicles.
Bureau of Motor Carrier Safety	Administers and enforces motor carrier safety regulations (formerly under the ICC) and the regulations governing the transportation of hazardous materials.

Figure 4. Department of Transportation: Organization and Responsibilities.
Source: Transportation Association of America, op. cit.

The Federal transportation regulatory agencies are arms of the legislative branch of the Government. They are NOT courts. They do have recourse to the courts in order to enforce their orders, although they exercise quasi-judicial powers, as well as quasi-legislative powers. Their members are appointed by the President with Senate approval at salaries of $38,000 with chairmen receiving an additional $2,000. Not more than a majority of one can be from any one political party.

INTERSTATE COMMERCE COMMISSION

The ICC was created in 1887 by the Act to Regulate Commerce. It currently consists of eleven members who serve terms of seven years. Its Chairman is appointed by the President, and its Vice Chairman is elected annually by the members. The following table indicates the types of domestic interstate carriers over which the Commission has economic and safety jurisdiction, as well as its other major functions.

Modes Regulated	Major Functions
Railroads (1887), Express Companies, Sleeping Car Companies (1906) Oil Pipe Lines (1906)* - Common carriers only Motor Carriers (1935) Private carriers and carriers of agricultural commodities exclusively are exempt, as are motor vehicles used by farm co-ops. Water Carriers (1940), Water carriers operating coastwise, intercoastal, and on inland waters of the U.S. Private carriers and carriers of liquid bulk or three or less dry bulk commodities in a single vessel are exempt. Freight Forwarders (1942) Non-profit shippers' associations exempt. *Gas Pipelines regulated by Federal Power Commission.	Regulates, in varying degrees by mode of transport, surface carrier operations, including rates, routes, operating rights, abondonment and mergers; conducts investigations and awards damages where applicable and administers railroad bankruptcy. Prescribes uniform system of accounts and records, evaluates property owned or used by carriers subject to the act; authorizes issuance of securities or assumption of obligations by carriers by railroad and certain common or contract carriers by motor vehicle. Develops preparedness programs covering rail, motor, and inland waterways utilization.

CIVIL AERONAUTICS BOARD

The CAB, as it exists today, is an outgrowth of the Civil Aeronautics Act of 1938, Presidential Reorganization Plans of 1940, and the Federal Aviation Act of 1958. There are five Board members, each serving terms of six years. The Chairman and Vice Chairman are appointed annually by the President.

Regulates	Major Functions
U.S. domestic and international air carriers Foreign air carrier operations to, from, and within the U.S.	Regulates carrier operations, including rates, routes, operating rights, and mergers; determines and grants subsidies. Assists in the development of international air transport, and grants, subject to Presidential approval, foreign operating certificates to U.S. carriers and U.S. operating permits to foreign carriers.

FEDERAL MARITIME COMMISSION

The present FMC was established by Presidential Reorganization Plan 7 of 1961, although most of its regulatory powers are similar to those granted its predecessor agencies by the Shipping Act of 1916 and subsequent statutes. The Commission consists of five members appointed to four-year terms by the President with Senate approval. The President designates the Chairman. The Vice Chairman is elected annually by the members.

Regulates	Major Functions
All U.S.-flag and foreign-flag vessels operating in the foreign commerce of the U.S. and common carriers by water operating in domestic trade to points beyond the continental U.S.	Regulates services, practices, and agreements of water common carriers in international trade. Regulates rates and practices of water common carriers operating in domestic trade to points beyond continental U.S.

Figure 5.   Federal Transportation Regulatory Agencies.
Source: Transportation Association of America, op. cit.

REFERENCES

Fair, Marvin L., and John Guandolo. *Transportation Regulation.* Dubuque: Wm. C. Brown, 1972.

Farris, Martin T. "Rationale: The Regulation of Motor Carriers." In *Modern Transportation: Selected Readings*, 2d ed., edited by Martin T. Farris and Paul T. McElhiney. Boston: Houghton Mifflin, 1973.

Flood, Kenneth U. *Traffic Management.* Dubuque: Wm. C. Brown, 1963.

Frederick, John H. *Commercial Air Transportation.* Homewood, Ill.: Richard D. Irwin, 1961.

Locklin, D. Philip. *Economics of Transportation*, 7th ed. Homewood, Ill.: Richard D. Irwin, 1972, chapter 10.

Luna, Charles. *The UTU Handbook of Transportation in America.* New York: Popular Library, 1971.

McDowell, Carl E., and Helen M. Gibbs. *Ocean Transportation.* New York: McGraw-Hill, 1954.

Nicholson, Joseph L. *Air Transportation Management.* New York: John Wiley & Sons, 1951.

Smith, Henry Ladd. *Airways.* New York: Russell & Russell, 1965.

United States, Civil Aeronautics Board. *Aeronautical Statutes and Related Material.* Washington, D.C.: Government Printing Office, 1970.

United States, Gilman Udell, Superintendent House Document Room. *Laws Relating to Shipping and Merchant Marine.* Washington, D.C.: Government Printing Office, 1968.

United States, Interstate Commerce Commission. *The Interstate Commerce Act together with Text of Supplementary Acts and Related Sections of Various Other Acts.* Washington, D.C.: Government Printing Office, 1968.

CHAPTER 9

Shipping Contracts

The purpose of this chapter is to describe the basic provisions of the bill of lading and similar shipping contracts. Although regulatory laws set forth some requirements for shipping contracts, the degree of responsibility that the carrier assumes under them varies greatly from mode to mode. Because of this, the shipper's selection of a transportation alternative may be affected by contract provisions as well as by factors such as cost, speed, and dependability.

Common carriers make a separate contract for each shipment that moves. The bill of lading is used by railroads, domestic freight forwarders, trucklines, and steamship companies, although not in identical form in each case. The railway express document is usually called an express receipt, and air freight shipments move with an air bill. Contract motor carriers make long-term (30- to 60-day) contracts, and the water and air modes use charters. Contract carriers keep track of individual loads with trip tickets, driver's manifests, or documents with similar names.

One of the most important matters covered by shipping contracts is what the carrier will or will not pay for in case the shipment is damaged or never reaches destination. A shipping contract, like any legally enforceable contract, is an agreement made by two parties who are legally competent to contract. It involves a lawful consideration that one party will give the other for the performance of a lawful act that is capable of performance. Thus, a shipping contract is not a one-sided thing in which the customer may demand performance from the carrier without giving consideration: the customer must pay the freight bill even if the goods are lost or damaged, or he violates the contract himself.

HISTORICAL DEVELOPMENT

Ancient commerce was mostly by ship, and not many people could read and write. Most shipping contracts were verbal agreements between the cargo owner and the master of the vessel, but very often the cargo owner or his representative went along to see that the goods were delivered. By about 1400 the custom of listing all of the cargo in the "ship's book" developed; this was very similar to listing it on the "ship's manifest" as is done today. At the same time, the courts, particularly in England, were beginning to define the duties and obligations of common carriers. Finally, in 1703, an English judge, Lord Holt, explained the liability of common carriers in the case of *Coggs* v. *Bernard*. He said:

> The law charges this person thus intrusted to carry goods, against all events, but acts of God, and of the enemies of the King. For though the force be never so great, as if an irresistible multitude of people should rob him, nevertheless he is chargeable. And this is a politic establishment, contrived by the policy of the law, for the safety of all persons, the necessity of whose affairs oblige them to trust these sorts of persons, that they may be safe in their ways of dealing; for else those carriers might have an opportunity of undoing all persons that had any dealings with them, by combining with thieves, &c., and yet doing it in such a clandestine manner as would not be possible to be discovered. And this is the reason the law is founded in that point.

Translated from its archaic language, this means that a common carrier must deliver goods in the same condition as he received them or pay for the loss or damage, except for two reasons. The exceptions were "acts of God," or natural happenings such as hurricanes over which the carrier has no control, and "enemies of the King," which essentially means the warlike act of a foreign power. This degree of liability is referred to as common-law liability.

For about 150 years, bills of lading remained very simple documents that acknowledged receipt of the goods and promised to deliver them in the same condition as received. As the Industrial Revolution progressed, however, the duty to pay for almost all loss and damage became a burden, and common carriers looked for a way to escape it.

The principal method English carriers used to reduce their liability was the released-value rate. They posted notices that they would not pay more than a certain amount per pound for loss or damage unless the shipper paid a higher rate. The practice soon became so widespread that all traffic moved on released-value rates, and carrier liability was negligible. Parliament passed the Railway and Canal Traffic Act of 1854, which required any agreement in advance as to the value of the goods to be in a signed, written document. It then became the custom to issue a bill of lading on every shipment, stating the amount to be recovered in event of loss. About this time also, the liability coverage of the ocean bill of lading began to differ greatly from the land bill. Water bills of lading are discussed subsequently.

Like their English counterparts, early American canals and railroads used bills of lading. Each carrier made up his own, so they were all different. This was fine as long as railroads were local affairs. When railroads joined together for long-distance traffic, lack of uniformity caused trouble. By 1900 shippers suffered with some other bill-of-lading problems as well. There was no law requiring a carrier to issue or sign a bill of lading, so he could conceivably refuse to do so. Released-value provisions were common, and sometimes appeared in very fine print. Carriers accepted liability only for incidents occurring on their own lines, and connecting carriers on through routes maintained that they were not parties to the contract issued by the origin carrier. Like other railroad abuses, these were corrected by government regulation.

The original Act to Regulate Commerce did not deal with the shipping contract, but subsequent amendments soon did so. The Carmack Amendment of 1906 required the carrier to issue a bill of lading and made the initial carrier liable for loss and damage on its own lines or those of a connecting carrier. The Cummins Amendments of 1915 and 1916 restricted the use of released-value rates essentially to cases where the value of the goods is hard to determine. Today, carriers must have advance approval of the I.C.C. to publish released-value rates. In 1916, the Pomerene Act gave the I.C.C. power to prescribe the form and content of bills of lading. In 1919, the Commission prescribed a uniform bill of lading to be used by all carriers. Since trucks were not regulated until 1935, this did not apply to them, but today trucklines use a uniform bill that is almost identical to the rail bill. The liability that carriers have under these bills of lading is not quite as extensive as common-law liability, but it is so complete that land carriers are sometimes said to be insurers of the goods. This degree of liability that they have is called bill-of-lading liability.

LAND BILLS OF LADING

An illustration of the Uniform Straight Bill of Lading is shown in Figures 6 and 7. This or a similar bill is used by railroads, domestic freight forwarders, and motor trucklines. Although we have been referring to it as a contract, it has three functions. It is a receipt, an evidence of title, and a contract of carriage.

First, the bill of lading is a receipt for the goods. This function of the bill may be considered separately from the contract terms and conditions of the bill. This distinction is necessary because, once it has been signed, a contract may not be altered without permission of both parties. With a freight shipment the condition of the goods may change after the bill has been made out. Careful notation on the receipt portion of the document indicates whether the damage occurred before or after the carrier took possession of the goods. The statement of receipt appears on the face of the bill near the top of the page. It reads as follows:

> RECEIVED, subject to the classifications and tariffs in effect on the date of the issue of this Bill of Lading, at _____, 19____, from _____, the property described below, in apparent good order, except as noted (contents and condition of contents of packages unknown), marked, consigned, and destined as indicated below, which said company (the word company being understood throughout this contract as meaning any person or corporation in possession of the property under the contract) agrees to carry to its usual place of delivery at said destination, if on its own road or its own water line, otherwise to deliver to another carrier on the route to said destination. It

(Uniform Domestic Straight Bill of Lading, adopted by Carriers in Official, Southern, Western and Illinois Classification territories, March 15, 1922, as amended August 1, 1930, and June 15, 1941.)

UNIFORM STRAIGHT BILL OF LADING

Original—Not Negotiable

Shipper's No...........

(To be Printed on "White" Paper)

Agent's No.............

Company

RECEIVED, subject to the classifications and tariffs in effect on the date of the issue of this Bill of Lading,

at.., 19...

from....................

the property described below, in apparent good order, except as noted (contents and condition of contents of packages unknown), marked, consigned, and destined as indicated below, which said company (the word company being understood throughout this contract as meaning any person or corporation in possession of the property under the contract) agrees to carry to its usual place of delivery at said destination, if on its own road or its own water line, otherwise to deliver to another carrier on the route to said destination. It is mutually agreed, as to each carrier of all or any of said property over all or any portion of said route to destination, and as to each party at any time interested in all or any of said property, that every service to be performed hereunder shall be subject to all the conditions not prohibited by law, whether printed or written, herein contained, including the conditions on back hereof, which are hereby agreed to by the shipper and accepted for himself and his assigns.

(Mail or street address of consignee—For purposes of notification only.)

Consigned to......................

Destination...State of.........................County of...........................

Route........................

Delivering Carrier....................................Car Initial.......................Car No...................

No. Pack- ages	Description of Articles, Special Marks, and Exceptions	*Weight (Subject to Correction)	Class or Rate	Check Column	Subject to Section 7 of conditions, if this ship- ment is to be delivered to the consignee without recourse on the consign- or, the consignor shall sign the following state- ment:
					The carrier shall not make delivery of this shipment without pay- ment of freight and all other lawful charges.
					.... (Signature of consignor.)
					If charges are to be pre- paid, write or stamp here, "To be Prepaid."
					....
					Received $............. to apply in prepayment of the charges on the property described hereon.
					.... Agent or Cashier.
					Per...................... (The signature here acknowl- edges only the amount prepaid.)

*If the shipment moves between two ports by a carrier by water, the law requires that the bill of lading shall state whether it is "carrier's or shipper's weight."

Note.—Where the rate is dependent on value, shippers are required to state specifically in writing the agreed or declared value of the property.

The agreed or declared value of the property is hereby specifically stated by the shipper to be not exceeding

Charges advanced:

......................................per.................

$......................

....Shipper. ....Agent.

Per.. Per....................................

Permanent postoffice address of shipper...............................

Figure 6. Uniform Straight Bill of Lading.
Courtesy: Uniform Freight Classification Committee.

CONTRACT TERMS AND CONDITIONS

Sec. 1. (a) The carrier or party in possession of any of the property herein described shall be liable as at common law for any loss thereof or damage thereto, except as hereinafter provided.

(b) No carrier or party in possession of all or any of the property herein described shall be liable for any loss thereof or damage thereto or delay caused by the act of God, the public enemy, the authority of law, or the act or default of the shipper or owner, or for natural shrinkage. The carrier's liability shall be that of warehouseman, only, for loss, damage, or delay caused by fire occurring after the expiration of the free time allowed by tariffs lawfully on file (such free time to be computed as therein provided) after notice of the arrival of the property at destination or at the port of export (if intended for export) has been duly sent or given, and after placement of the property for delivery at destination, or tender of delivery of the property to the party entitled to receive it, has been made. Except in case of negligence of the carrier or party in possession (and the burden to prove freedom from such negligence shall be on the carrier or party in possession), the carrier or party in possession shall not be liable for loss, damage, or delay occurring while the property is stopped and held in transit upon the request of the shipper, owner, or party entitled to make such request, or resulting from a defect or vice in the property, or for country damage to cotton, or from riots or strikes.

(c) In case of quarantine the property may be discharged at risk and expense of owners into quarantine depot or elsewhere, as required by quarantine regulations or authorities, or for the carrier's dispatch at nearest available point in carrier's judgment, and in any such case carrier's responsibility shall cease when property is so discharged, or property may be returned by carrier at owner's expense to shipping point, earning freight both ways. Quarantine expenses of whatever nature or kind upon or in respect to property shall be borne by the owners of the property or be a lien thereon. The carrier shall not be liable for loss or damage occasioned by fumigation or disinfection or other acts required or done by quarantine regulations or authorities even though the same may have been done by carrier's officers, agents, or employees, nor for detention, loss, or damage of any kind occasioned by quarantine or the enforcement thereof. No carrier shall be liable, except in case of negligence, for any mistake or inaccuracy in any information furnished by the carrier, its agents, or officers, as to quarantine laws or regulations. The shipper shall hold the carriers harmless from any expense they may incur, or damages they may be required to pay, by reason of the introduction of the property covered by this contract into any place against the quarantine laws or regulations in effect at such place.

Sec. 2. (a) No carrier is bound to transport said property by any particular train or vessel, or in time for any particular market or otherwise than with reasonable dispatch. Every carrier shall have the right in case of physical necessity to forward said property by any carrier or route between the point of shipment and the point of destination. In all cases not prohibited by law, where a lower value than actual value has been represented in writing by the shipper or has been agreed upon in writing as the released value of the property as determined by the classification or tariffs upon which the rate is based, such lower value plus freight charges if paid shall be the maximum amount to be recovered, whether or not such loss or damage occurs from negligence.

(b) As a condition precedent to recovery, claims must be filed in writing with the receiving or delivering carrier, or carrier issuing this bill of lading, or carrier on whose line the loss, damage, injury or delay occurred, within nine months after delivery of the property (or, in case of export traffic, within nine months after delivery at port of export) or, in case of failure to make delivery, then within nine months after a reasonable time for delivery has elapsed; and suits shall be instituted against any carrier only within two years and one day from the day when notice in writing is given by the carrier to the claimant that the carrier has disallowed the claim or any part or parts thereof specified in the notice. Where claims are not filed or suits are not instituted thereon in accordance with the foregoing provisions, no carrier hereunder shall be liable, and such claims will not be paid.

(c) Any carrier or party liable on account of loss of or damage to any of said property shall have the full benefit of any insurance that may have been effected upon or on account of said property, so far as this shall not avoid the policies or contracts of insurance: **Provided,** That the carrier reimburse the claimant for the premium paid thereon.

Sec. 3. Except where such service is required as the result of carrier's negligence, all property shall be subject to necessary cooperage and baling at owner's cost. Each carrier over whose route cotton or cotton linters is to be transported hereunder shall have the privilege, at its own cost and risk, of compressing the same for greater convenience in handling or forwarding, and shall not be held responsible for deviation or unavoidable delays in procuring such compression. Grain in bulk consigned to a point where there is a railroad, public or licensed elevator, may (unless otherwise expressly noted herein, and then if it is not promptly unloaded) be there delivered and placed with other grain of the same kind and grade without respect to ownership (and prompt notice thereof shall be given to the consignor), and if so delivered shall be subject to a lien for elevator charges in addition to all other charges hereunder.

Sec. 4. (a) Property not removed by the party entitled to receive it within the free time allowed by tariffs, lawfully on file (such free time to be computed as therein provided), after notice of the arrival of the property at destination or at the port of export (if intended for export) has been duly sent or given, and after placement of the property for delivery at destination has been made, may be kept in vessel, car, depot, warehouse or place of delivery of the carrier, subject to the tariff charge for storage and to carrier's responsibility as warehouseman, only, or at the option of the carrier, may be removed to and stored in a public or licensed warehouse at the place of delivery or other available place, at the cost of the owner, and there held without liability on the part of the carrier, and subject to a lien for all freight and other lawful charges, including a reasonable charge for storage

(b) Where nonperishable property which has been transported to destination hereunder is refused by consignee or the party entitled to receive it, or said consignee or party entitled to receive it fails to receive it within 15 days after notice of arrival shall have been duly sent or given, the carrier may sell the same at public auction to the highest bidder, at such place as may be designated by the carrier: **Provided,** That the carrier shall have first mailed, sent, or given to the consignor notice that the property has been refused or remains unclaimed, as the case may be, and that it will be subject to sale under the terms of the bill of lading if disposition be not arranged for, and shall have published notice containing a description of the property, the name of the party to whom consigned, or, if shipped order notify, the name of the party to be notified, and the time and place of sale, once a week for two successive weeks, in a newspaper of general circulation at the place of sale or nearest place where such newspaper is published: **Provided,** That 30 days shall have elapsed before publication of notice of sale after said notice that the property was refused or remains unclaimed was mailed, sent, or given.

(c) Where perishable property which has been transported hereunder to destination is refused by consignee or party entitled to receive it, or said consignee or party entitled to receive it shall fail to receive it promptly, the carrier may, in its discretion, to prevent deterioration or further deterioration, sell the same to the best advantage at private or public sale: **Provided,** That if time serves for notification to the consignor or owner of the refusal of the property or the failure to receive it and request for disposition of the property, such notification shall be given, in such manner as the exercise of due diligence requires, before the property is sold.

(d) Where the procedure provided for in the two paragraphs last preceding is not possible, it is agreed that nothing contained in said paragraphs shall be construed to abridge the right of the carrier at its option to sell the property under such circumstances and in such manner as may be authorized by law.

(e) The proceeds of any sale made under this section shall be applied by the carrier to the payment of freight, demurrage, storage, and any other lawful charges and the expense of notice, advertisement, sale, and other necessary expense and of caring for and maintaining the property, if proper care of the same requires special expense, and should there be a balance it shall be paid to the owner of the property sold hereunder.

(f) Property destined to or taken from a station, wharf, or landing at which there is no regularly appointed freight agent shall be entirely at risk of owner after unloaded from cars or vessels or until loaded into cars or vessels, and, except in case of carrier's negligence, when received from or delivered to such stations, wharves, or landings shall be at owner's risk until the cars are attached to and after they are detached from locomotive or train or until loaded into and after unloaded from vessels.

Sec. 5. No carrier hereunder will carry or be liable in any way for any documents, specie, or for any articles of extraordinary value not specifically rated in the published classifications or tariffs unless a special agreement to do so and a stipulated value of the articles are indorsed hereon.

Sec. 6. Every party, whether principal or agent, shipping explosives or dangerous goods, without previous full written disclosure to the carrier of their nature, shall be liable for and indemnify the carrier against all loss or damage caused by such goods, and such goods may be warehoused at owner's risk and expense or destroyed without compensation.

Sec. 7. The owner or consignee shall pay the freight and average, if any, and all other lawful charges accruing on said property; but, except in those instances where it may lawfully be authorized to do so, no carrier by railroad shall deliver or relinquish possession at destination of the property covered by this bill of lading until all tariff rates and charges thereon have been paid. The consignor shall be liable for the freight and all other lawful charges, except that if the consignor stipulates, by signature, in the space provided for that purpose on the face of this bill of lading that the carrier shall not make delivery without requiring payment of such charges and the carrier, contrary to such stipulation, shall make delivery without requiring such payment, the consignor (except as hereinafter provided) shall not be liable for such charges. **Provided, that,** where the carrier has been instructed by the shipper or consignor to deliver said property to a consignee other than the shipper or consignor, such consignee shall not be legally liable for transportation charges in respect of the transportation of said property (beyond those billed against him at the time of delivery for which he is otherwise liable) which may be found to be due after the property has been delivered to him, if the consignee (a) is an agent only and has no beneficial title in said property, and (b) prior to delivery of said property has notified the delivering carrier in writing of the fact of such agency and absence of beneficial title, and, in the case of a shipment reconsigned or diverted to a point other than that specified in the original bill of lading, has also notified the delivering carrier in writing of the name and address of the beneficial owner of said property; and, in such cases the shipper or consignor, or, in the case of a shipment so reconsigned or diverted, the beneficial owner, shall be liable for such additional charges. If the consignee has given to the carrier erroneous information as to who the beneficial owner is, such consignee shall himself be liable for such additional charges. On shipments reconsigned or diverted by an agent who has furnished the carrier in the reconsignment or diversion order with a notice of agency and the proper name and address of the beneficial owner, and where such shipments are refused or abandoned at ultimate destination, the said beneficial owner shall be liable for all legally applicable charges in connection therewith. If the reconsignor or diverter has given to the carrier erroneous information as to who the beneficial owner is, such reconsignor or diverter shall himself be liable for all such charges.

If a shipper or consignor of a shipment of property (other than a prepaid shipment) is also the consignee named in the bill of lading and, prior to the time of delivery, notifies, in writing, a delivering carrier by railroad (a) to deliver such property at destination to another party, (b) that such party is the beneficial owner of such property, and (c) that delivery is to be made to such party only upon payment of all transportation charges in respect of the transportation of such property, and delivery is made by the carrier to such party without such payment, such shipper or consignor shall not be liable (as shipper, consignor, consignee, or otherwise) for such transportation charges but the party to whom delivery is so made shall in any event be liable for transportation charges billed against the property at the time of such delivery, and also for any additional charges which may be found to be due after delivery of the property, except that if such party prior to such delivery has notified in writing the delivering carrier that he is not the beneficial owner of the property, and has given in writing to such delivering carrier the name and address of such beneficial owner, such party shall not be liable for any additional charges which may be found to be due after delivery of the property; but if the party to whom delivery is made has given to the carrier erroneous information as to the beneficial owner, such party shall nevertheless be liable for such additional charges. If the shipper or consignor has given to the delivering carrier erroneous information as to who the beneficial owner is, such shipper or consignor shall himself be liable for such transportation charges, notwithstanding the foregoing provisions of this paragraph and irrespective of any provisions to the contrary in the bill of lading or in the contract of transportation under which the shipment was made. The term "delivering carrier" means the line-haul carrier making ultimate delivery.

Nothing herein shall limit the right of the carrier to require at time of shipment the prepayment or guarantee of the charges. If upon inspection it is ascertained that the articles shipped are not those described in this bill of lading, the freight charges must be paid upon the articles actually shipped.

Where delivery is made by a common carrier by water the foregoing provisions of this section shall apply, except as may be inconsistent with Part III of the Interstate Commerce Act.

Figure 7. Uniform Straight Bill of Lading (reverse side). Courtesy: Uniform Freight Classification Committee.

Sec. **8.** If this bill of lading is issued on the order of the shipper, or his agent, in exchange or in substitution for another bill of lading, the shipper's signature to the prior bill of lading as to the statement of value or otherwise, or election of common law or bill of lading liability, in or in connection with such prior bill of lading, shall be considered a part of this bill of lading as fully as if the same were written or made in or in connection with this bill of lading.

Sec. **9.** (a) If all or any part of said property is carried by water over any part of said route, and loss, damage or injury to said property occurs while the same is in the custody of a carrier by water over the liability of such carrier shall be determined by the bill of lading of the carrier by water (this bill of lading being such bill of lading if the property is transported by such water carrier thereunder) and by and under the laws and regulations applicable to transportation by water. Such water carriage shall be performed subject to all the terms and provisions of, and all the exemptions from liability contained in the Act of Congress of the United States, approved on February 13, 1893, and entitled "An act relating to the navigation of vessels, etc.," and of other statutes of the United States according carriers by water the protection of limited liability, as well as the following subdivisions of this section; and to the conditions contained in this bill of lading not inconsistent with this section, when this bill of lading becomes the bill of lading of the carrier by water.

(b) No such carrier by water shall be liable for any loss or damage resulting from any fire happening to or on board the vessel, or from explosion, bursting of boilers or breakage of shafts, unless caused by the design or neglect of such carrier.

(c) if the owner shall have exercised due diligence in making the vessel in all respects seaworthy and properly manned, equipped, and supplied, no such carrier shall be liable for any loss or damage resulting from the perils of the lakes, seas, or other waters, or from latent defects in hull, machinery, or appurtenances whether existing prior to, at the time of, or after sailing, or from collision, stranding, or other accidents of navigation, or from prolongation of the voyage. And, when for any reason it is necessary, any vessel carrying any or all of the property herein described shall be at liberty to call at any port or ports, in or out of the customary route, to tow and be towed, to transfer, trans-ship, or lighter, to load and discharge goods at any time, to assist vessels in distress, to deviate for the purpose of saving life or property, and for docking and repairs. Except in case of negligence such carrier shall not be responsibile for any loss or damage to property if it be necessary or is usual to carry the same upon deck.

(d) General Average shall be payable according to the York-Antwerp Rules of 1924, Sections 1 to 15, inclusive, and Sections 17 to 22, inclusive, and as to matters not covered thereby according to the laws and usages of the Port of New York. If the owners shall have exercised due diligence to make the vessel in all respects seaworthy and properly manned, equipped and supplied, it is hereby agreed that in case of danger, damage or disaster resulting from faults or errors in navigation, or in the management of the vessel, or from any latent or other defects in the vessel, her machinery or appurtenance , or from unseaworthiness, whether existing at the time of shipment or at the beginning of the voyage (provided the latent or other defects or the unseaworthiness was not discoverable by the exercise of due diligence), the shippers, consignees and/or owners of the cargo shall nevertheless pay salvage and any special charges incurred in respect of the cargo, and shall contribute with the shipowner in general average to the payment of any sacrifices, losses or expenses of a general average nature that may be made or incurred for the common benefit or to relieve the adventure from any common peril.

(e) If the property is being carried under a tariff which provides that any carrier or carriers party thereto shall be liable for loss! rom perils of the sea, then as to such carrier or carriers the provisions of this section shall be modified in accordance with the tariff provisions, which shall be regarded as incorporated into the conditions of this bill of lading.

(f) The term "water carriage" in this section shall not be construed as including lighterage in or across rivers, harbors, or lakes, when performed by or on behalf of rail carriers.

Sec. **10.** Any alteration, addition, or erasure in this bill of lading which shall be made without the special notation hereon of the agent of the carrier issuing this bill of lading, shall be without effect, and this bill of lading shall be enforceable according to its original tenor.

Figure 7A. Uniform Straight Bill of Lading (reverse side, continued).
Courtesy: Uniform Freight Classification Committee.

is mutually agreed, as to each carrier of all or any said property over all or any portion of said route to destination, and as to each party at any time interested in all or any of said property, that every service to be performed hereunder shall be subject to all the conditions not prohibited by law, whether printed or written, herein contained, including the conditions on back hereof, which are hereby agreed to by the shipper and accepted for himself and his assigns.

Before he and the shipper sign at the bottom of the page, the carrier's agent must examine the pieces of the shipment to see that they are "in apparent good order." If they are not, he notes this fact on the face of the bill before signing it. It is assumed that the material in the packages is in good condition, but the bill protects the carrier from the necessity of opening and examining each piece.

Second, the bill of lading is evidence of some ownership interest in the goods. At one time, the custom was for the consignee to present the original bill of lading in order to claim the goods at destination. This meant, of course, that the shipper had to mail it to him in advance of the arrival of the shipment. Although presentation of the original bill is no longer required, mailing it to the consignee is still good practice so that he can tell how and when the goods will arrive. When the negotiable or order/notify bill of lading is used, the original bill is evidence of title and must be presented to the carrier before the shipment can be released.

Finally, the bill of lading is a contract of carriage. The receipt clause and the ten sections of terms and conditions on the back of the bill of lading state the contract responsibilities of the shipper and the carrier in detail.

The Uniform Straight Bill of Lading that is used by land common carriers in the United States is unique in the broad protection it gives to shippers. The carrier is not only responsible for loss and damage due to his own negligence, but must repay the cargo owner for any other loss that happens to the shipment, except a few causes completely beyond the control of the carrier.

Section 1 of the Uniform Straight Bill of Lading provides that the carrier will be liable for the property as at common law, with the following exceptions: the act of God, the public enemy, the authority of law, the act or default of the shipper, and natural shrinkage. The carrier is also not liable for any loss, damage, or delay due to inherent defect of the goods, or resulting from riots or strikes.

A synopsis of the other sections of the terms and conditions of the bill of lading follows:

Section 2 states that no carrier is bound to transport the property by any particular train or vessel, or in time for any particular market, or with other than reasonable dispatch. This section also provides that released-value rates may be used in cases permitted by law and sets forth instructions for filing freight claims with the carrier.

Section 3 provides that any cooperage or baling (repackaging) that is necessary will be done at the owner's expense.

Section 4 provides for storage or sale of both perishable and non-perishable goods that are refused or undeliverable.

Section 5 warns that carriers will not carry documents or specie or articles of extraordinary value unless a special agreement to do so is made and a stipulated value of the articles is endorsed thereon.

Section 6 provides that explosives may be destroyed by the carrier without liability when they are shipped without "full written disclosure to the carrier."

Section 7 deals with payment of freight charges and with the carrier's lien against the goods for the charges.

Section 8 provides for the substitution of bills of lading.

Section 9 provides that the provisions of the water bill of lading will apply if any part of the route is by way of water carrier. The provisions of the water or ocean bill of lading are set forth in modified form.

Section 10 stipulates that any changes in the bill of lading that are made after it is signed will be void.

Negotiable Bills of Lading

In rail transportation, there is a negotiable form of the bill of lading called the Uniform Order Bill of Lading. Order bills are also used in truck and water transport, but express receipts and air bills are not negotiable. The order bill of lading is also referred to as a negotiable bill of lading, a sight-draft bill of lading, or an order/notify bill of lading.

The negotiable bill makes possible the transfer of ownership of the goods after they have been shipped. Usually, the shipper consigns the goods to himself. The name of the party who is expected to purchase the goods is written on the "notify" line of the bill. This party can change if the goods are sold to someone else while en route.

One purpose of the negotiable bill of lading is to allow the shipper to recover the value of his goods before delivery. The original order bill of lading is a document of title to the merchandise. It can become collateral for a loan of money to the shipper. At destination, the consignee must surrender the original order bill to the carrier in order to take delivery of the goods. Thus, this document is also a means of guaranteeing that the merchandise will be paid for before delivery.

The Uniform Order Bill of Lading is very much like the straight bill in its appearance and in its terms and conditions. It is, however, printed on yellow paper. Negotiable bills of lading can be used only for direct shipments from one origin to one destination. Transit privileges and stops to complete loading or to partially unload cannot be used because the bill would have to be surrendered to the carrier at the first stop. Goods in the hands of the carrier may not be inspected by the consignee or other parties unless the inspection privilege is stated in the contract. In the event an original order bill of lading is lost or destroyed, possession of the shipment may be obtained through the presentation of a fiduciary bond in an amount double the invoice value of the goods or through a cash deposit of 125 percent of the invoice value. To obtain delivery by any other means is punishable by law, and the carrier is equally liable with the receiver of the goods.

As with other bills of lading, the carrier has the duty to issue the order bill of lading. However, the shipper usually prepares it. Three copies are made: the "original," the "shipping order," and the "memo."

As shown in Figure 8, several steps are followed in using the negotiable bill of lading. (1) The shipper takes the goods and the bill of lading to the carrier. (2) The carrier receipts for the goods and returns the "original" and "memo" copies to the shipper while retaining the "shipping order." (3) The shipper draws a draft on his customer, the consignee, and attaches the draft and an invoice for the goods to the original bill of lading. He then endorses the documents to his bank. (4)

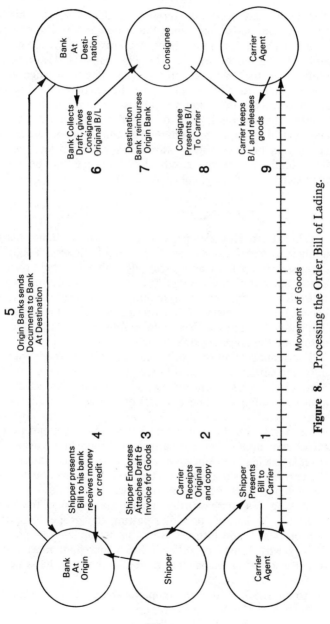

Figure 8. Processing the Order Bill of Lading.

Bank
At Desti-
nation

Consignee

Carrier
Agent

Bank Collects
Draft, gives
Consignee
Original B/L
6

Destination
Bank reimburses
Origin Bank
7

Consignee
Presents B/L
To Carrier
8

Carrier keeps
B/L and releases
goods
9

5
Origin Banks sends
Documents to Bank
At Destination

Shipper presents
Bill to his bank
receives money
or credit
4

Shipper Endorses
Attaches Draft &
Invoice for Goods
3

Carrier Receipts
Original
and copy
2

Shipper
Presents
Bill to
Carrier
1

Bank
At
Origin

Shipper

Carrier
Agent

Movement of Goods

The bank may lend him money on the goods at this point. (5) The shipper's bank sends the documents to the consignee's bank. (6) The destination bank presents the draft for collection and the consignee pays it. (7) The bank at destination then reimburses the bank at origin. (8) The consignee presents the original order bill of lading to the carrier. (9) The carrier receives the bill of lading and releases the shipment.

Note that possession of the original order bill is the key to claiming the shipment. Therefore, the original order bill of lading can be "negotiated" through several parties; the person who finally claims the goods does not need to be the same person they were originally sold to.

OCEAN BILLS OF LADING

When Lord Holt defined common-carrier liability, his ruling applied to water carriers as well as land carriers. Today, however, steamship lines are essentially liable for their own negligence, since both the law and the ocean bill of lading give them extensive exemptions from liability. This has occurred partly because of the desire to encourage the merchant marine by lightening the burden of freight claims, and partly due to the nature of the shipping operation.

The management of a shipping operation is fragmented, with different parties and even different firms performing the various parts of the work. Conceivably, a voyage can be conducted by a carrier company using a vessel chartered from another shipowner. Responsibility for vessel operation and management of its crew rests on the master, who is autonomous and not under direct control of either company during the whole voyage. When trouble occurs, the question arises as to who was at fault—the carrier, the shipowner, or the crew. This has been resolved through the doctrine of seaworthiness.

Making a ship seaworthy means making sure the vessel is physically as safe as possible, putting the proper supplies and fuel on board, and hiring a crew that is capable of operating it. This is why it may be difficult for a merchant marine captain to get a job after he has had a wreck—because he is no longer seaworthy.

About 1850, steamship companies began to put many clauses

in their bills of lading to get out of the full common-law liability that Lord Holt had put on them. Various cases went to the United States Supreme Court, which held that in the absence of a specific contract an ocean carrier has an absolute duty to make the ship seaworthy. Steamship lines then began to put clauses in bills of lading that went so far as to relieve them from the duty to make the ship seaworthy. Public reaction caused corrective legislation to be passed. The Harter Act of 1893 required that the carrier exercise due diligence to make the ship seaworthy, properly manned, and fit for cargo. It also required the carrier to issue a bill of lading upon demand of the shipper.

The Harter Act applied only to American vessels. Shipowners of foreign nations continued to insert clauses in their bills of lading exempting them from liability, often including negligence. Also, bills of lading stipulated maximum amounts of money that the shipowner would pay for loss or damage. These amounts varied from line to line. The customer was never sure how the terms of the contract differed from time to time. This situation was also difficult for the banker and the insurance underwriter. World-wide pressure developed for the adoption of a uniform bill of lading for all countries. In 1921 the leading maritime nations sent representatives to The Hague. This conference resulted in a set of rules for the carriage of goods by sea, which are known as The Hague Rules. Such international rules, however, cannot govern any nation unless they are made a part of the law of that nation. The principal maritime nations have each passed a law that is usually called the Carriage of Goods by Sea Act.

Carriage of Goods by Sea Act

Congress passed the American Carriage of Goods by Sea Act in 1936. This law sets forth the main terms of the ocean bill of lading. These terms differ from those of the land bill of lading. They apply, as stated in the preamble of the Act, to "every bill of lading or similar document . . . which is evidence of a contract for the carriage of goods by sea to or from ports of the United States, in foreign trade. . . ." They also apply to the bills of lading of domestic intercoastal, coastwise, and inland water carriers if such carriers so choose. If domestic carriers do not make their bills subject to the Carriage of Goods by Sea Act, they are still governed by the Harter Act.

COGSA specifies the duties of carriers as follows:

At the beginning of the voyage, the carrier is bound to exercise due diligence to make the ship seaworthy; properly man, equip and supply the ship, and make all parts of the ship in which cargo is carried safe for the cargo.

The carrier is to properly and carefully load, handle, stow, carry, keep, care for, and discharge the cargo.

Upon demand of the shipper, the master or his agent shall issue a bill of lading to the shipper after the goods are received.

COGSA prohibits the carrier from putting any clauses in the bill that relieve him from liability for his own negligence. The allowable exemptions from liability are extensive, however. They are as follows:

Neither the carrier nor the ship shall be responsible for loss or damage arising or resulting from—

a. Act, neglect, or default of the master, mariner, pilot, or the servants of the carrier in the navigation or in the management of the ship;

b. fire, unless caused by the actual fault or privity of the carrier;

c. perils, dangers, and accidents of the sea or other navigable waters;

d. act of God;

e. act of war;

f. act of public enemies;

g. arrest or restraint of princes, rulers, or people, or seizure under legal process;

h. quarantine restrictions;

i. act or omission of the shipper or owner of the goods, his agent or representative;

j. strikes or lockouts or stoppage or restraint of labor from whatever cause, whether partial or general: provided, that nothing herein contained shall be construed to relieve a carrier from responsibility for the carrier's own acts;

k. riots and civil commotions;

l. saving or attempting to save life or property at sea;

m. wastage in bulk or weight or any other loss or damage arising from inherent defect, quality, or vice of the goods;

n. insufficiency of packing;

o. insufficiency or inadequacy of marks;

p. latent defects not discoverable by due diligence; and

q. any other cause arising without the actual fault and privity of the carrier and without the fault or neglect of the agents or servants of the carrier, but the burden of proof shall be on the person claiming the benefit of this exception to show that neither the actual fault or privity of the carrier nor the fault or neglect of the agents or servants of the carrier contributed to the loss or damage.

COGSA also provides that in no case shall the carrier be liable for more than $500 per package or customary freight unit. Steamship bills of lading and tariffs often provide for a greater amount if a higher freight rate is paid.

Marine Insurance

Because of the extensive exemptions from liability allowed in the water bill of lading, the purchase of insurance is necessary. Thus, the cost of marine insurance must always be included when comparing water transport as a shipping alternative.

Marine insurance is the oldest form of insurance, having been used for about 700 years. Several forms are available to provide protection for vessels, the freight they are earning or the cargo they are carrying. The wording of marine insurance policies is archaic, so that the average businessman may need some professional help to make sure he is buying adequate coverage. Agents of marine insurance underwriters are found in principal cities. Today, marine insurance has been expanded into "inland" marine insurance to protect against carrier liability exemptions in all forms of transport.

Face of the Water Bill of Lading

The general appearance of a marine bill of lading is the same as the land bill of lading, but there are many specific differences.

In foreign commerce, the custom is to mark goods with a symbol such as a star or a diamond, in addition to the usual name and address. These symbols are called "marks" and are used so goods can be identified by people who cannot read the writing. Marks are placed on the bill so it can be matched to the cargo.

Steamship lines often use some copies of the bill of lading as freight bills. They machine-produce many copies of the bill, typing rates and charges in the space provided, and mail the bill to the customer as an invoice.

Freight charges on water bills are usually due and payable as soon as the bill is receipted. The "freight earned" clause of the contract makes these charges payable in full whether or not the voyage ever commences or is completed. Another clause gives to the carrier the right to change the voyage from what was originally intended in any manner he wishes or to cancel it entirely.

Freight claim provisions also differ from land bill of lading procedures. The time limits for making inspections, filing claims, and starting lawsuits are much shorter than in land transportation.

The ocean bill of lading also provides that the carrier's liability shall be several. "Several" essentially means "individual," and this clause means the steamship line will not accept liability for anything that happens to the shipment while it is in the hands of a connecting carrier.

THE AIR FREIGHT CONTRACT

Air freight carriers use a document called an air waybill or an air bill instead of a bill of lading. Physically, it is a half-sheet, or smaller, piece of paper. It has a receipt clause and spaces for shipping information, but it does not have any terms and conditions. All contract terms and conditions are set forth in the freight tariffs of the air carriers. The shipper is presumed to be familiar with these tariffs.

The Federal Aviation Act has no provisions relating to the air-carrier shipping contract, liability for air freight, or freight claim procedures. Probably because air freight shipments are small and volume is not heavy, little case-law about air freight liability has been recorded. The air carriers are developing liability provisions much like those of the water carriers.

Working Rule of Liability

Since there are no official rules, some interested parties have summarized what seem to be the practical rules of air freight liability: (1) Air freight carriers are liable only for loss and damage caused by their own negligence and on their own lines. (2) They may limit this liability to a stated released value per shipment or per pound. (3) The filed tariff is conclusive evidence of the contract of carriage, and the shipper is presumed to be familiar with it in detail.

Valuation of shipments. Like the Railway Express Agency, the air cargo carriers will accept shipments only on a released-value basis. If the shipper does not specify otherwise, the goods are accepted on the released value of $50 per shipment or 50 cents per pound on shipments of over 100 pounds. The carrier will reimburse the customer for a higher value only if a higher freight rate has been paid. The rate is usually increased 10 cents for each hundred dollars, or fraction thereof, by which the stated value of the goods is increased. These valuations will vary for different commodities and between different carriers, however. The usual practice is for the shipper to obtain in-transit insurance for the excess valuation and the risks not covered by the air carrier.

Exemptions from liability. The main provisions of the air freight contract may be found in the *Official Air Freight Rules Tariff*. Although the provisions of this tariff are presented as shipping rules, they are in effect contract provisions, since the customer agrees to them in using the air bill. The exemptions from liability incorporated into the air freight contract can be listed as follows:

1. Perils of the air.
2. Act of God.
3. Act of war.
4. Act of public enemies.
5. Authority of law.
6. Quarantine.
7. Act or default of consignor, consignee, or owner.
8. Strikes, riots, and civil commotions.
9. Defect or inherent vice of the shipment.
10. Violation by the customer of any rules contained in the *Official Air Freight Rules Tariff*.
11. Delay.

CONTRACT-CARRIER LIABILITY

Unlike common carriers, for-hire carriers who operate on a long-term contract or some form of cargo charter do not issue bills of lading. Nor does the law set forth the liability of contract carriers. The courts have generally held that the government cannot interfere with the right of individuals to make contracts with each other unless it is necessary for the protection of the public as a whole. Thus the question of who will pay how much for what loss or damage must be set forth in the contract between the shipper and the contract carrier. The amount of liability he must assume will probably affect the rate the carrier charges.

REFERENCES

Fair, Marvin L., and John Guandolo. *Transportation Regulation.* Dubuque: Wm. C. Brown, 1972.

Flood, Kenneth U. *Traffic Management.* Dubuque: Wm. C. Brown, 1963.

McElhiney, Paul T., and Charles L. Hilton. *Introduction to Logistics and Traffic Management.* Dubuque: Wm. C. Brown, 1968.

Miller, John M., and Fritz R. Kahn. *Law of Freight Loss and Damage Claims.* Dubuque: Wm. C. Brown, 1961.

Way, William, Jr. *Elements of Freight Traffic.* Washington, D.C.: Regular Common Carrier Conference, A.T.A., 1956.

Winter, William D. *Marine Insurance.* New York: McGraw-Hill, 1952.

CHAPTER 10

Freight Rates
and Tariffs

The purpose of this chapter is to familiarize the business student with the establishment and publication of freight rates. Many freight tariffs are in use in the United States, and they contain thousands of freight rates. Mistakes is assessing rates are often made because of the large number of alternative routings and the large numbers of commodity descriptions that are available. The misconception prevails that freight rates are difficult to look up. This is untrue. Freight tariffs may be tedious, but they are simple to use. On the majority of shipments, the rate clerk finds the correct rate quickly the first time he looks for it.

In a short chapter, treatment of rates cannot be exhaustive, so only essential topics are covered. The elements of three areas of interest about rates are covered: rate terminology, establishment of rates, and rate publication. The emphasis of the chapter is upon the freight rate system used in the railroad and trucking industries.

RATE TERMINOLOGY

Freight rates are prices that are charged for the transportation of property. They are published in formal price lists or catalogs known as *tariffs*. Freight rate tariffs must be approved by and on file with the appropriate regulatory agency. Freight rates may include all or only part of the service necessary for a through movement. For instance, a rate may include pickup and delivery service or it may cover only a "station-to-station" or a "dock-to-dock" movement. Some tariffs give only accessorial charges for some additional service the customer can buy, such as weighing, loading, or protective services.

Railroad and motor truck rates are usually charged in cents per hundred pounds. Steamship rates are usually quoted in dollars per ton; several different tons are used including the short ton, long ton, metric ton, and measurement ton. Air freight rates are published as cents per pound up to 100 pounds and then as dollars per hundred pounds.

Traditionally, rates have been different for different commodities as well as increasing with distance. With the increasing use of containers there is a trend toward the publication of rates on a dollar-per-container basis regardless of container contents; these rates vary only with distance.

Rates Based on Volume

The matter of heavy-loading rate incentives was discussed in Chapter 5. A review of the concept is appropriate here. Railroad and motor freight carriers traditionally have had two basic scales of volume-related rates—LCL or LTL rates for shipments not requiring an entire vehicle, and CL or TL rates for full carloads or truckloads. Usually, there is a substantial spread between these two categories. Trucklines usually give additional spreads or weight-breaks in LTL rate scales. For instance, if one looks up an LTL rate in a truck tariff he discovers that the rate decreases a few cents at, perhaps, the 2,000-pound level and again at the 6,000-, 12,000-, and 20,000-pound levels. Freight tariffs also contain a rule dealing with the application of rates on volume shipments. Usually this rule reads something like, "When the charges accruing on a shipment based on actual weight exceed the charges computed on a rate based on a greater unit of minimum weight, the latter shall apply." This rule takes care of the "weight-break" situation. That is, if it is cheaper to say that something is heavier than it actually is, it is all right to do this.

Rates Affected by Type of Journey

Some freight rate terms come from the way the journey is made up. A *local* rate is one for a haul entirely on the lines of one carrier. When carriers were small, a local rate really applied only in one locality, because the carriers did not go very far. However, on the huge systems of today a local rate conceivably could reach across the ocean. The test is that only one carrier is involved.

When two or more carriers agree to establish a through route, the rate that they charge for the combined haul is called a *joint* rate. Usually a joint rate is also a through rate, but it can be made up of the local rates of both carriers added together. Only one of the carriers would send a bill to the customer, however.

A *through* rate is a single-factor rate that covers the shipment all the way from origin to destination. It can be local, all on the lines of one carrier, or it can be joint, with two or more carriers sharing the revenue. The test is that the through rate is published as a single amount for the entire line-haul.

When there is no through rate published from a certain origin to a certain destination, it may be necessary to build a rate by putting together a *combination of local rates*. This may involve just one carrier, or on a transcontinental basis it might necessitate combining local rates from two or more carriers. Section 4 of the Interstate Commerce Act contains the "aggregate of intermediates rule," which states, "It shall be unlawful for any common carrier [by rail or inland water] to charge any greater compensation as a through rate than the aggregate of intermediate rates." This means that the through rate should always be the same as or lower than the combination of locals. If it is higher, the combination of locals applies. This is one way many rate auditors have made savings for their customers —by discovering a legal, alternative combination of locals that is lower than the through rate the carrier has applied.

Systems of Rate Publication

If a separate rate were published for every commodity that could move on every possible haul, the freight rate situation would be a lot more complicated. The problem of simplifying tariffs has led to two basic rate systems, *class rates* and *commodity rates*.

Class rates. The class rate system was the earliest attempt of commercial carriers to simplify freight rates. Early wagonlines and bargelines posted rates that applied to *classes* of commodities rather than to the commodities themselves. Products were grouped together by their transportation characteristics and a rate published for the whole group rather than for each separate commodity. Transportation characteristics are those aspects of a good that affect the cost of transporting it. Size, bulkiness or density, and value of the article are such characteristics; also such things as the quantity of the freight that moves at one time, the regularity of the movement, the direction of movement, and the perishability of the goods. These and similar factors were considered by early transport men to produce a listing of goods called a *classification*. This list sorted all goods into about four major groups, which were numbered 1, 2, 3 and 4 and called *class ratings*. The carrier then provided only four rates between the towns on his route and did not need to list a separate rate for each and every commodity offered to him. These were referred to as the first-class rate, the second-class rate, and so on.

Since many commodities are covered by each *class rating*, a *class rate* is, in a sense, an average rate for a range of articles with similar transportation characteristics. With the class rate system, one can find a rate for any commodity between any two points on the railroad network or the truckline network of the United States. However, much of the freight traffic and freight revenue is generated through *commodity rates*.

Commodity rates. Class rates apply on products that have similar transportation characteristics but not necessarily similar physical characteristics. Frequently, however, there is something about a product that makes it special. A carrier can often afford to charge much less than the established class rate for hauling a commodity if it moves in large quantities, or if he can be assured a regular movement, or if he needs the traffic to fill unused capacity, or for backhaul. In such cases, *commodity rates* are published. Commodity rate tariffs list articles directly by name and show the rates for them on a point-to-point basis. They are limited in scope and generally apply only over the routes where the majority of a particular traffic moves. A basic shipping rule, published in the rules of the *Uniform Freight Classification*, requires that when both a class and a commodity rate are published for a certain commodity over a certain route, the commodity rate must be used instead of the class rate. Some tariffs take exception to this and allow the lower of the two rates to apply. Generally, however, the commodity rate must be used. Sometimes, when a carrier has a monopoly on a movement or when it is undesirable traffic, the commodity rate will be higher than the class rate. This is done when the carrier cannot afford to haul the product at the class rate and has nothing to gain by encouraging a volume movement of the traffic.

Other modes do not use quite the same system of class and commodity rates as the railroads and trucklines. Steamship lines usually do not use the class rate method at all but publish only commodity rates. If a product is offered to them for which no rate is published, it is placed in a category known as "freight, all kinds." Such a rate is higher than those for specific goods.

REA Express utilizes a simple classification that involves only three classes. All items move at the first-class rate, except food-stuffs, which are second class, and printed matter, which is third class. The express agency also has general and specific commodity rates for many things.

Air freight carriers use two types of rates—general commodity rates and specific commodity rates. Air freight general commodity rates are sometimes referred to as class rates or first-class rates; they consist of a single rate between each set of cities. This rate applies to all articles that move unless a specific commodity rate is shown for the product.

HOW RATES ARE ESTABLISHED

Section 6 of The Interstate Commerce Act requires "That every common carrier . . . shall file with the Commission . . . and print and keep open to public inspection schedules showing all the rates, fares, and charges for transportation." Section 6 further states, "No change shall be made in the rates, fares, and charges . . . except after thirty days notice to the Commission and to the public." All tariffs and changes in them must be in the form prescribed by the Commission.

Thousands of rate changes are made every year, and most of them are approved by the Interstate Commerce Commission as a matter of routine. But the I.C.C. has the power to disapprove of rates in three ways. First, if a new tariff or change does not meet the requirements established by Section 6 of the Act, the I.C.C. may reject it until it is done properly. Second, the I.C.C. may investigate and suspend any rate that violates the requirements of the Act about reasonableness or non-discrimination.

Third, the I.C.C. can investigate and suspend in response to a worthwhile protest received from someone in the public—a carrier, shipper, association, or citizen. After its investigation, if the Commission doesn't approve of the rate in question it can prescribe "the just and reasonable . . . rate . . . to be charged." Considering the large number of rate changes that are put through, the Commission does this in relatively few cases.

Once a freight rate or tariff is properly filed and approved by the I.C.C., it has the effect of a law. The only legal rate that may be charged is the published rate, and both the carrier and the shipper are presumed to know what it is and are obliged to use it. The receipt clause of the bill of lading also makes the tariff a part of the shipping contract. The shipper has the duty to understand the freight tariff, and the carrier is not responsible for erroneous rate quotations made verbally or in writing other than in the tariff.

Setting the Rate

The purpose of the foregoing discussion was to show that the government does *not* set the rates. For the most part, rate changes are either negotiated between carriers and shippers or proposed by the carriers. Shipper-carrier negotiation is to set rates for new products, new plant locations, or changed shipping conditions. Carriers seek rate changes to meet competition or perhaps to try to keep up with inflation.

Although the Interstate Commerce Act says the carrier shall "print" the freight tariffs, most freight tariffs today are created and published by carrier-owned, third-party, nonprofit associations. These are called freight bureaus, associations, or committees; in the steamship industry they are called conferences. For instance, cross-country rail rates are published by the Trans-Continental Freight Bureau. There are about fifteen such agencies each in the rail and truck modes. An agency has responsibility for a particular geographic region and generally publishes one set of tariffs used by all the carriers in that area. (In the air freight industry, one bureau publishes most of the tariffs, but C.A.B. policy discourages the carriers from all using exactly the same rate.)

Carriers delegate the authority to make freight tariffs to their rate bureaus by issuing powers-of-attorney to the bureaus as prescribed in Section 5a of the Interstate Commerce Act. A carrier may be a member of more than one rate association, and does not necessarily use every tariff published by each association. When a carrier does use a particular tariff he must execute a document called a *concurrence* to show that he is a participating carrier in that tariff. Tariffs issued by rate bureaus or associations are called *agency tariffs*. Most carriers also issue some tariffs of their own; usually these are for local hauls or specific commodity rates. A tariff that is issued by the carrier itself is called an *individual tariff*.

Antitrust protection. In most American industries, if the pricing specialists of all the different firms got together and issued a consolidated price list, the federal government would quickly accuse them of collusion in restraint of trade. However, cooperative rate-making is permitted in the transportation industry. For many years, although they do not conform to the Sherman Antitrust Act of 1890, rate bureaus were tolerated by the Department of Justice as long as each carrier had the right of independent action and could publish his own rates without prejudice when he disagreed with the rate bureau. In 1948, cooperative rate-making was exempted from antitrust regulation by the *Reed-Bulwinkle Act*.

Some form of cooperative rate-making is a necessity in our regulated transportation industry, for several reasons. First, the purpose of interstate commerce regulation is to eliminate destructive competition, stabilize rates, and yet ensure fair treatment for the customer. Second, the law requires and encourages the carriers to form networks of through routes; they must cooperate extensively to do this. Third, due to the number of points served and number of commodities carried, rate publication is complex enough without having each carrier publish his fragment of it in individual tariffs.

Proposing rate changes. Proposals for new or different rates can be submitted to a rate bureau by a carrier or by a shipper. Each bureau has a standard form for presentation of such proposals. Each bureau also has a *standing rate committee*, made up of full-time employees of the bureau, which publishes *dockets*, or schedules, of proposals that it will consider. If an interested party requests it, a public hearing will be held. If the standing rate committee approves a proposal, the new rate will be published in the appropriate tariff. This tariff is then sent to the I.C.C. for its acceptance.

If the standing rate committee disapproves the proposal, it is sent to an appeals committee within the bureau for further consideration. The appeals committee is made up of traffic executives of the member carriers. Generally, a good practice is for the shipper desiring a rate change to ask his carrier to file the proposal. Then if it is not accepted, the shipper can modify it and file it again as a shipper proposal. Finally, if the proposal has real merit and meets all of the tangible and intangible requirements of the Interstate Commerce Act, the shipper can ask a carrier to publish the rate by independent action.

HOW RATES ARE PUBLISHED

The freight rate tariffs of the various modes are similar in form. This is probably because the other regulatory bodies have followed the leadership of the Interstate Commerce Commission. In 1891, the I.C.C. began publishing tariff circulars prescribing the exact form in which tariffs were to be constructed. Today, the Commission publishes several circulars for different types of carriers and services. The Federal Maritime Commission also publishes a circular, and tariff specifications are found in the Economic Regulations of the Civil Aeronautics Board.

Tariff circulars specify such things as the size and type of paper that may be used, the size of type, the reference marks to be used, and whether the tariff may be looseleaf or bound in a pamphlet. Since the requirements vary for different types of carriers, the author of a freight tariff should read the correct tariff circulars before starting to make up a tariff.

A person who becomes familiar with the tariffs of one type of carrier finds it easy to read the rate books of any mode because the information is generally arranged in the same way and in the same order. I.C.C. tariff circulars, for instance, require the following divisions in a rate tariff:

—Title Page
—Table of Contents
—List of Participating Carriers
—Alphabetical List of Commodities
—Alphabetical List of Stations
—Geographical List of Stations

—Explanation of Symbols, Reference Marks, and
  Abbreviations
—List of Exceptions to Governing Classification
—Rules and Regulations
—Statement of the Rates
—Routing Provisions.

HOW TO FIND A RATE

Figures 9 through 21 on pages 172–184 show some examples
of tariff pages. A step-by-step examination of these pages can
convey the general idea of what is involved in looking up a
freight rate. There is no set procedure that must be followed in
checking out a freight rate; what is done first will depend upon
the expertise of the person doing it. However, one should never
depend upon his memory of what the rate was the last time he
looked it up, because changes are made so frequently they can
go unnoticed. A logical set of steps that could be followed is set
forth below. Each step is discussed briefly, and then an example
using the sample tariff pages is presented.

Steps in Rate-Checking

The first problem in tariff interpretation is to make sure that
one has the proper tariffs on hand. Only a few "helper" tariffs
such as the classification or the explosives and dangerous
articles tariffs are national in scope. Rate tariffs each cover a
limited geographical area or route; perhaps the I.C.C. is the
only organization that has anywhere near all the tariffs, and
theirs take over a mile of shelf space. Possibly the best way
for an industrial user to find the right tariffs is to ask the
carrier. This does not mean that the carrier will cheerfully
provide a copy, because tariffs are expensive and mostly available only by subscription. When the books are assembled,
several steps should be followed:
  1. Refer to the appropriate classification; determine the
     proper description and classification of the article to
     be shipped.
  2. Refer to the proper class rate tariff.
  3. Determine whether the class rate tariff (or sometimes a
     separate helper tariff) takes exception to the class rating
     provided by the governing classification.

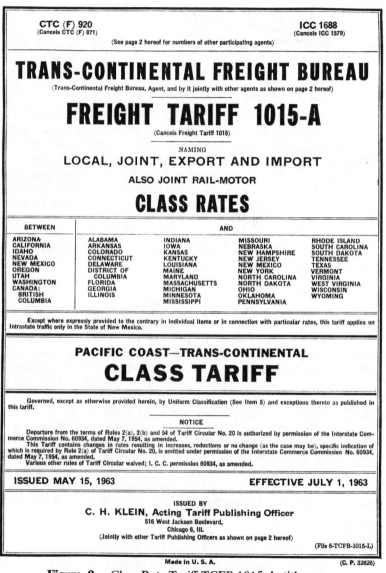

Figure 9.   Class Rate Tariff TCFB 1015-A, title page.

TARIFF 1015-A

POINTS IN ARIZONA, BRITISH COLUMBIA, CALIFORNIA, IDAHO, NEVADA, NEW MEXICO, OREGON, UTAH AND WASHINGTON TO AND FROM WHICH RATES APPLY

POINTS	RAILROAD LOCATION	BASIS APPLICABLE (See Item 212)	SEE ITEM	WESTERN GATEWAYS (See Item 214)
CALIFORNIA	AT&SF (SantaFe)...	South Coast...........	615	1, ⑤1B, ⑤1G, 1U, 2A, 2H, 2P, 2R, 2T, 2U, 2W, 2DD, 2EE, 2FF, 2GG, 2HH, 2JJ, 2KK, 2LL, 30E
	LAJ...............	South Coast...........	......	36
Los Angeles........	⑥PE(SPLines)....	South Coast...........	615	28, 28H, 28L, 28R, 28V, 29, 29D, 29G, 29K, 29L, 29X, 29Y
	SP...............	South Coast...........	615	13, 13B, 13C, 13D, 13G, 13H, 13L, 13M, 13T, ⑥13W, 13BA, 13BC, 30E, 30X
	UP...............	South Coast...........	615	7, 7A, ⑥7C, ⑥7D, ⑥7E, ⑥7F, 7G, 8C
⑥Los Angeles........ (50th Street)	SP...............	South Coast...........		13, 13B, 13C, 13D, 13G, 13H, 13L, 13M, 13T, ⑥13W, 13BA, 13BC, 30E, 30X
Los Angeles Harbor (East San Pedro, San Pedro and Wilmington)............	AT&SF (SantaFe)...	South Coast...........		1, 1B, 1J, 1V, 2B, 2J, 2P, 2R, 2T, 2U, 2W, 2DD, 2EE, 2FF, 2GG, 2HH, 2JJ, 2KK, 2LL, 30E
	SP...............	South Coast...........		13, 13B, 13C, 13D, 13G, 13H, 13L, 13M, 13U, 13W, 13Y, 13BA, 13BC, 30E, 30X
	UP...............	South Coast...........		7, 7B, 7C, 7D, 7E, 7F, 7G, 8C
Los Angeles Harbor (Wilmington, San Pedro, East San Pedro and McDonald)..........	PE(SPLines).......	South Coast...........		28, 28H, 28L, 28R, 28V, 29, 29D, 29G, 29K, 29L, 29X, 29Y

POINTS IN EASTERN DEFINED TERRITORIES FROM OR TO WHICH RATES APPLY	GROUP BASIS APPLICABLE

MISSOURI:

Points shown in Open and Prepay Station List, located on lines of carriers parties hereto, not otherwise provided for below.

GROUP E

Adrian	Chitwood	Holmes	Leeds	Noel	Seneca
Agency	Cisco Spur	Horton	Lee's Summit	North Kansas	Sheffield
Amazonia	Cleveland	Huber	Le Vance Spur	City	Sheldon
Amoret	Corning	Hume	Liberal	Oronogo	South Lee
Amsterdam	Craig	Hy-Tex	Link	Panama	State Hospital
Anderson	Deerfield	Iantha	Lisle	Parkville	Spur
Archie	Dodson	Iatan	Little Blue	Passaic	Stotesbury
Armour	Drexel	Independence	McElhany	Peculiar	Sugar Creek
Arthur	East Joplin	Inter-Contin	(Fort	Phelps	Swope Park
Asbury	East Leaven	ental Spur	Crowder)	Pierce City	
Atlas	worth	Irwin	Martin City	Pleasant Hill	Thoms
Avan	East Opolis	J. & G. Jct.	Melville	Porto Rico	Tiger
B. C. Jct.	Eve	Jasper	Merwin	Prospect	Tipton Ford
Bee Creek	Exeter	Jaudon	Metz	Purdy	
Belton	Farley	Jeffreys	Milo	Quinn	Vale
Belvidere	Faucett	Joplin	Minden	Racine	
Beverly	Forbes	Kansas City	Minden Mines	Raytown	Waco
Bigelow	Forest City	Kansas City	Missey Spur	Red Bridge	Waldron
Boston	Fort Crowder	(Centropolis	Monett	Red Plant	Washburn
Bronough	(McElhany)	Station)	Mordaunt	Reeds	Watson
Butler	Fortescue	Kansas City	Moundville	Richards	Webb City
Butterfield	Goodman	(Grand Ave.)	Mulberry	Rich Hill	Webb City-
Cagle	Granby	Kansas City	Napier	Rinehart	Carterville
Camp Clark	Grand View	(Leeds	Nassau Jct.	Ritchey	Wentworth
Carl Jct.	Greenwood	Station)	Neosho	Rushville	West Joplin
Carterville-Webb	Gulfton	Kansas City	Nevada	Ruth	Weston
City	Hannon	Stock Yards	Nevada	St. Joseph	West Platte
Carthage	Harrelson	Kenmoor	Storehouse	St. Joseph	Wightman
Carthage Quarry	Harrisonville	Knights	New Alms Spur	Water Works	Willow Brook
Spur	Hawley	Lamar	Niles	Sarcoxie	Wimmer
Carytown	Haydite	Lanagan	Nishnabotna	Seligman	Winthrop
Centropolis	Hercules	Langdon	Nodaway		Woodruff
					Wrightoe Spur

GROUP F

Figure 10. Class Rate Tariff TCFB 1015-A, page 168.

TARIFF 1015-A

SECTION 1—PART A—APPLICATION OF RATE BASES

Item	BETWEEN (See Item 110) AND Points on pages 123 to 203 in following Groups (See Item 110)	NORTH COAST TERRITORY (See Item 215)				SOUTH COAST TERRITORY (See Item 220)				
		NORTH COAST	CASCADE	PRAIRIE OR VALLEY	SPOKANE	SOUTH COAST	KELSO	SIERRA	NIPTON	LAS VEGAS OR RENO
		RATE BASES APPLICABLE (For rates, see Section 2)								
675	A................	995	956	915	878	995	956	936	915	878
	B................	912	875	840	805	912	875	858	840	805
	C, C-1...........	870	836	801	768	870	836	819	801	768
	D................	829	796	763	731	829	796	780	763	731
	E................	787	756	725	695	787	756	741	725	695
	E-1..............	787	756	725	695	......	......	......	......	......
	F................	746	717	686	658	746	717	702	686	658
	G................	705	677	649	622	705	677	663	649	622
	H................	829	796	763	731	705	677	663	649	622
	I................	663	636	611	585	②663	③636	624	②611	③585
	J................	639	613	588	563	②639	③613	601	②588	③563
	J-1.............	{①639 / ②705}	613	588	563					
	J-E.............	{①590 / ②673}	561	533	505	......				
	K, K-1...........	995	956	915	878	995	956	936	915	878
	L................	912	875	840	805	912	875	858	840	805
	M................	870	836	801	768	870	836	819	801	768
	N................	779	748	718	686					

SECTION 2
CLASS RATES IN CENTS PER 100 POUNDS

RATE BASES NUMBERS	400	300	250	200	175	150	125	110	100	92½	85	77½	70	65	60	55
742...........	3396	2547	2123	1608	1486	1274	1061	934	849	785	722	658	504	552	509	467
743...........	3400	2550	2125	1700	1488	1275	1063	935	850	786	723	659	595	553	510	468
744...........	3404	2553	2128	1702	1489	1277	1064	936	851	787	723	660	596	553	511	468
745...........	3408	2556	2130	1704	1491	1278	1065	937	852	788	724	660	596	554	511	469
746...........	3416	2562	2135	1708	1495	1281	1068	939	854	790	726	662	598	555	512	470
747...........	3420	2565	2138	1710	1496	1283	1069	941	855	791	727	663	599	556	513	470

50	45	40	37½	35	32½	30	27½	25	22½	20	17½	16	14½	13	RATE BASES NUMBERS
425	382	340	318	297	276	255	233	212	191	170	149	136	123	110	 742
425	383	340	319	298	277	255	234	213	191	170	149	136	123	111	 743
426	383	340	319	298	277	255	234	213	192	170	149	136	123	111	 744
426	383	341	320	298	277	256	234	213	192	170	149	136	124	111	 745
427	384	342	320	299	278	256	235	214	192	171	149	137	124	111	 746
428	385	342	321	299	278	257	235	214	192	171	150	137	124	111	 747

248

Figure 11.   Class Rate Tariff TCFB 1015-A, page 248.

SUBJECT TO INCREASES IN RATES AND CHARGES AS PROVIDED IN ITEM X-281.

C.T.C.(F) 7   I.C.C. 7

(For Federal Maritime and State Commission Nos. and Cancellations, see page 2)

UNIFORM CLASSIFICATION COMMITTEE, AGENT

UNIFORM
FREIGHT CLASSIFICATION 11⁻

RATINGS,
RULES AND REGULATIONS

THIS TARIFF IS APPLICABLE ONLY IN CONNECTION WITH TARIFFS
SPECIFICALLY SUBJECT HERETO

NOTICE

The provisions published herein will, if effective, not result in an effect on the quality of the human environment.

ISSUED JULY 14, 1972   **EFFECTIVE SEPTEMBER 8, 1972**

J. D. SHERSON
Tariff Publishing Officer
Room 1106
222 South Riverside Plaza
CHICAGO, ILL. 60606

Copyright 1972 by J. D. Sherson

Made in U.S.A.   (K-23691)

Figure 12. Uniform Freight Classification, title page.
Courtesy: Uniform Freight Classification Committee.

UNIFORM FREIGHT CLASSIFICATION

INDEX TO ARTICLES

STCC No.	Article	Item
40 211 52	Truck wheels,locomotive or rwy car, old,having value only for remelting purposes.	82960
35 515 60	Trucks and drainers,combined, bottle.	92700
37 413 58	Trucks and motors combined, locomotive.	82850
37 428 75	Trucks and motors combined,rwy car	82850
35 371 78	Trucks and tractors combined, platform or warehouse,noibn, motor	93440
37 999 10	Trucks: Automobile-wrecking,without body,two-wheeled.	9280
37 992 55	Brush-burning,iron,horse-drawn or trailer.	93130
35 321 43	Coal-cutting-machine conveying, SU.	63690,†63710
37 112 15	Driving for freight vehicles or fire apparatus	93340
37 422 74	Dry kiln,noibn,rwy,iron.	81810,†81820
37 992 30	Farm or freight,noibn,horse-drawn,completely KD	92900
37 992 31	Farm or freight,noibn,horse-drawn,ot completely KD.	92900
37 151 15	Farm or freight,noibn,trailer, ot motor,completely,KD.	92900
37 151 16	Farm or freight,noibn,trailer, ot motor,ot completely KD	92900
35 371 26	Form metal,printers'	79990,†80070
19 313 20	Gun-lifting.	73325
37 993 15	Hand,noibn	92670,†93290
35 371 62	Hand,with basket-work bodies.	93140
35 371 66	Hand,with canvas-basket bodies.	93150
35 371 71	Hand,with fibreboard or chemically-hardened fibre bodies,KD	93160
35 371 70	Hand,with fibreboard or chemically-hardened fibre bodies,SU	93160
35 371 74	Hand,with steel bodies,bodies nstd.	93170
35 225 73	*Hay-curing,two-wheeled	3210,†4050
35 371 46	House movers',iron or wood, ot motor vehicle.	92940
35 371 50	Lift,hand.	92950
35 371 78	Lift,motor	93440
37 413 57	Locomotive,without motors,KD	82840
37 413 56	Locomotive,without motors,SU	82840
37 992 42	Logging,horse-drawn or trailer, KD	92960
37 422 15	Logging,rwy,not moved on own wheels.	81260
35 371 54	Nose,hand.	92990
35 371 78	Platform or warehouse,noibn, motor	93440
37 151 25	Platform trailer,ot motor,each weighing 5,000 lbs or over.	93010
37 428 74	Rwy car,without motors,KD.	82840
37 428 73	Rwy car,without motors,SU.	82840
37 992 58	Steam boiler,horse-drawn or trailer,steel.	93180
37 112 10	Tongue or transport,noibn, other than hand	4000,†4050
37 114 20	Tractor,(driving trucks for freight trailers),army tractor tank recovery,armored	73330
37 151 25	Trailer,platform,ot motor,each weighing 5,000 lbs or over.	93010
35 371 26	Waste metal,printers'	79990,†80070
35 899 48	Wheeled and mop wringers combined.	92980
35 314 14	Wrecker,for towing or hauling disabled vehicles (cranes,ot revolving,mounted on auto-mobiles).	60700

STCC No.	Article	Item
35 227 18	Trumbols,rice (rice polishers)	59800,†59810
24 416 15	Trunk box material,wooden,in shooks or panels,noibn.	97940
24 411 70	" boxes,wooden,in the white, nnstd	97950
24 411 71	" boxes,wooden,in the white, nstd	97950
26 497 34	" cover paper,printed.	75400
31 611 22	" handles,leather.	48550
24 419 81	" lids,wooden,SU	97960
26 497 34	" lining,paper,printed	75400
31 611 31	" lockers,army	92270
24 999 85	" slats,wooden,finished.	97820
24 999 86	" slats,wooden,in the white.	97820
24 419 80	" top material,wooden,in the white,nstd.	97970
24 419 81	" tops,wooden,SU	97960
24 419 81	" trays,wooden,SU.	97960
34 619 68	" trimmings,noibn,iors or tin	50960
39 998 86	" trimmings,noibn,metal,ot iors or tin	†49771,50970
	Trunks:	
35 599 13	Cigar pressure,steel and wood combined	26855
39 998 59	Containing articles not specifically provided for in trunks,when contents consist of articles rated Class 125 or lower	92405
39 998 60	Containing articles not specifically provided for in trunks,when contents consist of articles rates higher than Class 125.	92405
31 611 64	Nnstd,or in nests of two.	92390
31 611 65	Nstd in nests of three or more	92390
34 411 68	Toy	45130,†45210
35 599 58	Truss bars,iors	δ
34 411 56	Truss hoops,coopers'	90750
	Trusses:	
34 411 56	Iors.	55170
39 313 45	Piano,finished.	69950
39 313 50	Piano,in the white.	69960
24 331 26	Roof,wooden,KD.	58200
24 331 25	Roof,wooden,SU or in SU sections.	58200
38 421 46	Surgical	32590
25 421 47	Tub covers,display,noibn.	31340
24 983 15	" covers,laundry,wooden.	78140
24 419 73	" covers,noibn,wooden,with rims or handles	97480,†98040
34 421 56	" enclosures,glass or plastic combined with metal	78320
34 619 60	" fasteners,wooden, steel	49410,†49781
34 819 65	" fasteners,noibn,steel, wire.	49410,†49781
30 619 53	" plugs (stoppers),rubber or rubber and metal combined.	78550
34 611 70	" shapes,washing machine	δ 78420
30 712 40	Tube fittings,plastic	77788
38 113 30	Tube holders,test,metal	52140
38 113 35	Tube holders,test,wooden.	52150
30 115 15	Tubeless tire liners (blow-out shields)	56815
01 319 10	Tubers,artichoke,fresh or green,ot cold-pack	41840
01 319 90	*Tubers,edible,fresh or green, noibn,ot cold-pack	42210
01 912 90	Tubers,noibn,florist stock.	39100

For explanation of reference marks,see top of page 17; for abbreviations,see last page of this Classification.

399

Figure 13.   Uniform Freight Classification, page 399.
Courtesy: Uniform Freight Classification Committee.

UNIFORM FREIGHT CLASSIFICATION   93325-93490

ITEM	ARTICLES	Less Carload Ratings	Carload Minimum (Pounds)	Carload Ratings
	VEHICLES,MOTOR (Subject to Item 93315)-Concluded: Automobiles,see Notes 1,2,4,5 and 6,Items 93321 to 93326,incl. (Subject to Item 93320)-Concluded:			
93325 93326	NOTE 5.-Axles may protrude from boxes or crates. NOTE 6.-In every case the minimum weight shall be that provided for the car used. If a single shipment is loaded in or on (as the case may be) more than one car,the lading of each car shall be subject to the minimum weight provided for the car which contains it. The carriers do not obligate themselves to supply cars of inside length in excess of 50 feet 8 inches.			

93330	Chassis,SU,wheels on or off,with or without seat cabs,loose or in packages:
	In closed or open top cars of inside length,or on flat cars of platform length,viz.:
	  In cars not exceeding 50 feet 8 inches in length. . . . . . .
	  In cars exceeding 50 feet 8 inches in length. . . . .
		150
		150
			12,500
			20,000
				85
				85

93335	Chassis,KD,LCL,in boxes or crates; CL,loose or in packages:
	In closed or open top cars of inside length,or on flat cars of platform length,viz.:
	  In cars not exceeding 50 feet 8 inches in length. . . . . . .
	  In cars exceeding 50 feet 8 inches in length. . . . .
		100
		100
			12,500
			20,000
				85
				85

93340	Freight,including tractors (driving trucks for freight vehicles or fire apparatus),loose or in packages:
	In closed or open top cars of inside length or on flat cars of platform length,viz.:
	  In cars not exceeding 50 feet 8 inches in length. . . . . . .
	  In cars,exceeding 50 feet 8 inches in length. . . . .
		150
		150
			12,500
			20,000
				85
				85

93350	Passenger,including ambulances or hearses,loose or in packages:
	In closed or open top cars of inside length,or on flat cars of platform length,viz.:
	  In cars not exceeding 50 feet 8 inches in length. . . . . . .
	  In cars exceeding 50 feet 8 inches in length. . . . .
		150
		150
			12,500
			20,000
				100
				100

93353	Snow tractors or snow trailers:
	In closed or open top cars of inside length,or on flat cars of platform length,viz.:
	  In cars not exceeding 50 feet 8 inches in length. . . . . . .
	  In cars exceeding 50 feet 8 inches in length. . . . .
		150
		150
			12,500
			20,000
				100
				100

93365	Carts,golf-club bag,motor propelled,KD: Without batteries,in boxes. . . . . With batteries,in boxes	125 85	24,000R 24,000R	45 45
93370	Chairs,rolling or invalid,motor propelled,without batteries: SU,in boxes or crates . . . . Folded or collapsed,in boxes or crates.	200 125	10,000R 24,000R	100 55
93372	Children's automobiles or children's automobile chassis,with or without motors: SU,in boxes or crates . . . . KD,in boxes or crates	150 100	12,000R 12,000R	85 85
93375	Coal,concrete,earth,ore or stone hauling or dumping vehicle chassis,SU,wheeled or crawler type,with or without seat cabs (low speed vehicles not suitable for general highway transportation).	. . . . . .	24,000R	45
93380	Coal,concrete,earth,ore or stone hauling or dumping,(low speed vehicles not suitable for general highway transportation),wheeled or crawler type,with seat cabs	100	24,000R	45
93390	Floats,pageantry,loose or in packages	200	10,000R	100
93400	Half-tracks,army,with or without ramps (runways).	100	24,000R	45
93405	Mail pickup and delivery,three-wheeled,SU,in crates; also CL,loose,securely braced in car	150	10,000R	85
93410	Motorcycles; motor scooters; or electric cars,noibn,see Note 8,Item 93411; two-wheeled or three-wheeled: SU,in boxes,crates or Package 273 . . . . KD,in boxes or crates	100 100	16,000R 24,000R	70 55
93411	NOTE 8.-Applies only on battery-powered electric cars,such as are used on golf courses or for messenger or light-delivery work,industrial or commercial.			
93420	Motorcycles,two-wheeled or three-wheeled,in mixed CL,with motorcycle side cars,or motorcycle or motorcycle side car chassis parts,noibn,see Note 9,Item 93421.	. . . . . .	16,000R	70
93421	NOTE 9.-Weight of side cars and motorcycle or motorcycle side car chassis parts must not exceed 50% of weight on which freight charges are assessed.			
93425	Snow or ice,noibn,see Note 9½,Item 93426,in boxes or crates or Package 1451: With skis,runners or windshields attached . . . . With skis or runners detached,without windshields or with windshields detached	200 100	12,000R 24,000R	85 45
93426	NOTE 9½.-Ratings apply on vehicles equipped with runners,skis or traction treads with net weight not exceeding 1,000 pounds.			
93430	Snow plows,power,self-propelling,see Rule 33 and Note 10,Item 93432,loose or in packages	150	12,000R 24,000R	85 45
93432	NOTE 10.-Section 2 of Rule 34 is not applicable.			
93440	Trucks or tractors or trucks combined,platform or warehouse,noibn,or lift trucks,loose or in packages.	85	24,000R	45
	VEHICLE PARTS:			
93445	Axle boxes or skeins,iron,loose or in packages.	70	36,000	40
93480	Axle or spring clips,couplings or staples,noibn,LCL,in bags,barrels	70	36,000	40
93490	or boxes; CL,in packages	70	36,000	40

For explanation of abbreviations,numbers and reference marks,see last page of this Classification; for packages,see pages following rating section.

876

Figure 14.   Uniform Freight Classification, page 876.
Courtesy: Uniform Freight Classification Committee.

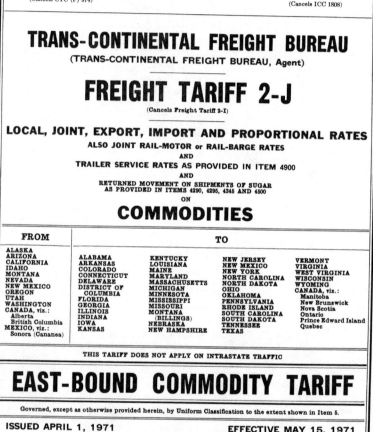

SUBJECT, EXCEPT AS OTHERWISE PROVIDED HEREIN, TO INCREASE IN RATES AND CHARGES AS
PROVIDED IN ITEMS X-259, X-262, X-265 AND X-267

A reissue of this tariff will become effective not later than May 15, 1972

CTC(F) 977
(Cancels CTC (F) 974)

ICC 1822
(Cancels ICC 1808)

TRANS-CONTINENTAL FREIGHT BUREAU
(TRANS-CONTINENTAL FREIGHT BUREAU, Agent)

FREIGHT TARIFF 2-J
(Cancels Freight Tariff 2-I)

LOCAL, JOINT, EXPORT, IMPORT AND PROPORTIONAL RATES
ALSO JOINT RAIL-MOTOR or RAIL-BARGE RATES
AND
TRAILER SERVICE RATES AS PROVIDED IN ITEM 4900
AND
RETURNED MOVEMENT ON SHIPMENTS OF SUGAR
AS PROVIDED IN ITEMS 4290, 4295, 4345 AND 4500
ON

COMMODITIES

FROM	TO			
ALASKA ARIZONA CALIFORNIA IDAHO MONTANA NEVADA NEW MEXICO OREGON UTAH WASHINGTON CANADA, viz.: Alberta British Columbia MEXICO, viz.: Sonora (Cananea)	ALABAMA ARKANSAS COLORADO CONNECTICUT DELAWARE DISTRICT OF COLUMBIA FLORIDA GEORGIA ILLINOIS INDIANA IOWA KANSAS	KENTUCKY LOUISIANA MAINE MARYLAND MASSACHUSETTS MICHIGAN MINNESOTA MISSISSIPPI MISSOURI MONTANA (BILLINGS) NEBRASKA NEW HAMPSHIRE	NEW JERSEY NEW MEXICO NEW YORK NORTH CAROLINA NORTH DAKOTA OHIO OKLAHOMA PENNSYLVANIA RHODE ISLAND SOUTH CAROLINA SOUTH DAKOTA TENNESSEE TEXAS	VERMONT VIRGINIA WEST VIRGINIA WISCONSIN WYOMING CANADA, viz.: Manitoba New Brunswick Nova Scotia Ontario Prince Edward Island Quebec

THIS TARIFF DOES NOT APPLY ON INTRASTATE TRAFFIC

EAST-BOUND COMMODITY TARIFF

Governed, except as otherwise provided herein, by Uniform Classification to the extent shown in Item 5.

ISSUED APRIL 1, 1971

EFFECTIVE MAY 15, 1971
(Except as otherwise provided herein)

ISSUED BY
FRED OFCKY, TARIFF PUBLISHING OFFICER
516 West Jackson Boulevard, Chicago, IL 60606

(File 6-2-M)

(Printed in U. S. A.)   G.-W.   82-244

Figure 15.   East-Bound Commodity Tariff TCFB 2-J, title page.

TARIFF 2-J

TABLE OF CONTENTS

6

Figure 16. East-Bound Commodity Tariff TCFB 2-J, page 6.

TARIFF 2-J

		RULES AND OTHER GOVERNING PROVISIONS
		SPECIAL RULES AND REGULATIONS **UNLIMITED**
ITEM	**SUBJECT**	**APPLICATION**
585 (Con- cluded)	Package Requirements	**Note 1.**—Unless otherwise provided, rates on articles in barrels or drums apply on the same articles in drums or in bulk shipping containers made of cord fabric and rubber combined complying with the specifications in Rule 40 of the Uniform Classification. **Note 2.**—Unless otherwise provided, rates on articles in wooden boxes apply on the same articles in fibreboard, pulp-board or double-faced corrugated fibreboard boxes with or without wooden frames, or fibre barrels, drums or pails, provided the requirements and specifications named in Rule 41 of Uniform Classification or authorized for shipment involved in individual items thereof are fully complied with. If, contrary to this provision, articles in such packages not fully complying with the requirements and specifications of Rule 41 of Uniform Classification or authorized for shipment involved in individual items thereof have been accepted and come into carriers' possession for transportation, the freight rate shall be increased 20 per cent (See Items 755 to 764) on less than carload shipments and 10 per cent (See Items 755 to 764) on carload shipments (Subject to Exception 1). **Note 3.**—The term "container cars" means cars that are described in the Official Railway Equipment Register ICC RER 379 as follows: "LF"........A flat car equipped to handle one or more demountable containers for transportation of commodities not under refrigeration. "LFA"......A flat car equipped with a container or containers for the purpose of transportation of commodities immersed in liquids or gases. "LFR"......A flat car supplied with a power unit and equipped to handle one or more demountable containers for transportation of commodities under refrigeration. "LG"........An open top car equipped to handle one or more demountable containers for the transportation of commodities not under refrigeration. "XU"........A house car with removable superstructure to be used for special loading. **Exception 1.**—The freight rate on shipments destined to points taking K-1 rates shall be increased 25 per cent (See Items 755 to 764) on both carload and less than carload shipments. **Exception 2.**—Class rates apply to points taking Group K-1 rates on articles in kinds of packages not specified in tariff. **Exception 3.**—The provisions of paragraph (g) hereof do not apply in connection with rates named in this tariff which provide only for shipments in compressed bales.
590	Package Requirements	(The provisions of this item do not apply to points taking Group A, A-1, K, K-1, K-2, L, L-1, M or M-1 rates; Group B, B-1 and C rates are subject to Item 11735) When an article in LCL quantity is loaded in the same car with a carload shipment and is covered by the same bill of lading, such article may be in any package authorized for a carload of the article between the same points (or it may be loose when the carload rate between the same points provides the article may be loose) and forwarded at the lowest less than carload rate, class or commodity, authorized on the article in the form (not package) in which shipped (See Note 1). **Note 1.**—This provision deals only with package requirements and not with different rates or ratings dependent on the form (not package) in which the article is shipped, such as whether knocked down or set up, nested or not nested, size of package, etc.
595	Points in Group A to N, etc.	For list of points taking Group A, A-1, B, B-1, C, C-1, C-2, C-3, C-4, D, D-1, D-3, D-4, E, E-1, E-2, E-3, E-4, E-5, E-6, F, G, H, I, J, K, K-1, K-2, L, L-1, M, M-1 or N rates or points in Groups 1 to 26, see pages 174 to 360 of TCFB Freight Tariff 5-B, ICC 1674.
600	Points taking Rate Basis 1 or 4 Rates, etc.	For list of points taking Rate Basis 1 or 4 rates or arbitraries higher and points taking Notes 1 to 373 basis for rates, see Column B on pages 8 to 156, and Column E on pages 157 to 173, of TCFB Freight Tariff 5-B, ICC 1674.
605	Prohibited and Restricted Articles via Water Routes	Rates applying in connection with the AA, COCD, GTW and PCP are subject to the Rules and Regulations governing Prohibited and Restricted Articles as published in CTRTB Tariff 631, ICC 4083, CTC(F) 1983.
610	Prohibited and Restricted Articles via Lake Lines	**RATES AUTHORIZED HEREIN AS APPLYING IN CONNECTION WITH** **NORTHERN NAVIGATION CO., ARE SUBJECT TO THE** **RESTRICTIONS NOTED IN ITEM 615** ①—Articles shown in Item 615, bearing reference "①" indicate that shipments thereof will not be received or transported on any terms. ②—Articles shown in Item 615, bearing reference "②" enumerated in the Restricted List indicate that shipments of the character referred to must not be tendered for transportation without first ascertaining whether they can be handled or can be handled without being subject to damage or deterioration and without endangering other freight. Such special authority must be received from Northern Navigation Co., through Agent of initial carrier at point of origin of shipment or through Northern Navigation Co. direct and no rates shall be quoted until such special authority has been given by the Northern Navigation Co.

Figure 17.   East-Bound Commodity Tariff TCFB 2-J, page 171.

TARIFF 2-J

SECTION 2—GENERAL COMMODITY RATES

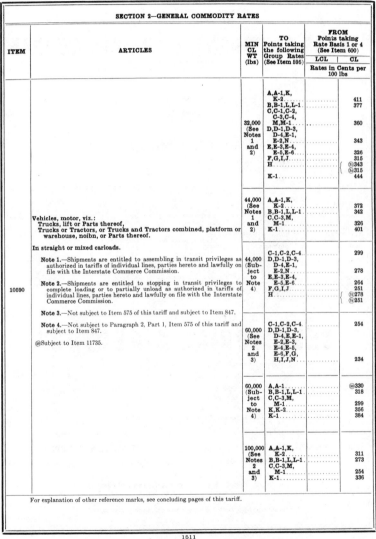

ITEM	ARTICLES	MIN CL WT (lbs)	TO Points taking the following Group Rates (See Item 595)	FROM Points taking Rate Basis 1 or 4 (See Item 600) LCL	CL
				Rates in Cents per 100 lbs	
		32,000 (See Notes 1 and 2)	A,A-1,K, K-2	....	411
			B,B-1,L,L-1	....	377
			C,C-1,C-2, C-3,C-4, M,M-1	....	360
			D,D-1,D-3, D-4,E-1, E-2,N	....	343
			E,E-3,E-4, E-5,E-6	....	326
			F,G,I,J	....	315
			H	....	(51)343 (54)315
			K-1	....	444
	Vehicles, motor, viz.: Trucks, lift or Parts thereof, Trucks or Tractors, or Trucks and Tractors combined, platform or warehouse, noibn, or Parts thereof.	44,000 (See Notes 1 and 2)	A,A-1,K, K-2	....	372
			B,B-1,L,L-1	....	342
			C,C-3,M, M-1	....	326
			K-1	....	401
	In straight or mixed carloads.				
	Note 1.—Shipments are entitled to assembling in transit privileges as authorized in tariffs of individual lines, parties hereto and lawfully on file with the Interstate Commerce Commission.	44,000 (Subject to Note 4)	C-1,C-2,C-4. D,D-1,D-3, D-4,E-1, E-2,N	....	299
	Note 2.—Shipments are entitled to stopping in transit privileges to complete loading or to partially unload as authorized in tariffs of individual lines, parties hereto and lawfully on file with the Interstate Commerce Commission.		E,E-3,E-4, E-5,E-6	....	278
			F,G,I,J	....	264
					251
	Note 3.—Not subject to Item 575 of this tariff and subject to Item 847.		H	....	(51)278 (54)251
10590	Note 4.—Not subject to Paragraph 2, Part 1, Item 575 of this tariff and subject to Item 847.	60,000 (See Notes 2 and 3)	C-1,C-2,C-4. D,D-1,D-3, D-4,E,E-1, E-2,E-3, E-4,E-5, E-6,F,G, H,I,J,N	....	254
	(50)Subject to Item 11735.				234
		60,000 (Subject to Note 4)	A,A-1	....	(50)330
			B,B-1,L,L-1	....	318
			C,C-3,M, M-1	....	299
			K,K-2	....	356
			K-1	....	384
		100,000 (See Notes 2 and 3)	A,A-1,K, K-2	....	311
			B,B-1,L,L-1	....	273
			C,C-3,M, M-1	....	254
			K-1	....	336

For explanation of other reference marks, see concluding pages of this tariff.

Figure 18. East-Bound Commodity Tariff TCFB 2-J, page 1511.

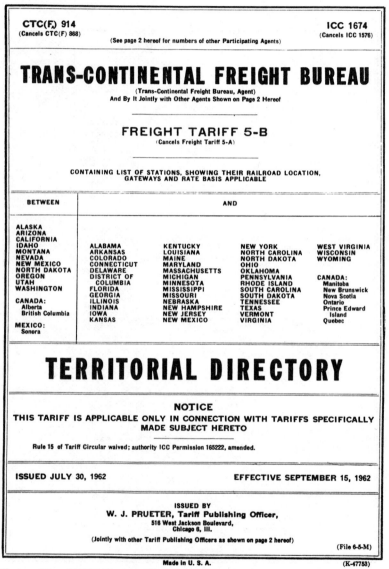

Figure 19.   TCFB Freight Tariff 5-B (Territorial Directory), title page.

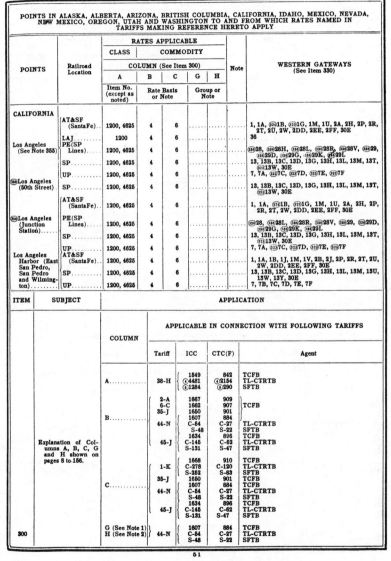

Figure 20. TCFB Freight Tariff 5-B (Territorial Directory), page 51.

TARIFF 5-B

POINTS IN EASTERN DEFINED TERRITORIES FROM OR TO WHICH RATES NAMED IN TARIFFS
MAKING REFERENCE HERETO APPLY

MISSOURI—Continued

POINT	Rates Applicable (See Note)	POINT	Rates Applicable (See Note)	POINT	Rates Applicable (See Note)	POINT	Rates Applicable (See Note)
J & G Jct.		Livingston		Neosho	1	Raytown	
Jasper	1	Lockwood	5	Netherlands	2	Red Bridge	
Jaudon		Logan		Nevada		Red Plant	1
J. B. Jct.		Lopez		Nevada Storehouse	1	Reeds	
Jedburg	5	Lorwood	2	New Alms Spur		Reeds Spring	5
Jefferson Barracks	6	Loughboro		Newburg		Republic	
Jeffreys	1	Lowry City		New Castle	5	Richards	1
Jeffriesburg	5	Low Wassie	5	New Fountain Farm		Rich Hill	
Jennings	6	Ludwig		New Madrid	2	Richland	5
Joplin	1	Lumtie		New Offenburg		Rinehart	1
Jury	5	Lutesville	2	Niangua	5	Risco	
Kancon		Luther	6	Nichols		Ristine	2
Kansas City		McBride	2	Niles		Ritchey	1
Kansas City (Centropolis Station)		McCoy		Nishnabotna	1	Rivermines	2
Kansas City (Grand Avenue)	1	McElhany (Fort Crowder)	1	Nodaway		Riverside	5
Kansas City (Leeds Station)		McMullin	2	Noel		Rives	2
Kansas City Stock Yards		Macomb	5	North Clinton	5	Robert Ave (Carondelet)	6
Keeners	5	Madie	5	North Des Arc	5	Robertson	6
Kenmoor	1	Maes Spur	6	North Kansas City	1	Robertsville	5
Kennett	2	Malden	2	Northview	5	Rockview	2
Kenoma	5	Mansfield	5	Norwood		Rockville	
Kewanee	2	Maplewood	6	Octa	2	Rogersville	5
Keysville	5	Marbleton	2	Oetters	5	Rolla	
Kimmswick		Marionville	5	Ogborn	2	Rombauer	2
Kinder	2	Marlo		Olden	5	Rosati	
Kirkwood (MoPac)	5	Marquand	2	Old Orchard	6	Rosebud	5
Kissick	5	Marquette		Old Rock	1	Round House	
Knights	1	Marshfield	5	Olivette	6	Rush Tower	2
Knob Lick	2	Marston	2	Opal	5	Rushville	
KO&G Jct.	1	Martin City	1	Oran	2	Ruskin	1
		Marvel Cave	5	Oronogo	1	Ruth	
		Maryland Heights	6	Osceola		St. Albans	5
		Matthews	2	Owenmont	5	St. Clair	
				Owensville			

Note 1.—Group F rates apply (Subject to Items 205 and 340).

Note 2.—{(a) Group E-3 rates (Subject to Item 340) (except as provided in paragraph (b) below), apply.

Note 5.—{(a) Group E-3 rates (Subject to Items 205 and 340) (except as provided in paragraph (b) below), apply.

Note 6.—{(a) Group E-4 rates (Subject to Items 205 and 340) (except as provided in paragraph (b) below), apply.

Note 7.—{(a) Group E-5 rates (Subject to Item 340), apply except as provided in paragraph (b) below.

(Concluded on following page)

For explanation of reference marks, see concluding pages of this tariff.

Figure 21. TCFB Freight Tariff 5-B (Territorial Directory), page 224.

4. Determine the rate basis number that the class rate tariff assigns to the particular journey from the origin to the destination with which you are dealing.

5. Cross-reference the rate basis number and the class rating on the appropriate rate page of the class rate tariff to find the applicable class rate.

6. In the class rate tariff, check the routing section, if there is one, to see over what route the rate applies, or if it applies over the route you wish to use.

7. Refer to the proper commodity rate tariff.

8. Determine whether the class and commodity rates in the tariffs you are using are "alternating" or "non-alternating."

9. Refer to "list of commodities" in the commodity tariff and find item listing rates for specific named commodity; determine if rates apply between desired origin and destination points.

10. Compare class and commodity rate if alternation is allowed.

Refer to appropriate classification. A *classification* is a freight tariff that is essential to the class system of rate publication. Classifications contain shipping rules and regulations, descriptions of commodities, packing requirements, and other information. Their most important function, however, is to classify into a few categories all the products that are shipped. These categories are called class ratings. A class rating is not a price for transportation service. It is merely the designation of the group into which a commodity falls. A rate or price must then be found for it from one town to another. Since commodities are arranged in the classification tariff under "generic" headings or in "families," ratings can be obtained even for unlisted articles by taking the general rating for the generic group or by taking the rating for the article to which they are most similar. Classification is so extensive a task that products and their ratings are listed in these large books separately from the rate tariffs.

Several classifications are in use in the United States today. Some of them apply only to specific regions; all of them apply only to specific tariffs. Therefore, one must first refer to the class rate tariff to determine which classification the tariff is governed by. The two classifications that are most nearly nation-wide in scope are the *Uniform Freight Classification* of the railroads and the *National Motor Freight Classification, 100-Series* of the trucklines. These volumes use the same system of classification.

Commodities are listed in alphabetical order in the index near the front of the classification. This index assigns an "item number" to each commodity. In the main body of the book, the item numbers are arranged in numerical order. Generally, articles are listed under "generic headings," which group products together in families. At the item number location, a uniformly acceptable shipping description is given for the article and a class rating is assigned. Assignment of class ratings depends upon shipping characteristics of the product. High-value, light and bulky, poorly-packed goods take high ratings; low-value, dense and heavy, well-packed goods take low ratings. The classification system begins with a basic class rating of 100, representing 100 percent. Goods with extremely high-cost shipping characteristics are rated in multiples of Class 100, being assigned ratings such as Class 150, Class 200, or Class 400. Goods with low-cost shipping characteristics are assigned ratings ranging downward from 100, such as Class 85, Class 70, Class 55, and so on. Approximately 31 classes are used. In rail transportation, the class rates (prices) in the freight rate tariff bear the same percentage relationship to each other as the class ratings. Therefore, if a person knows the class rate for one class rating between two cities, he can estimate the rates for other classes. This procedure is only good for "ballpark" estimates, however, and cannot be depended upon for precision. In the trucking industry, class rates have only an approximate percentage relationship to each other.

Figures 12, 13, and 14 on pages 175, 176, and 177 show sample pages from the Uniform Freight Classification.

Refer to the proper class rate tariff. Once the class rating for the product has been determined, one must look in a class rate freight tariff to find the rate that applies to that rating. Obviously, the tariff used must apply to the geographic area containing the desired origin and destination. One is not always so lucky as to find both points in the same publication; one may have to construct a rate over a common junction-point found in two tariffs. In such cases, the tariffs must be compatible, making provision for joint rather than purely local rates, and they must apply to the same traffic (intrastate vs. interstate).

Exceptions to classification. Our previous discussion showed that carriers frequently desire to treat some commodity specially and give it a different class rate level from what the classification calls for. One way of doing this is to publish an exception to the classification. For instance, the classification assigns LTL shipments of fruit-juice powder or crystals in boxes a class rating of Class 70. An individual carrier or group of carriers might wish to handle this at the same rate level at which grocery products are moving—say Class 55. So, an exception reducing the product to that rating will be published in the exceptions section of the class rate tariff.

Determine rate basis number. The rate basis system is another simplifying device that is used in class rate tariffs. Frequently the freight rates between different sets of towns will be the same. Tariff bulk can be reduced by using rate basis numbers instead of individual city names. If the same rates apply between more than one set of stations, the same rate basis number can be assigned to both hauls without repeating the entire scale of rates. Figure 11 on page 174 shows an example of a tariff page assigning rate basis numbers between towns.

Cross-reference rate basis and class rating. Once the class rating identifying the commodity and the rate basis number identifying the journey have been located, determination of the class rate is a simple matter of cross-referencing the two on a coordinate system. Figure 11 on page 174 illustrates this. Once the rate is determined one must make sure it applies over the route he wishes to use. This is done by referring to the routing section of the tariff.

Commodity rate tariff. Often more than one commodity rate tariff is in effect for the same route or geographic areas as the class rate tariff one is using. Some commodity tariffs apply on "general commodities" and include several or many unrelated products; some are for "specific commodities" and apply only to a small group of related products. In the motor truck industry, class and commodity rates are sometimes published in the same tariff volume.

Once one has found the appropriate commodity rate tariff, its use is simpler than the class rate tariff. This is because the classification step is omitted. Rate bases are not used, either, but cities may be assigned group numbers which require interpretation. Commodity rates, again, may be restricted to certain routes.

Using Rate Tariffs: An Example

The Figures (9 through 21) to which we have been referring are excerpts from four different railroad freight tariffs. Each of these tariffs is a sizable paperbound book. The student should note that a title page from each of these volumes has been included to aid him in visualizing the necessity of handling and referring to different publications. In the following exercise, reference is made to the page numbers of these tariffs rather than to the Figure numbers with which they have been identified in this book.

Let us assume that we are an industrial firm in Los Angeles, California, which is going to ship lift trucks to a distributor in Kansas City, Missouri. The lift trucks weigh 5,000 pounds each. We want to know what the railroad freight charges will be and how many lift trucks we should ship at one time. We consult the freight tariffs discussed below. (The student should turn to the appropriate tariff and follow each step as it is explained. It may help to refer to the list of steps in rate-checking on pages 171 and 185.)

Uniform Freight Classification.   We find that class rates between California and Missouri are published in *Trans-Continental Freight Bureau Tariff* (TCFB) 1015-A. The title page of this tariff (see text page 172) also tells us it is governed by the *Uniform Freight Classification.*

We turn to the *Uniform Freight Classification* (see text page 175). In the index on page 399 of the tariff we find that "Trucks: Lift, motor" are assigned Item number 93440.

We find Item number 93440 in the sideline of tariff page 876 (this is shown on text page 177). Item 93440 tells us that "Trucks or tractors, or truck and tractors combined, platform or warehouse, noibn, or lift trucks, loose or in packages" take ratings of Class 85 in LCL quantities or Class 45 if a carload of at least 24,000 pounds is shipped. (The R following the 24,000 in the Carload Minimum column indicates that the product may be bulky, requiring a larger-than-average car.)

Class Rate Tariff TCFB 1015-A. We now know that lift trucks take Class 85 LCL or Class 45 in 24,000-pound carloads. Armed with this information, we turn to Class Rate Tariff 1015-A (see text page 172). We find no exceptions to the ratings given us by the Uniform Classification, so we are next interested in finding the rate basis to apply. Page 168 of Tariff 1015-A (text page 173) shows us that the "Basis Applicable" to Los Angeles is "South Coast." Page 168 also shows us that the "Group Basis Applicable" to Kansas City, Missouri, is "Group F." On the top of page 248 of the tariff (text page 174) we are able to coordinate "Group F" from the sideline points and "South Coast" from the headline points to find that the Rate Basis applying from Los Angeles to Kansas City is 746. We can now use the Class Ratings and the Rate Basis to find the rates applicable.

To save space, the pages showing the class rates have also been excerpted on tariff page number 248. Under Section 2 on page 248, we find Rate Basis 746 listed in the sidelines for both sets of classes shown. Following it across the page at the appropriate level, we find that the Class 85 rate is 726¢ per hundred pounds. We also find that the Class 45 rate is 384¢ per hundred pounds. This means that if we shipped one lift truck weighing 5,000 pounds it would move at the 726¢ rate for a total of $363.00. If we shipped 24,000 pounds of lift trucks, the rate would be 384¢ for a total of $921.60. This information is summarized again subsequently.

East-Bound Commodity Tariff TCFB 2-J. In order to see if a more attractive commodity rate is in effect, we refer to Tariff 2-J published by the same bureau as our class rate tariff. The title page (text page 178) tells us that it applies on commodities moving from California to Missouri. On page 1511 of this tariff (see text page 181) we find Item 10590, which lists rates for "Vehicles, motor, viz.: Trucks, Lift or Parts thereof," etc. We are unable to interpret these rates, however, as the names of towns are not shown. In the Table of Contents of the tariff (tariff page 6, text page 179) we find that "Points in

Groups A to N, etc.," and "Points taking Rate Basis 1 or 4 rates" are explained in Items 595 and 600 on page 171 of the tariff. When we turn to these Items on page 171 they refer us to TCFB Freight Tariff 5-B.

TCFB Freight Tariff 5-B.   The title page of Territorial Directory 5-B is found on page 182 of this text. Interpreting the material on page 51 of this tariff, we find that Los Angeles is Rate Basis 4. Similarly, page 224 of the tariff shows us that Kansas City takes Group F rates. This information enables us to refer again to Item 10590 of the Commodity Tariff (see text page 181).

Item 10590 of Commodity Tariff.   Rates in Item 10590 of Tariff 2-J (tariff page 1511, text page 181) apply from Rate Basis 1 or 4, which includes Los Angeles. We are interested in rates applying to Group F. By careful searching among the letters in the "To" column, we find that there is a rate on 32,000 pounds of lift trucks of 315¢ per hundred pounds. On 44,000 pounds the rate is 251¢ and on 60,000 pounds the rate is 234¢. We now have enough information that we can make an analysis to determine the optimum number of lift trucks to ship. Table 2 on page 191 summarizes the rates we have found and their effects on the unit cost of the lift trucks. The step of checking the routing over which these rates will apply has been omitted from this problem in the interest of simplicity.

Table 2. Summary of Lift Truck Rates.

Number of Trucks Shipped	Weight of Shipment (lbs.)	Freight Rate	Source of Rate	Total Charges	Cost Per Truck
1	5,000	726	LCL Class 85	$ 363.00	$ 363.00
2	10,000	726	LCL Class 85	726.00	363.00
3	15,000	726	LCL Class 85	1089.00	363.00
But if three lift trucks were shipped as 24,000 pounds, the rate would be:					
4	24,000	384	CL Class 45	921.60	307.20
	20,000 as 24,000	384	CL Class 45	921.60	230.40
5	25,000	384	CL Class 45	960.00	192.00
6	30,000	384	CL Class 45	1152.00	192.00
But if six lift trucks were shipped as 32,000 pounds, the rate would be:					
7	32,000	315	Commodity rate 32000# Min. Wt.	1008.00	168.00
	35,000	315	Commodity rate 32000# Min. Wt.	1102.50	157.50
8	40,000	315	Commodity rate 32000# Min. Wt.	1260.00	157.50
But if eight lift trucks were shipped as 44,000 pounds, the rate would be:					
9	44,000	251	Commodity rate 44000# Min. Wt.	1104.40	138.05
	45,000	251	Commodity rate 44000# Min. Wt.	1129.50	125.50
10	50,000	251	Commodity rate 44000# Min. Wt.	1255.00	125.50
11	55,000	251	Commodity rate 44000# Min. Wt.	1380.50	125.50
12	60,000	234	Commodity rate 60000# Min. Wt.	1404.00	117.00

CHAPTER 11

Dealing with Carriers

Previous chapters have presented many facts about our commercial transportation system. The purpose of this chapter is to discuss several activities related to making a shipment. These activities are examined in the chronological order in which they might appear in the shipping process.

ORDERING SERVICE

Most transportation service can be ordered informally by telephone. When volume is large and there are penalties for keeping equipment overtime, written orders are preferred.

Pickup of Small Shipments

Small shipments usually move by truckline, air freight, United Parcel Service, or REA Express. Generally a telephone call to the city dispatcher of these carriers is sufficient for them to stop the pickup truck at the shipper's door. Timing is important, as many small-lot carriers have their truck fleets deliver in the morning and pick up in the afternoon. Each truck has a regular route, and dispatchers do not like to have a truck backtrack once it has passed the customer who calls in late. Since trucks have regular routes, arrangements can be made for daily stops. Most carriers do this free if the customer ships regularly. United Parcel Service will stop every day regardless of outbound volume for a fee of about $2 per week.

On full trailerload shipments the shipper should keep written records of the size of trailer ordered, and the times the order was placed and the trailer delivered. This permits auditing of bills for detention charges.

Shippers sometimes find that they are receiving too much pickup and delivery service and that shipping facilities are congested by trucks. If the account is an important one, most carriers will make some efforts to comply with a schedule set up by the customer to alleviate this. Also, one carrier, such as a city transfer company, can be hired to do all of the shipper's pickup and delivery work. Line-haul carriers will sometimes pay allowances to the cartage company chosen by the customer. Usually, however, such arrangements are more expensive and less efficient than dealing directly with the line-haul carrier.

Railroad Service

Rail service also can be ordered informally by calling the car desk or car clerk who works for the local freight agent. Such orders should always be confirmed in writing on car requisition forms furnished by the railroad. Cars come in different types and sizes, and misunderstandings can result in extra charges.

The person who orders rail cars for outloading should be familiar with the rules of the *Uniform Freight Classification* that deal with cars. The minimum weights for carloads shown in the classification are set for "standard" boxcars 40 feet 7 inches or less in length. When a shipper needs a larger car, the minimum carload weight required increases as the length of the car increases. However, when the shipper orders a 40-foot car and the railroad supplies a larger one, the required minimum does not increase. Thus, a notation of the size of car ordered and the size of the car furnished must be made on the bill of lading and railroad waybill to protect against overcharge. Other rules also apply when freight is light and bulky, extra long, or when more than one car is required. A customer who ships a reasonable volume will probably find that the railroad freight salesman is often eager to help him with preparing the bill of lading and securing cars.

Customers are expected to leave cars clean and in good order when they finish using them. The next shipper often is irritated when the railroad delivers him an empty that the previous user has left dirty and full of protruding nails. Because of this, cars must always be carefully inspected, cleaned, and prepared before loading to prevent damage to the shipment.

Booking Marine Cargo Space

In conventional ocean freighters, preplanning of stowage is essential to efficiency and safety. Cargo must be loaded to give the ship a certain weight and balance; it must also be possible to get it off the ship at the various ports of call. Therefore, shiplines like to book cargo in advance and to schedule the time it will arrive for loading.

The first step in booking space is to telephone the carrier to see if space will be available on a certain vessel scheduled to sail on a certain date. If so, the carrier will send the shipper a *booking memo* or a *freight contract*. If the contract form is used, it commits the carrier to have space available for the customer. Next, a *shipping permit* or *dock receipt* is issued, authorizing the merchandise to be brought to the pier at a certain time. Finally, when the cargo is placed aboard, the carrier signs the bill of lading. A written record of promised delivery times is very important. For example, if delivery to port is by rail car, the steamship company may delay unloading and incur rail demurrage charges. If the delay is the fault of the shipline, it must absorb these charges. For customers located inland, the ocean freight forwarder performs these services for a fee.

Since ocean containers have come into use, booking for a particular vessel is not so important. Stowage of container vessels does not have to be preplanned as much as hand-stowed vessels. Therefore, the container can often be scheduled to go out on the first available vessel. Written commitment from the carrier is still essential.

In the Atlantic container trade, European and British container-ship lines have established a separate company, known as the Consortium, that provides joint container service. The shipper books with the Consortium, which in turn books the container out on an available vessel. In the Pacific, the Japanese lines use a so-called Space Charter System. Each carrier reserves space for some of its containers on the vessels of every other carrier. Thus, each company has some space available on each outbound schedule, and the shipper books with the individual company.

ROUTING OF SHIPMENT

When he is ordering transportation service, the shipper must also consider the route it will follow and where it will arrive in the destination area. The ease with which the consignee can receive the shipment is very important, because unsatisfactory delivery may cause him to switch his buying to a competitive supplier. Thus, unsatisfactory transportation can wreck the whole marketing program for a product. Selection of the delivering carrier, therefore, is always important.

In air transport and especially in water transport, when one selects the origin carrier, generally he is also selecting the destination carrier, as these modes usually do not connect to form networks.

Trucklines join together to provide through movements, but they have no obligation to let the shipper pick which carriers join together. Trucklines will usually honor a shipper's request for a particular delivering carrier, however.

Since 1910, American shippers by railroad have had the legal right to specify which carriers shall join together in a route to move a shipment and at which junction points the carriers shall transfer the shipment. This is subject to the limitation that in the absence of specific instructions, the origin carrier can expect a line-haul (rather than merely a switching move), and the limitation that no carrier on the route shall be forced to carry the shipment for substantially less than the length of its line that lies between the termini of the route.

In both the motor truck and rail fields, attractive rates are frequently tied to a specific route. In such cases, careful selection of route ensures savings in costs. When "open routing" is allowed and the rate is the same for all carriers, savings in time or the courtesy and general efficiency of the carriers may be important to consider.

PACKING AND LOADING

While transportation service is being ordered, the merchandise must be properly packed for loading. Persons inexperienced in shipping seldom realize the damage that can result from the moving, shifting, jolting, and chafing that occurs in transportation. Much more is involved than setting an article in a carton and then stacking the cartons in a transportation vehicle. The goods must be packed and loaded so that they are not free to move and so that they cannot be damaged by external objects.

Because the shipper must pay freight charges on the weight of the container as well as the merchandise, he is tempted to underpackage. Inadequately packaged shipments are often tendered to carriers on the assumption that if the carrier accepts it he is thereby approving the package and must pay for the material if it is damaged. This is false economy. First, carriers set up specific package requirements, which they wish to have followed. Detailed package descriptions are given in both the *Uniform Freight Classification* and the *National Motor Freight Classification*. Penalty charges are provided for non-conforming packages found in transportation. Of course, carriers do not always apply these penalties, but when damage occurs, the carrier may reject the freight claim if it is clear that the shipment was improperly packed. Even if the carrier pays the claim, the shipper is still the loser, as the purpose of transportation is delivery of shipments and not generation of freight claims.

Many large companies have packaging departments or subdepartments that research packing problems and design containers. Also, new packing and loading materials such as styrofoam carton liners, fiber-glass pads, and inflatable dunnage are continually developed. However, the principles of proper packing and loading are seldom taught to the employees who actually do the shipping work. Many firms could profit by creating a short course in packing and loading for such employees.

DEMURRAGE

Closely related to the loading process is the subject of demurrage. Demurrage originated as a penalty that shipowners charged against charter customers who kept the ship for unloading for a longer time than called for in the contract. Today it is also in use by railroads and motor carriers.

Railroads allow the customer a *free time* for loading or unloading a car after it is delivered. This time is 48 hours, beginning with the first 7 AM after the car is placed. When free time expires, the customer is charged $10 per day for holding the car. The charge increases to $20 and then $30 per day if the car is held for an extended time. Saturdays, Sundays, and holidays are not charged. Because of this and the 7-AM beginning point, the time and day when a car is placed can greatly affect the total uncharged time and the total charges that result. Currently, about 46 percent of all cars are being released within 24 hours and about 68 percent within 48 hours. Another feature of railroad demurrage that requires careful management is the concept of *constructive placement*. When the customer's sidings are full, the rail carrier may place the car elsewhere, such as on a public team track, and demurrage will be figured as though it had been placed at the customer's plant. Railroads offer volume shippers an *average demurrage agreement* whereby the user earns credits for releasing cars early. These are applied against debits charged for keeping cars past free time. Loading and unloading accounts must be kept separately, and credits on one do not apply against debits of the other.

The trend in recent years has been to raise demurrage charges so that shippers will find it too expensive to use cars for storage. In 1971, the I.C.C. approved increases from $5 per day (for the first four days) to $10. The average car is still in the hands of the shipper or consignee, rather than the railroad, for about 20 percent of its time. The extremely liberal allowances of free time encourage this unproductive use of equipment.

Motor trucklines use *detention charges* rather than demurrage. Free time allowed is much shorter, sometimes being stated in minutes. Motor-carrier detention charges are not uniform and vary from tariff to tariff. Some carriers only remember to assess the charges when a shipper habitually over-detains equipment. When motor-carrier tariffs call for detention charges, the customer should require the carrier's drivers to sign in or punch the clock so that the exact moment of equipment delivery can be recorded.

CONTROL OF SHIPMENTS EN ROUTE

Business firms who buy and sell goods from and to each other often do so on unduly short lead-times. Goods are frequently ordered on short notice, the supplier is rushed to fill the order, and the shipping situation becomes a crash program. At such times, the whole burden of a successful physical-distribution program falls upon the transportation company, and the wisdom of having chosen a reliable carrier becomes evident. When the goods are in the hands of the carrier, direct control of the movement is no longer in the hands of the shipper, and there is little he can do, indirectly, to exercise control. There are, however, some ways in which he can affect the shipment. These include reconsignment and diversion, stoppage in transitu, tracing, and expediting.

Reconsignment and Diversion

The right of changing the consignee and/or destination of a shipment was discussed in Chapter 5. Reconsignment and diversion are usually planned in advance. The carrier charges a fee for performing the service.

Stoppage in Transitu

Often referred to simply as *stoppage in transit*, this right of the shipper should not be confused with stopping in transit for partial loading or unloading, or with transit privileges. Stoppage in transitu refers to the right of the shipper to stop the shipment before it can be delivered if he learns that the consignee is insolvent and cannot pay for the merchandise. Some carriers demand that the shipper indemnify them against damage suits before they will do this. This is because the carrier may be held guilty of conversion if he withholds delivery but it turns out that the consignee is solvent.

Tracing

The purpose of tracing is to find out where a shipment is. Much tracing could be avoided if shippers would give consignees useful advance information. The original bill of lading should always be sent to the consignee, and copies of purchase orders and related documents should show accurate carrier and routing information. Sometimes shippers are late in meeting shipping deadlines and are reluctant to admit it. When the consignee lacks adequate information, a bad situation is made worse.

Modern railroads and trucklines use centralized data-storage banks to record information on all shipments. When so equipped they are capable of telling a customer exactly where a carload, truckload or even a less-than-truckload is at a certain time. For active shippers, railroads often query their computers on a daily (or oftener) basis to prepare a *passing report*, which can be sent or telephoned to the customer.

Although the computer has brought a high degree of efficiency to tracing, businessmen should not trace shipments unless the reason is important.

Expediting

The Latin meaning of "expedite" is "to free one caught by the foot." This archaic meaning would be appropriate in transportation if expediting meant an attempt to get a stalled or delayed shipment moving again. However, when business firms try to expedite a shipment they are usually trying to get faster service than what the carrier would ordinarily give them. This sort of expediting is not very effective, for at least two reasons.

First, the concept of reasonable dispatch is clearly established and is set forth in Section 2 of the bill of lading contract that the shipper signs. The carrier is not obligated to deliver the shipment any faster than he usually delivers most shipments. He has this provision in writing in the contract and is not likely to go beyond the contract provision.

Second, there is some question whether the carrier could alter the contract by giving a written promise to deliver sooner than usual. This would constitute discrimination unless he stood ready to do it for every customer, which would be unlikely.

The best way to expedite a shipment is to plan carefully in advance for its transportation. This probably will mean selecting a fast, high-priced carrier rather than trying to force premium service from a low-priced carrier. However, judicious and courteous use of tracing can do much to prevent "foul-ups"; the carrier usually notices the customer who displays an interest in what is going on. Some firms have used personal expediting to speed orders from suppliers. When an important order is due to be sent them, the company sends a man to the supplier's plant. He observes the packing and shipping procedure. If necessary, he follows the shipment to the carrier's terminal and watches the loading process. Usually any delays in the process are discovered in the shipper's plant before the material reaches the carrier. An example of personal expediting is that of a large engineering company. A shipment of delicate refinery machinery was being made from Pennsylvania to Texas by special train. A representative of the engineering company's traffic department joined the train at origin and rode it to destination, making sure that connections were made properly with no unnecessary switching moves.

Trucklines are usually more willing than railroads to promise some kind of expedited service. This may be done to impress a new customer. No company expects to be asked to expedite every shipment a customer makes, however.

Freight Claims

Unfortunately, at the end of many transportation movements there is a freight claim. An inefficient carrier may pay out as much as 3 percent of its gross annual revenue in loss and damage claims. An efficient carrier is seldom able to reduce these payments below ½ percent of annual revenue.

Freight claims arise when the shipping contract is violated. There are several causes of action for them, among which are loss, damage, delay, and overcharge.

When there is shortage to all or part of a shipment or when contents are damaged, the carrier is liable to pay for it under his common-law duty to deliver unless he can claim one of the exemptions from liability set forth in the bill of lading. Loss and damage are possibly the most frequent type of claim the average businessman will have.

A claim for delay may arise when a carrier fails to transport a shipment with reasonable dispatch under the terms of Section 2 of the bill of lading. Such claims are relatively rare and fairly hard to establish. This is because the claimant must prove that there has been a definite loss of market value in the goods. With goods such as agricultural products that are sold in a commodities market, such loss of value is easy to demonstrate. Manufactured products, however, usually are worth the same amount even when they arrive later than the consignee planned.

The receipt clause of the bill of lading makes the contract "subject to classifications and tariffs in effect on the date of issue of this Bill of Lading." This means that the legal rate shall be charged. When the carrier does not apply the correct rate, a contract violation takes place. If he charges too high a rate there is cause for an overcharge claim. If the rate charged is too low, the carrier is legally obliged to send the customer a balance-due bill. Overcharge claims arise very frequently; usually they are sent to the rate department of the carrier rather than to the claim department.

I.C.C. Jurisdiction

Regulatory bodies such as the Interstate Commerce Commission do not have authority to pass on the merits of loss or damage claims. Claims involve violations of the shipping contract, and action to collect them must be taken in the courts. The I.C.C. is limited to enforcing the Interstate Commerce Act. For example, the Commission would be interested if a carrier unnecessarily paid a claim to a shipper in order to attract future business, since this might constitute rebating in violation of the Act.

The Interstate Commerce Act states that the origin carrier shall be liable to the lawful holder of the bill of lading for any loss, damage, or injury caused by it or any carrier over whose line the shipment passes. Claims may also be filed with the destination carrier, or with any intermediate carrier if damage can be proved to have occurred on the intermediate line.

Time for Filing

The Interstate Commerce Act also provides that no carrier shall set a period of less than 9 months for the customer to file a freight claim, or a period of longer than 2 years after the claim is turned down for starting a lawsuit. Therefore, claims against railroads, trucklines, and domestic freight forwarders must be filed within 9 months after delivery or when delivery should have occurred. The period for air carriers is the same, except that it is stated as 270 days. Water carriers, however, have a much shorter claim-filing period stated in their bills of lading. Generally, water-carrier claims must be filed within 3 months of the delivery date and suits instituted within one year of claim refusal. Water carriers also want to be notified of obvious damage before the goods are removed from the pier, and advised of concealed damage within 3 days of delivery.

Submitting Loss and Damage Claims

Although the I.C.C. cannot interfere in the handling of any freight claim, it can make rules for the handling of all freight claims. The matter was investigated in a proceeding known as *Ex parte 263*. The order written in this proceeding became effective in July, 1972. Appendix E to this order formalized a set of freight claim rules to be followed by all carriers under I.C.C. control. The following discussion is based on these rules.

Inspection.   Action on a loss or damage claim begins when the carrier delivers a shipment in short or injured condition. Shortage may be of an entire shipment, one or more pieces, or consist of pilferage from one carton. Damage may be obvious or concealed. Inspection begins with receipt of the merchandise by the consignee, before he signs the delivery receipt. If the receipt is signed "clear," the presumption is that there was no obvious damage to the shipment by the carrier. Therefore, the receiver must inspect it carefully and note obvious damage on the delivery receipt. Appendix-E rules allow the carrier to refuse any notations that do not specifically describe the damage. In other words, comments like "2 cartons bad order" or "all cartons dirty" would be useless.

Many carriers like to have an inspector from the claims department go out and examine all shipments on which claims will be filed. When damage is concealed and not found until unpacking, this is mandatory. The carrier is to be notified of concealed damage as soon as it is discovered or within 15 days of delivery. The container and its contents are to be preserved as received until they are inspected. The carrier is required to make the claim inspection within 5 days of the request to do so, but if he fails to make an inspection, the consignee must do so and record all information to the best of his ability. If a shipment looks as though it has been pilfered, a joint inventory of the contents must be made by the carrier and the consignee. An example of a typical freight-claim inspection report is shown in Figure 22.

Legally, a consignee cannot refuse to accept a shipment just because it is damaged. Like insurance, freight claim procedure is designed only to restore what has been lost, not to create a profit for the loser. A damaged shipment can be refused only when it is clearly and totally unusable for its intended purpose.

Filing the claim.   Claims will not be paid unless they are submitted in writing. A claim can be a simple business letter, but it must clearly identify the shipment, state who is liable, and request a specific amount of money. The best practice is to use

INSPECTION REPORT OF LOST OR DAMAGED MERCHANDISE

CARRIER _____ Date _____ 19_____ Report Number _____

Freight Bill No._____ Date _____ Consignee _____

Shipper _____ Address_____

Origin _____ City _____ State _____

Billed as _____

Date Delivered _____ Date Inspection Called For _____ Date Unpacked _____

Does the freight bill or bill of lading show that shipment was released at a specific value?_____ Yes _____ No _____ If yes quote _____

Were there any indications that shipment had prior transportation to origin point shown above? _____ Explain_____

Was merchandise received in original container?_____ Show original point of shipment if known_____

Import merchandise?_____ If yes, does merchandise appear to have been inspected prior to reshipment?_____ Explain _____

NATURE OF INSPECTION: Loss _____ Damage _____ Visible _____ Concealed _____

Were goods unpacked before the inspection was made?_____ Were containers and packaging available at point of inspection? _____

Does consignee claim exception taken at time of delivery?_____ Could damage to contents have been noted by consignee at time of delivery?_____ Explain

PACKING: Container _____ New____ Reused ____ Wired ____ Corded ____ Strapped ____ Nailed _____

Glued _____ Stapled _____ Taped _____ Gross weight of loaded container or package _____ dimensions _____

Box Maker's certificate_____ Container markings: directional _____ glass _____ fragile _____ HWC _____ others _____

How were goods packed?_____

SPECIFIC STATEMENT OF ARTICLES LOST OR DAMAGED: Total number of articles inspected _____

Invoice or Purchase Order # _____ Date_____ Discounts or Terms_____

Consignee's suggested disposition of salvage pending carriers approval _____

Inspector_____ X_____

➤ THIS INSPECTION REPORT IS NOT A CLAIM ◀

NOTE: This report is subject to the terms and conditions of the Bill of Lading and is not an admission of liability, nor a claim, against the carrier.

Upon your request carrier will forward claim blanks and other necessary forms to properly present your claim.

FCS-19A

Figure 22. Claim Inspection Report.

the *Standard Form for Presentation of Loss and Damage Claim*; an example of this form is shown in Figure 23.

The claim must be accompanied by several other documents so that the carrier can trace the history of the shipment and determine the value of the merchandise. First, the original bill of lading and the paid freight bill must be included. If they are not, a bond of indemnity must be sent along to protect the carrier against two claims being filed on the same merchandise. Next, a copy of the original invoice for the goods is included to show the value of the goods. If repairs have been made, a copy of this bill must be sent. A copy of the inspection report must be sent as well, and finally any other documents pertinent to the claim.

In general, the amount of the claim is limited to the invoice value of the goods less any trade discounts. The claim may include a prorated share of the freight charges if they have been paid.

Acknowledgment.   Appendix-E rules require carriers to acknowledge freight claims within 30 days and to reject them, pay them, or make a compromise offer within 120 days. In case he cannot meet the 120-day requirement, the carrier will give the claimant a report about it every 60 days.

Overcharge Claims

Many modern business firms audit all freight bills either before or after payment to make sure that the proper rates have been applied and that the arithmetic is correct. This auditing is done by rate men in the traffic department or by an outside traffic consulting firm. In a preaudit, bills are usually paid on the corrected basis. In postauditing, overcharge claims must be prepared. Again, the best procedure is to use the *Standard Form for Presentation of Overcharge Claims* shown in Figure 24. Perhaps the most important element of an overcharge claim is the tariff reference where the allegedly correct rate has been found. If necessary, a statement stating the reasoning and procedure in finding the rate should be attached to the claim in addition to the other documents required. As stated previously, overcharge claims are usually sent to the carrier's rate department, or the rate-and-tariff section of the carrier's traffic department.

STANDARD FORM FOR PRESENTATION OF LOSS AND DAMAGE CLAIM
(Read Instruction on Back Before Filling in This Form)

To: ....
............................(Name of Carrier)............................

............................(Date)............................

............................(Street Address)............................

............................(Claimant's Number)............................

............................(City, State)............................

............................(Carrier's Number)............................

This claim for $............... is made against your company for ☐ Damage ☐ Loss in connection with the following described shipment:

(Shipper's Name)	*(Consignee's Name)*
(Point Shipped From)	*(Final Destination)*
(Name of Carrier Issuing Bill of Lading)	*(Name of Delivering Carrier)*
(Date of Bill of Lading)	*(Date of Delivery)*
(Routing of Shipment)	*(Delivering Carrier's Freight Bill No.)*

If shipment reconsigned en route, state particulars: ....

If shipment moved from warhousing or distribution point, indicate name of initial shipper and point of origin, and, if known, name of prior carrier or carriers and prior billing reference:...
....
....

DETAILED STATEMENT SHOWING HOW AMOUNT CLAIMED IS DETERMINED
(Number and description of articles, nature and extent of loss or damage, invoice price of articles, amount of claim, etc. ALL DISCOUNT and ALLOWANCES MUST BE SHOWN.)

Total Amount Claimed	

The following documents are submitted in support of this claim:
☐ Original Bill of Lading   ☐ Original invoice or certified copy
☐ Original paid freight bill or other carrier document bearing notation of loss or damage if not shown on freight bill.
☐ Carrier's Inspection Report Form (Concealed loss or damage).   ☐ Shippers concealed loss or damage form.
☐ Consignee concealed loss or damage form.   ☐ Other particulars obtainable in proof of loss or damage claimed:
....

(Note: The absence of any document called for in connection with this claim must be explained. When impossible for claimant to produce original bill of lading, or paid freight bill, a bond of indemnity must be given to protect carrier against duplicate claim supported by original documents.)
Remarks: ....
....

The foregoing statement of facts is hereby certified as correct.

............................(Claimant's Name)............................

............................(Address)............................

No. FCS 18

Figure 23. Form for Loss and Damage Claims.

A.T.A. Standard Form F.C.S. 7

Standard Form for Presentation of Overcharge Claims.

(Name of person to whom claim is presented)   _(Address of claimant)_   _(Claimant's Number)_ **

(Name of Carrier)   _(Date)_   _(Carrier's Number)_

(Address)

This claim for $_____is made against the carrier named above by_____
(Amount of claim)   _(Name of claimant)_
for Overcharge in connection with the following described shipments:

Description of shipment_____

Name and address of consignor (shipper)_____

Shipped from_____, To_____
City, town or station   _City, town or station_

Final Destination_____ Routed via_____
City, town or station

Bill of Lading issued by_____Co.;   Date of Bill of Lading_____

Paid Freight Bill (Pro) Number_____;

Name and address of consignee (Whom shipped to)_____

If shipment reconsigned en route, state particulars: _____

Nature of Overcharge_____
Weight, rate, or classification, etc.

DETAILED STATEMENT OF CLAIM

Note.—If claim covers more than one item taking different rates and classification, attach separate statement showing how overcharge is determined and insert totals in space below.

	No. of Pkgs.	Articles	Weight	Rate	Charges	Amount of Overcharge
Charges Paid:						
		Total				
Should have been:						
		Total				

Authority for rate or classification claimed._____
(Give, so far as practicable, tariff reference, I. C. C. number, effective date and page or item.)

IN ADDITION TO THE INFORMATION GIVEN ABOVE, THE FOLLOWING DOCUMENTS ARE SUBMITTED IN SUPPORT OF THIS CLAIM*

( ) 1. Original paid freight ("expense") bill.
( ) 2. Original invoice, or certified copy, when claim is based on weight or valuation, or when shipment has been improperly described.
( ) 3. Original bill of lading, if not previously surrendered to carrier, when shipment was prepaid, or when claim is based on misrouting or valuation.
( ) 4. Weight certificate or certified statement when claim is based on weight.
     5. Other particulars obtainable in proof of Overcharge claimed.†

Remarks _____

The foregoing statement of facts is hereby certified to as correct.

(Signature of Claimant)

** Claimant should assign to each claim a number, inserting same in the space provided at the upper right hand corner of this form. Reference should be made thereto in all correspondence pertaining to this claim.
* Claimant will please place check (x) before such of the documents mentioned as have been attached, and explain under "Remarks" the absence of any of the documents called for in connection with this claim. When for any reason it is impossible for claimant to produce original bill of lading, if required, or paid freight bill, claimant should indemnify carrier or carriers against duplicate claim supported by original documents.
† Claims for overcharge on shipments of lumber should also be supported by a statement of the number of feet, dimensions, kind of lumber, and length of time on sticks before being shipped.
Claims based on rates quoted in letters from traffic officials should be supported by the original or copies of such letters.

Figure 24.   Form for Overcharge Claims.

Overcharge claims must be presented to the carrier within 3 years of the cause of action. Carriers prefer to deal with them as soon as possible, however, rather than to have the claimant wait and submit them in large bunches.

PAYMENT OF FREIGHT CHARGES

Perhaps one might consider that the last activity in the processing of a freight shipment is payment for satisfactory service. Here again, transportation-industry procedure differs somewhat from the credit and payment arrangements the businessman encounters elsewhere.

Shipments may be forwarded either on a prepaid basis, where the shipper pays the charges, or on a collect basis, where the consignee pays the charges. In land transportation, the shipment will move collect if not otherwise stated on the bill of lading. In water transportation, it will move prepaid unless other arrangements are made. In either case, charges are due at once or after a very short lead-time. The carrying of a 30-day account with monthly statements is extremely rare in the transportation industry.

The Interstate Commerce Act provides that the carrier shall not deliver or relinquish possession of freight until all tariff rates and charges have been paid, except under such rules and regulations as the Commission shall prescribe. The I.C.C. has allowed the carriers to establish periods for the payment of freight charges. If a firm has a good credit rating, railroads will allow 120 hours (or 5 days) after delivery for payment of freight charges. The regulations are more lenient for motor-truck, inland-water, and domestic-freight-forwarder carriers. These companies are allowed 7 days after delivery to render a freight bill. The customer is then allowed 7 days to pay it.

Many motor trucklines factor their accounts receivable in order to receive cash immediately. The factoring agent is a third-party firm usually called "Transport Clearings" or a similar title. Every day, this agency buys the good-credit freight bills of its member carriers for a small discount and, in turn, bills the customers for the charges owing. Such agencies are often very aggressive in dealing with shippers and receivers, and do not necessarily observe the full 14-day period allowable under I.C.C. regulations.

REFERENCES

Association of American Railroads. "I.C.C. Proposes Change in Demurrage Payments," and "New Demurrage System Urged in Study for FRA." *Information Letter*, no. 2041 (25 October 1972).

Bryan, Leslie A. *Traffic Management in Industry*. New York. Dryden Press, 1953.

Gecowets, George. "A Distribution Manager's Guide to Handling Claims." *Handling and Shipping*, vol. 13, no. 10 (October 1972).

Kneiling, John G. "The Rolling Stock Riddle." *Trains*, vol. 28, nos. 4–7 (February, March, April, May, 1968).

Morton, Newton, and Frank H. Mossman. *Industrial Traffic Management*. New York: Ronald Press, 1954.

National Motor Freight Traffic Association, Inc. *Supplement 32 to National Motor Freight Classification A-12*. Washington, D.C.: American Trucking Associations, Inc., 1972.

CHAPTER 12

Transportation Economics

This chapter deals with some of the economic reasons for transportation practices and activities that have been discussed in the earlier parts of this book. As in other fields of business and economic endeavor, a consideration of both the macro-economics of transportation and the microeconomics of transportation is appropriate.

Transportation macroeconomics considers the broad effects of transportation upon our economy. Such matters as the relation of transportation to the development of natural resources, the location of industry, the encouragement of industry, and the interrelation of market areas can properly be discussed in this connection.

Transportation microeconomics deals with the relationship of transportation to the individual business firm or industry. It includes the problem of maximizing profits within a transportation firm. The matter of setting remunerative rates by transportation companies is another problem in transportation micro-economics.

TRANSPORTATION'S EFFECT ON THE ECONOMY

Geographical Separation of Production and Consumption

The purpose of economic activity is the satisfaction of human needs and wants. The first step in this activity is production, which can be accomplished by extraction (as in mining), agriculture, or manufacturing. The last step, of course, is consumption. Production and consumption are tied together by distribution. A major part of the distribution activity is transportation. One can see that a good transportation system is vital to a nation's economy because it makes geographical separation of production and consumption possible. When transportation systems are primitive and inefficient, people must grow or make everything that they need pretty close to home or go without.

Encouragement of Industry and Lower Prices

As a by-product of the separation of production and consumption, improved transportation also encourages industrial development. As transport routes spread out geographically around a production point, they widen the market that can be served. The volume of production can thus be increased, and mass production techniques employed. This, in turn, can enable lower prices to be charged for the goods being produced.

Transportation can also be credited with tending to equalize prices in the market area where goods are being consumed. If a locally produced commodity is in short supply, its price will of course tend to rise. However, if a competitive or substitutable product can be shipped in cheaply from a distant point, the price-rise will not be so extreme. On the other hand, if too much of a good is produced locally, a glut of the market will develop, and the price will fall. With improved transportation, the excess production can be shipped to other markets, thus stabilizing the price received by local producers.

Regional Specialization and Natural Resources

As the national transportation system and economy develop together, more and more separation of production and consumption is possible. Since local production no longer needs to be dedicated to producing multiple products exclusively for local use, each region of the country can begin to specialize in producing the thing it does best.

This has an effect on the way in which natural resources are developed. Petroleum and mineral deposits, stands of timber, and farmlands can only be exploited if their products can be brought to market. Thus, the state of development of a country's transportation system may well determine the state of development of its natural resources. Improved transportation permits areas having particular natural resources to specialize in developing these as industries. Local needs can be shipped in from other producing areas, and local production can be shipped out in exchange.

LOCATION OF INDUSTRY

Improved transportation not only encourages the development of industries, but also plays a major role in determining where they will be located.

Obviously, extractive industries must be located where the natural resource is found in or on the earth. Thus, transportation cannot determine where a coal mine is to be located, but the way transportation facilities are expanded may determine which coal deposits can be tapped and which cannot. However, the more important consideration is where the raw material is located.

Some manufacturing industries also tend to locate near the source of their raw materials, but there are usually several other factors to be considered in finding the optimum location for a factory or plant. In addition to raw material supply, these may include the availability of a large labor supply or of skilled labor, the cost of land and the level of taxes, and the availability of power to run the factory. The decision must certainly consider the cost of hauling the raw materials and supplies to the factory, as well as the cost of shipping the finished product to market.

Thus, the cost of transportation is one of the important determinants of where industries will be located. A compromise will be made between the cost of shipping raw materials to the factory and the cost of shipping the finished product to market. A location will be chosen where aggregate transport costs tend to be the lowest. Transportation costs do not necessarily include only direct dollar charges and costs. Speed, convenience, and condition of product may be factors to consider as well. Thus, even though direct transportation costs are low, if delivery time to market is slow or if damage or deterioration of the product occur, then the effective cost of transportation is higher than the obvious monetary cost.

If transportation cost is the determining factor in plant location, the solution to the problem is related to whether the goods lose weight or gain weight during manufacture. When the product becomes lighter as it is processed, the factory will probably be located near the source of raw material. When the product becomes heavier as it goes through the plant, the plant will probably be located close to the market.

Weight-Losing and Weight-Gaining Materials

The often-cited classic example of weight-losing and weight-gaining products is that of wine and beer. The raw material for wine, of course, is grapes. In the wine-making process only the juice of the grapes is finally used; the stems, skins, and pulp do not appear in the final product. Therefore, it would not pay to ship anything but the juice to market, and the winery is located near the vineyards.

One of the main components of beer, on the other hand, is water. Water is a heavy commodity, and an adequate supply is found in nearly every market area. Therefore, in order to save the freight on shipping water, breweries are usually located in the market area.

Two other points in the wine and beer example are worthy of emphasis. One is that grapes are a perishable commodity that is subject to deterioration in transit. Deterioration, thus, is an indirect transport cost. A generality is that processing of perishable raw materials tends to take place near their source. The other point is that the water that is added to beer is a *ubiquitous* commodity—that is, it is found nearly everywhere. Another generalization is that products containing ubiquitous raw materials tend to be manufactured near the market.

Tapering Rates and Transit Privileges

Not all industries locate either at the source of raw materials or at the market. Many of them are found somewhere in between the two. This may be because it is the place where the aggregate of freight rates on raw materials and the freight rates on finished products is the lowest. Or it may be an accident of industrial development. The plant may have been put in one location to serve a certain market only to find a better market developing nearby and the whole locational pattern changing as economic development progressed. Due to the tapering principle of freight rates, such a plant may find itself at a disadvantage in comparison to factories located either at the raw-material source or at the market.

The tapering principle of freight rates was discussed at the end of Chapter 2. The earlier discussion pointed out that amortization of terminal costs over the line-haul makes it possible for the cost per mile to decrease as the length of the line-haul increases. Transportation charges are usually assessed on the basis of the weight shipped, but they are also related to distance. For instance, it may cost 284 cents per hundred pounds to ship steel fencing material from Chicago to Deming, New Mexico, a distance of about 1,500 miles. And it may cost 254 cents per hundred pounds to ship the same commodity from Kansas City to Deming, a distance of about 1,000 miles. Thus, the rate per hundred pounds increases with the distance. On a mileage basis, however, the rate from Chicago is about 19/100 cents per mile while the rate from Kansas City is about 25/100 cents per mile. Thus, the rate per mile decreases. This is due to the fact that terminal and other startup costs are the same in both instances but can be amortized over more miles on the Chicago haul. It is also due to the fact that some economies of scale are realized on the longer line-haul movement.

The way in which the tapering principle can put an intermediately located producer at a disadvantage can be illustrated as follows. Assume we have a raw-material-producing point called RM and a market area called MA. Half-way between them is an intermediate city or point called IP. Assume also for purposes of simplicity that the freight rate on raw materials is the same as the rate on the finished product. Assume the rates and distances are as follows:

Journey Segment	*Freight rate per 100 pounds*	*Distance in miles*
from RM to IP	80 cents	100
from IP to MA	80 cents	100
from RM to MA (non-stop thru IP)	145 cents	200

The transportation cost to a producer located at RM or MA is 145 cents per hundred pounds, and it is immaterial at which point he is located because the rates on the raw material and the finished product are the same. For a producer located at IP, however, the total transportation cost to market is 160 cents per hundred pounds; thus he has a rate disadvantage of 15 cents per hundred pounds.

The subject of transit privileges was discussed briefly in Chapter 5. In the above example, the producer located at IP could benefit from a transit privilege that would allow him to bring in a raw material from RM, transform it into a finished product at IP, and then ship it to MA, all on the through 145-cent rate. When the raw material is not transformed into an entirely different product, railroads often establish such privileges to encourage industries at intermediate points. Thus, wheat may be stopped at an intermediate point and made into flour, or oil-field pipe may be stopped at a wrapping plant and coated with a preservative covering. Complete equalization of costs is not possible because the carriers make a flat charge for each car-load that is stopped and processed. Because of the volume, however, the effect of this charge is minimal compared to the disadvantages of paying two short-haul rates.

Blanket Rates

Another effect of the tapering principle is that it aids in the establishment of "blanket" or "group" rates. Especially on long hauls it will be found that freight rates from or to a distant point are the same from a whole group of cities in one region. One reason for this is that after startup costs have been amortized over a large number of miles, the differences in costs of serving different points in the same region are not great. Therefore, for competitive reasons, minor differences in costs can be averaged and the same rate charged to or from all places in a related geographical area. The effect this has upon the location of industry is to cause decentralization of producing facilities (or receiving facilities) throughout the area that is covered by the blanket rate.

RATE PROBLEMS OF THE
TRANSPORTATION CARRIER

In Chapter 1, transportation was partly defined as the movement of goods from where they are not needed to where they are needed. In traditional economic language this is the activity of giving them place utility because moving the goods makes them more useful in one place than in another.

The creation of place utility illustrates the concept of "derived demand." The demand for transportation service derives from the demand at destination for the product that is to be moved. If there is heavy demand for the product, there is probably heavy demand for transportation to move it to where it is needed. If there is no demand for the product, there probably will be no demand for transportation to move it.

Our transportation system is designed and equipped to move all sorts of products in and between all parts of the nation. Yet the demand for it depends upon the demand for each of the many products that it is prepared to carry. This makes the determination of demand for transportation a very complex matter. Although there is an aggregate demand for all transportation services in our economy, a transportation carrier cannot price his service on the basis of aggregate demand. This is because the demand for each product he hauls is different and the demand for his service is only secondary to the demand for each product that he carries.

Demand is important to the carrier because it determines the quantity of his service that the public will purchase at a given price at a given time. Usually the amount of service the public is willing to buy will increase if the carrier lowers his rates; conversely, the quantity the public is willing to buy will decrease if he raises his rates. However, the transportation company is, in effect, dealing with a whole group of different publics because the basic demand for each product he carries is different. Therefore, when he is setting rates, the carrier must consider the demand for each product itself as well as the demand that product may have for transportation.

The goal of the carrier is to set all of his rates so that he will maximize his total revenues and his profits. To do this he tries to set the rate on each product so that a maximum profitable movement of it will be encouraged. He refrains from setting individual rates so high that they discourage movement of a commodity that it is profitable to move. Ideally, the carrier looks for situations in which a small decrease in rates will cause a large increase in traffic. He seeks to avoid raising rates where a small rate increase will cause a large number of customers to stop shipping with him. However, there are some commodities on which the carrier might be able to raise rates very substantially without discouraging traffic at all. Of course, he probably would like to identify the latter situation so that rates could be increased. All of these possible effects of rate changes are related to the *price elasticity of demand.*

Elasticity of Demand

Demand is said to be highly elastic when a small decrease in price causes a relatively large increase in sales, or vice versa. Demand is said to be highly inelastic when an increase or decrease in the price causes virtually no change in the amount sold.

Because of the concept of derived demand, the elasticity of demand for transportation service is closely related to the demand for the good itself. However, there are some limits on transportation pricing that may not apply in the pricing of the good itself. Generally, the demand for the necessities of life is relatively inelastic while the demand for luxuries is relatively elastic. It would seem that a carrier would run less chance of discouraging traffic when raising rates on a necessity than on a luxury. On the other hand, luxuries are frequently high-priced goods; since high-priced goods usually pay only a small portion of their own total value for transportation service, their demand for transportation may be relatively inelastic. In the same vein, the necessities of life frequently are low-value goods that contribute a proportionately higher part of their own value for transportation service. Thus, the demand for transportation of low-value necessities may be relatively elastic. Another facet of the situation is that if the shipper can pass a freight rate increase on to the consumer, his demand for transportation is likely to be more inelastic that if he cannot. Ultimately, the relative elasticity or inelasticity of demand for the services of a particular transportation carrier is determined by what his competitors charge. If he raises his rate for a given service above that of a competitive carrier or mode, the public will immediately be willing to buy less of his service and more of his competitor's service.

Discriminatory Pricing

Carriers recognize different price elasticities of demand by discriminating between different commodities, and in the passenger business by discriminating between different classes of service. The practice of providing first-, second-, and third-class passenger service is an example of the attempt to tap different elasticities of demand. For instance, in the earlier days of air travel only one class of service was offered to the public. Flying was regarded by many as an expensive means of transport to be used by the wealthy and by celebrities, and only in personal emergencies by common folk. For some time, apparently, people who could afford the price were sufficient in number to fill the seats available. When new equipment provided additional capacity, the "coach" class was introduced. As equipment size continued to grow, the "economy" section was added. Each of these steps was an attempt to introduce a price-break to attract people who previously could not afford to fly, but without diluting the higher-priced traffic already served. In order to prevent a cascading of traffic down into the low-price categories, each innovated class of service had to appear less desirable (in terms of seating configuration, food service, and other comforts) than the class of service above.

In freight transportation, the discrimination, of course, is between commodities. Different rates are charged on vegetables from what are charged on machinery. Rates on wheat are different from rates on coal. An important reason is that the demand each product has for transportation is different from the demand for transportation of every other product.

In both the passenger pricing situation and the freight rate situation, an argument can be made that the transportation characteristics of the traffics are different. This implies that the costs of handling them are different—as indeed they are. However, one must not overlook the primary role played by price elasticity of demand in causing different rates for different customers who are receiving very similar services.

Limits to Rate-Setting

Value of service. The price elasticity of demand for transportation is reflected in the concept of "the value of the service." By "value of service" is meant the worth in monetary terms of a particular service to a particular shipper. This value sets the upper limit on what a transportation carrier may charge when setting a freight rate for a product. In days of railroad monopoly, it signified the amount a road could charge without discouraging a customer from shipping altogether. Today, in the face of competition from many carriers of several modes, it means the amount a carrier can charge without either causing the shipper to switch to another carrier or to stop shipping altogether. Thus, to the individual transportation company, "value of service" represents the highest rate that can be charged without preventing a product from moving over its line. In other words, "value of service" places an upper limit on a carrier's rate-setting ability.

Cost of service.   Where on the one hand a shipper cannot afford to pay more for transportation than what the service is worth to him, on the other hand the carrier cannot afford to charge less for the service than what it costs him to provide it. The alternatives to the recovery of full costs in the long run are bankruptcy or government subsidy, or perhaps even government ownership of the carrier. Because transportation is a vital force in the economy, carriers must be allowed and encouraged to set their rates in such a way that their plant and equipment do not deteriorate when the costs of maintaining and replacing them are not met. Perennial questions in freight rate-making, however, are: how are costs to be defined, which costs should be covered, and can any costs be ignored in the short run? This leads to the subject of differential pricing, or as it has also been called, incremental-cost pricing.

Differential pricing.   Differential pricing or incremental-cost pricing is a method of setting rates for a product or service that recovers less than the full cost of the operation. This is because it provides for only the variable costs of the operation plus part or none of the fixed costs.

The reader is probably aware that variable costs are those that increase or decrease as the volume of business increases or decreases. These include such things as labor, materials that go into the product, and fuel to run the machinery. Fixed costs are expenditures that must continue even if the business is not operating. These include such items as plant investment, insurance on the plant, minimal standby salaries and wages, security costs, and minimum maintenance.

A simple example of differential pricing perhaps is more realistically constructed assuming a hypothetical manufacturing company rather than a transportation company. (Product line and pricing can be less complex, and price-setting is not as closely regulated by the government as it is in transport.) Let us assume a manufacturing company that makes one product— say, a household refrigerator. The management has established a certain volume of production and has priced the product based on an existing level of demand. The demand is being met fully. Price and resulting revenue are sufficient to cover all variable costs of production and all fixed costs of the plant. However, management recognizes that full plant capacity is not being utilized. In this situation, management may seek to use excess plant capacity by tapping another level of price elasticity of demand without disturbing the volume of the product being sold at the current price. They can do this by utilizing excess plant capacity to produce goods, competitive to their own, that will be sold to and through a large marketing firm— say, a mail-order house. This merchandise will be labeled with the mail-order-house brand. It can be priced to the mail-order house on the basis of covering only the variable costs, since the fixed costs have already all been covered by sales of the company's own brand. This can be also referred to as incremental-cost pricing because the price is based only on the increment of cost incurred in producing an additional lot of merchandise.

Differential pricing by railroads. For many years, railroad economists have made a strong argument that differential pricing can be applied to the making of railroad freight rates. Railroads are an industry that is characterized by an extremely large set of fixed costs in relation to variable costs. This is because there are thousands of miles of track, thousands of locomotives, and millions of freight cars, which must be paid for whether they are doing anything or not. Railroads are also characterized by having a lot of excess capacity or underutilized capacity. Very frequently they must pull empty cars across their lines in order to have them available for loads at the other end. Since the empty cars must be returned anyway, the railroad would be ahead if it could sell this unused space even at a bargain rate (this is sometimes referred to as pricing on a "backhaul" basis). This rate could be much lower than the "regular rate" because only the additional cost of getting the car loaded and switched into the train and the cost of pulling the loaded weight need be included. No amount would have to be collected for fixed costs, because the empty returning car was not contributing to these in the first place.

Railroad economists have taken this concept and have married it to the fact that different products have different price elasticities of demand for transportation. They have come up with a rationale for pricing railroad service on a "out-of-pocket" or incremental-cost basis; that is, by covering only the variable costs of transportation plus a partial contribution to fixed costs. The argument is that many commodities are of such low value that they cannot afford expensive transportation. If the railroad can identify these commodities, they can be priced on an incremental-cost basis, thereby conferring a benefit both on the railroad and the public. The railroad will have utilized unused capacity and maximized revenue (even if it did not cover all costs), and the public will have enjoyed wider distribution of a useful product that otherwise could not have been moved. Undoubtedly, this is a good practice in the short run, because it does generate revenue and some small contribution to fixed costs from space that otherwise would have traveled empty.

The railroad industry, however, is rather inflexible and is subject to more long-run than short-run forces. Once rates for a product are published in freight rate tariffs, they have the force of law, and they tend to develop "traditional" relationships to freight rates on other products. Thus, a traffic that was underpriced in order to use excess capacity and maximize revenues in the short run may linger on to demand much-needed space in the long run. Since the railroad is a common carrier, it must continue to accept this unprofitable traffic although conditions have changed and its cars are now filled with high-revenue traffic. Adherence to incremental-cost pricing, therefore, probably has contributed in part to the low-return-on-investment position in which railroads have found themselves for several decades.

Effects in the trucking industry. The practice of differential or incremental-cost pricing by railroads has been stressed above because it is a recurring issue in rail rate-making. Generally, the argument for or against differential pricing does not arise in the trucking industry. This is because costs in motor transportation are largely variable in nature and must be covered on every haul. To put it simply, if the trucker does not receive enough revenue to cover labor, fuel, and a contribution toward the payment on the vehicle, he cannot afford to accept the traffic. Individual trucking companies do, however, set rates on a backhaul basis very similar to the example above where railroad cars must return empty. When a truckline has a profitable haul in one direction, it may be tempted to set the return rates to cover just the cost of loading the truck plus the cost of fuel for the return trip. In the long run, this has the same danger as rail incremental-cost pricing. In the complexity of day-to-day operation one tends to forget which was the original, profitable haul and which was the backhaul. The result can be that rates are eventually lowered to attract backhaul in both directions.

EFFECT OF GOVERNMENT REGULATION AND POLICY

This chapter has reviewed some of the effects of transportation macroeconomics and microeconomics. The way in which these effects are controlled and channeled can have much to do with the way in which a country's industrial and transportation systems will develop. Since for-hire carriers are generally economically regulated in the United States, the federal and state governments are both in a position to guide this development.

CONCLUDING REMARK FOR THE BOOK

This book was intended for the student of business administration who has had little exposure to commercial transportation. If he has read the foregoing chapters, he should have acquired some knowledge of the fundamentals of our transportation system and how to use it. This will put him far ahead of the average person entering the business world but it won't make him an expert. Expertise in transportation can be developed through study in depth of each of the interest areas presented, in addition to others that will appear to the interested researcher.

REFERENCES

Association of American Railroads. "The Role of Cost in Minimum Pricing of Railroad Services." In *Modern Transporta-*

tion: Selected Readings, 2d ed., edited by Martin T. Farris and Paul T. McElhiney. Boston: Houghton Mifflin, 1973.

Locklin, D. Philip. *Economics of Transportation*, 7th ed. Homewood, Ill.: Richard D. Irwin, 1972.

Norton, Hugh S. *Modern Transportation Economics*. Columbus: Charles E. Merrill Books, 1963.

Sampson, Roy J. "The Case for Full Cost Rate Making." In *Modern Transportation: Selected Readings*, 2d ed., edited by Martin T. Farris and Paul T. McElhiney. Boston: Houghton Mifflin, 1973.

Sampson, Roy J., and Martin T. Farris. *Domestic Transportation*, 2d ed. Boston: Houghton Mifflin, 1971.

Westmeyer, Russell E. *Economics of Transportation*. Englewood Cliffs, N.J.: Prentice-Hall, 1952.

Index